'PLEASE SIR, SKOOL ISN'T WERKING'

PRAISE FOR MIKE KENT'S WRITING

THE RABBIT'S LAID AN EGG, MISS!
This book will raise a smile in any reader, but it will ring several bells for anyone involved in education. Mike Kent has obviously been there and printed the T-shirt. First published in 2006, it is still valid in its hilarious depiction of the reality of running a modern school, caught between the Scylla of challenging children (and their equally challenging parents) and the Charybdis of inspectors and educational authorities, who are mostly blissfully ignorant of the sharp end!
B. Sherunkle: Former Chair of Governors

This collection of Mike Kent's popular *Times Educational Supplement* columns is highly addictive, giving tantalising glimpses of life as a primary school headteacher. I became totally engrossed in sharing his humour, poignancy, frustration and joys. It will revitalise test-driven, demoralised teachers and will remind parents of the sort of education they really want for their children.
Emily G: Teacher

Absolutely brilliant! Snippets of some very entertaining aspects of school life in an inner London primary school that will have the reader giggling non-stop! It is a joy to read Mike Kent's books. His love of teaching and school life shines through and you certainly don't have to be a teacher to enjoy them.
Julie Jenkins: Social Worker

I loved this. I am a parent who was looking for insights into how primary schools work and how teachers think. It made me wish my children could go to his school. Quite a few laugh out loud moments. My only criticism? It was too short!
N. Stoker: Parent

TALES FROM THE HEAD'S ROOM
Humour, heroism, common sense and inspiring humanity shine through Mike Kent's writing. 'Tales From The Head's Room' demonstrates how, against all the odds, it is possible to create a centre of educational excellence, where both children and staff enjoy the learning process.
Emma Davis: Trainee Headteacher

I thoroughly enjoyed reading Mike Kent's school anecdotes. Each chapter is relatively self-contained and well suited for dipping into if you have a busy lifestyle. We need more school leaders like him. I hope his book inspires more potential school leaders to trust their judgement and ignore some of the loopier government initiatives!
Robert Butler: Senior Teacher

This book is such a joy! Encouraging children to learn is what education is about and Mike doesn't let the nonsense get in his way. Heads or tails, whichever way it lands, you are going to get a highly entertaining read and have a good laugh.
Kim Kool: Lecturer, Goldsmith's University

I opened this book and then could not put it down! This is a must for anyone who has ever worked in a primary school or for that matter anyone with the slightest interest in education. Mike Kent's stories are hilarious but also convey the hard work, effort and dedication that teachers put into our young people to give them a great education. A great read!
Stupot: Director, The Blue Elephant Theatre.

A LIFE AT THE CHALKFACE
An excellent read! Technology brings many changes but children remain the same. I taught Infants for thirty five years and no work could have been more satisfying. I live now with many wonderful memories and this book was a re-visit to the classroom and its unforgettable memories. Thank you!
E.R. Melville: Teacher

A brilliant book that brought back such wonderful memories of working at Mike's school. An absolutely amazing head teacher. After eighteen years I still haven't found a headteacher to match Mike Kent.
Karen Thompson: Teacher

This book is a beautifully warm, emotive and honest account of life in an inner London primary school. A wonderful insight into the varied life of a headteacher, and all the characters and situations that the author encountered in his career. Prepare to laugh and cry as this book recounts the high and low points of a career in primary education.
Rachel McMutrie: Parent

Mike Kent was obviously the kind of head teacher we would all have liked to have been. Although he does not pull any punches when he describes the trials, tribulations and stresses of headship, this book is clearly written by someone for whom headship was not just a job, but a joy and a privilege. There must be a great many people, now in their 20s, 30s and 40s, who have very fond memories of their time at his school.
Michael Evans: Headteacher

Life as a headteacher doesn't come with an unreservedly positive recommendation, but for Mike Kent it was the best job in the world. 'A Life At The Chalkface' is a love letter to thirty eventful years in a job he found endlessly challenging and fascinating. In a world of league tables and assessment spreadsheets, this book stands out as a testament to all that is best in primary education.
Lucy Edkin: Educational Columnist

Mike Kent is a rare talent. He writes beautifully and has spent most of his life in schools, first as a pupil, then as a teacher and deputy head, and finally thirty years as a headteacher in South London. So here is a rich tale, filled with meaningful insights and revealing anecdote, all set against the backdrop of school life. Read, and enjoy, his story.
Sir Tim Brighouse: Former Commissioner for London Schools

AMAZING ASSEMBLIES FOR PRIMARY SCHOOLS
This book is a must-buy for any imaginative, forward looking primary school.
John Lord: Headteacher

The activities are simple and easy to prepare and I will be using them immediately, just as long as I contact the fire brigade first!
Richard Dax: Primary Headteacher

Mike Kent's broad experience as a headteacher and thought-provoking columnist and writer has given him the skills to produce this book, full of practical ideas to make school assemblies exciting and interesting learning experiences.
John T Morris, JTM Educational Consultants.

As a busy headteacher, this book is just what I need to capture the imaginations of children of all ages at the start of the day.
Anita Asumadu: Headteacher

NINE TILL THREE AND SUMMERS FREE
When I pick up a book, whether it be factual or fiction, I want to be entertained as well as informed. I want to be able to read it without having to go back and re-read because I've not understood. I want the words to flow naturally as if in direct conversation. Well, I love reading Mike Kent's books because this is how he writes. He is a natural, and he writes with much humour too. Such an entertaining read, poignant, funny and informative. I just loved it. His best book yet!
Charlotte Russell, teacher.

Mike Kent is a familiar voice in education. For fifteen years he was a leading columnist on the Times Educational Supplement, entertaining countless readers with stories of life as a primary headteacher, all told with his trademark warmth and humour. Nine Till Three… charts the beginning of Mike's journey into the teaching profession during the sixties. The picture of college life that he paints is all brought to life in glorious and amusing technicolour. Whether you were a regular reader of Mike's weekly column or just somebody interested in education, this book is a real treat that is definitely not to be missed.
Jo Brighouse, Educational Journalist.

What a delightful book! A must for anybody in teaching, or anybody even slightly interested in education.
Loleta Pilgrim, retired Deputy Headteacher.

As with all Mike's books, a riveting read and a very amusing reminder of attitudes and practices in sixties teacher training.
Terry Powell, Teacher and Drama Specialist.

I WAS A TEENAGE TREACLE TIN
The title makes the mind boggle, but it makes much more sense by the time you've become engrossed, which doesn't take long! I've read all of Mike's

books and each one seems more entertaining than the last. I love reading, and have a few books on the go, but I always finish Mike Kent's books first, while the others remain languishing on the bedside table. What more do you need to know? Except that this book is comforting, cheering, occasionally shocking, and just so downright readable!
Charlotte Russell, teacher

Mike Kent's memoir is a thoroughly enjoyable experience. His wonderful anecdotes about his formative years in fifties London make for a heartwarming historical document. His stories, especially about his introductions to cinema and music, both passions I share with him, brought many smiles to my face. Mike has a rare talent. He's an economical writer who still paints vivid pictures from his memories. He's truly able to capture a time and a place and that's no small feat. Highly Recommended.
Paul Cruttenden, Hi-Fi Specialist

Another amazing treat from the wonderfully talented Mike Kent. He writes beautifully and effortlessly and no matter your age or generation the stories resound in each and every one of us. I laughed and cried (with laughter too) Thank you Mr Kent.
Kathy Doyle, Special Educational Needs Co-ordinator

A wonderful memoir of life in the 1950's, filled with funny and heartwarming tales of tricks and capers that had me laughing out loud.
Vicki Haselgrove, teacher

I really enjoyed reading this. Mike has an incredible recall of events which takes you right there with him, and with such a great sense of humour too. It's an excellent reminder of how our childhood shapes us. A really good read.
Andrew W, teacher

Beautifully written and a fascinating insight into how life was for the generation before my own. Funny, heart-warming and a pleasure to read. Another gem in the array of books Mike has written. This book will not disappoint.
Charlotte Trendell, media make-up artist

'ME GLASSES BUST AGAIN, SIR!'
Such an uplifting and thoughtful account of children and teachers lives in a London primary school. Mike Kent's humorous observations and comments are spot-on. They convey a lifetime's experience yet still retain a joyous enthusiasm and love of the profession. *Angela Lord, Teacher*

Another book by Mike Kent that I couldn't put down. Hilarious and so true to life diary of life in a South London primary school. *Sandra Quilter, Senior School Admin Officer*

Whether you are a teacher, parent or have no connection with educational establishments, this account of teaching in an inner city primary is impossible to put down.

It has charm and poignancy; the stories of the children, parents and staff are told honestly, empathetically and without sentimentality. The book will make you laugh out loud, and maybe shed a tear too. Overcoming the infuriating barriers by officialdom, which impact on children's learning not one bit, reflect the author's deep respect for the children and staff he works with, in a school which is so clearly a joyful place to be. The book is a gem. Buy it for anyone who has ever been to school! *Sue Gale, Teacher.*

Nobody.... Nobody.... says it better than Mike Kent... a truly inspirational teacher, writer and headteacher. He simply tells how it is, in real life, at the chalkface. Unlike Mike, very few school leaders dare to speak truth to education ministers and Ofsted inspectors. His love of children, basic life skills, literacy, mathematics, the arts, his school community plus his belief in and respect for all his school staff inspired me to strive to emulate his unwavering philosophy. It should be as he says ... all about the children and their teachers! *Richard Dax, Headteacher*

'PLEASE SIR, SKOOL ISN'T WERKING'

A Close Look At Our Education System

MIKE KENT

Copyright © 2024 Mike Kent

The moral right of the author has been asserted.

Apart from any fair dealing for the purposes of research or private study, or criticism or review, as permitted under the Copyright, Designs and Patents Act 1988, this publication may only be reproduced, stored or transmitted, in any form or by any means, with the prior permission in writing of the publishers, or in the case of reprographic reproduction in accordance with the terms of licences issued by the Copyright Licensing Agency. Enquiries concerning reproduction outside those terms should be sent to the publishers.

Troubador Publishing Ltd
Unit E2 Airfield Business Park
Harrison Road, Market Harborough
Leicestershire LE16 7UL
Tel: 0116 279 2299
Email: books@troubador.co.uk
Web: www.troubador.co.uk

ISBN 978-1-83628-102-3

British Library Cataloguing in Publication Data.
A catalogue record for this book is available from the British Library.

Printed and bound in Great Britain by 4edge Limited
Typeset in 11pt Minion Pro by Troubador Publishing Ltd, Leicester, UK

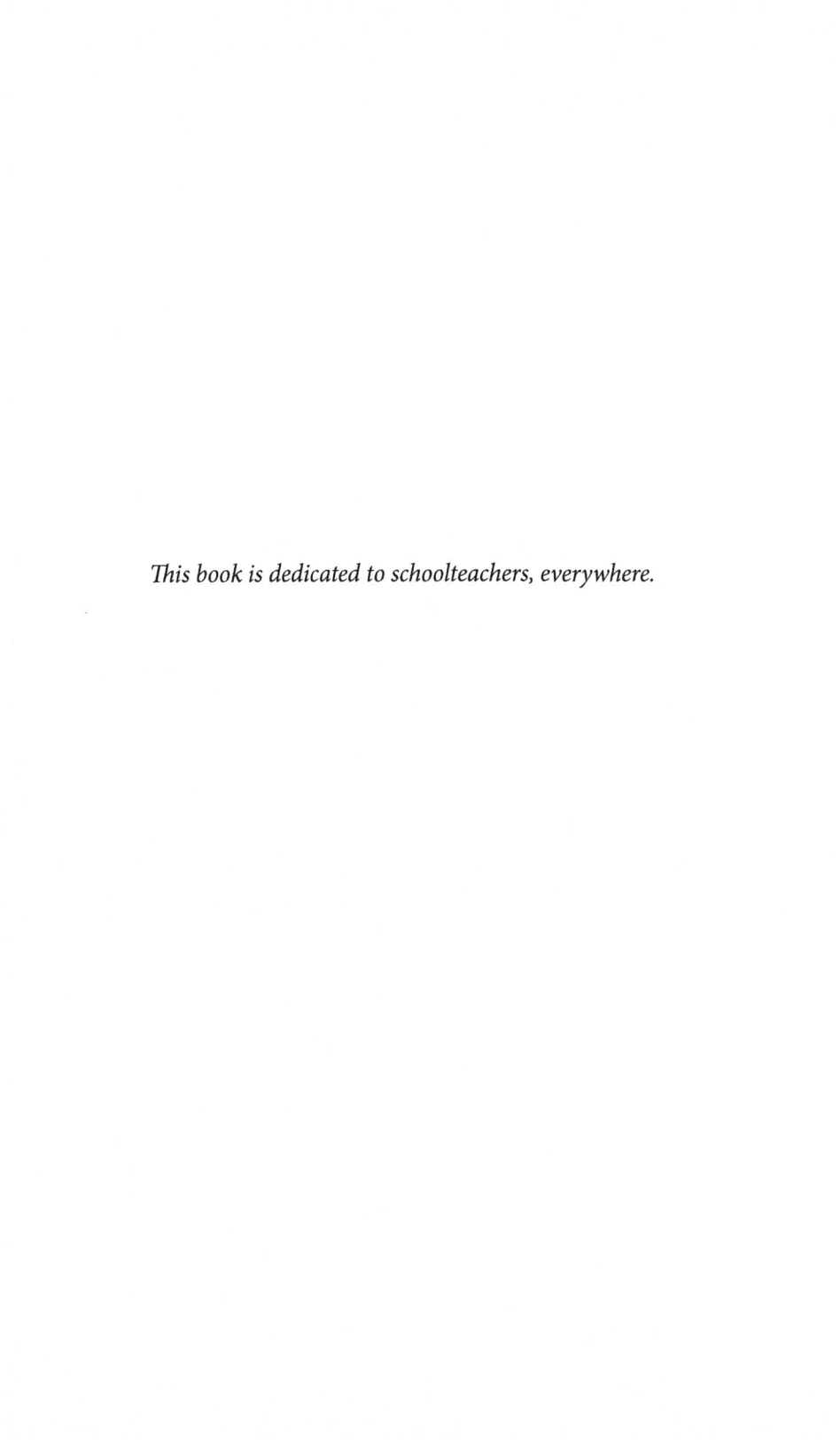

This book is dedicated to schoolteachers, everywhere.

CONTENTS

1	**Foreword**	1
2	**Follow My Leader** But What Makes A Good School Leader?	5
3	**Is Charlie Just Being... Naughty?** Children's Behaviour In School	24
4	**Can We Have A Decision, Please?** Schools And Their Governing Bodies	51
5	**Elf n' Safety** Avoiding Harm In School	70
6	**There'll Be Another One Along In Five Minutes** Fads, Fashions and Failings In Educational Policy	87
7	**How's He Getting On, Mr Brown?** The Curriculum, Children's Achievement, and Monitoring It	113
8	**I Can Just Look It Up OnLine** The Pace Of Technology	139

9	**Testing, Testing!** Children And The Standard Attainment Tests	158
10	**Mrs Smith Is In The Office Again!** What Parents Expect From Schools	178
11	**Horses For Courses. And Teachers** Professional Development	200
12	**Is Charlie Just Being… Naughty… Again?** The Rise In Children With Additional Needs	216
13	**Sorry, I'm Snowed Under** Teachers' Workload	237
14	**Who Inspects The Inspectors?** The Ofsted Problem	256
15	**Afterword**	286

1
FOREWORD

During the week that I retired from headship and the career that I had loved for nearly fifty years, I discovered a very old, faded photograph in a battered frame at the bottom of a cupboard. I'd forgotten all about it. The photo had been taken in a classroom at my school in 1913, just before the first world war.

The classroom looks as if it hasn't seen a lick of paint for many years. Tiered rows of raggedly dressed children stare passively towards the blackboard at the front of the room. Many have grubby faces and dirty hands, not one of them is smiling and one boy appears to have fallen asleep on his desk. There are more than forty children in the class. There is a map of the British Empire on the wall and a crucifix, but little else. A master, moustached and dour, stands halfway up the rows, looking stiffly at the camera.

There is a scruffy wooden teacher's desk at the front of the room with a pile of dilapidated books, and out of sight, undoubtedly a cane and a chair with a dunce's cap as well. In the right hand corner of the bottom tier sits a boy with the delightful name of Reginald Nightingale. Reginald is different from all the other children in the class. He is black, and I know his name because, as an older man, he returned to the school for a short time to work as the premises officer's assistant.

If Reg could see his classroom now, he'd be amazed. There are just twenty three children in it, and they have far more freedom to move about and chat to each other than Reg ever did. Other than answering a question fired at him from the master, Reginald probably wasn't allowed to speak at all. The children now sit in groups at tables, which can be moved and re-arranged depending on the activity taking place. The classroom walls are flooded with children's art work, 3D models, topic displays and colourful information charts for improving work quality. The teacher moves around the room, helping, explaining, assisting, and rarely sitting down.

Reg would find the children friendly and welcoming, but he'd be shocked at their physical size, and probably think many were teenagers. He'd notice the teacher smiled at him too, and he'd find her warm and encouraging, though he'd soon discover she was strict about work and behaviour standards. No cane exists, of course, but Reg would find her lessons so interesting he wouldn't want to muck about anyway. And undoubtedly he'd be impressed by the sheer range of learning that takes place, especially with the additional activities outside class time. He could make a boat, play an orchestral instrument, become a film buff in *Film Club*, write a play, learn to dance, join chess group, try some gardening, cook a pie, become a magician, make some pottery, do some woodwork, become an artist…

Reg would still find traces of things that have survived across the years. A small board at the front of the classroom, but now a smooth white, with dry markers instead of dusty chalk. The children still write in books, but now they make attractive covers for them, using a wide variety of colourful writing media, and the books and folders come in many shapes and sizes. The children still learn multiplication tables and maths rules, but now have clever apparatus to assist them. And they still learn to read of course… but with a vast array of interesting reading books readily available in their class library and the extensive school library.

Reg would be astonished at the classroom's electronic wizardry. The interactive whiteboard, where Mount Vesuvius can be instantly shown as well as talked about. The ability to play a sequence from a famous film, in high quality definition, or a documentary especially made for children, showing what life was like in Shakespeare's time.

The chance to enjoy music, properly, on good equipment. The opportunity to don headphones and escape into a private world of storytelling and drama. And, at the click of a button, the ability to harness vast amounts of information from the internet, because there are several computers in the room.

The classroom I've described is, of course, what an ideal primary school classroom should be. It's the classroom you or I would like our own children, or any other child to experience. We want children to enjoy their school careers with enthusiasm and motivation. We want their teachers to thoroughly enjoy working with each other and have a passion for the job, in schools where the headteacher and senior staff are dedicated to helping young children grow from their earliest years of discovery into interesting teenagers and ultimately useful, caring citizens. All children are unique, and we want to celebrate that by nurturing their individual talents and abilities. And if they have additional needs we want them met with sympathy and understanding.

But in education, as in any other public service, so much can so easily go wrong. We have moved a very long way from the experiences Reg would have had at school, but every decade has brought problems for schools and education in general. Much of this has been caused by unwise and sometimes incomprehensible decisions from successive governments, a much maligned and disliked school inspection system, vested interests, incompetence from secretaries of state, obstructive governing bodies, a data led method of assessing children and schools, a huge reduction in essential arts provision, a curriculum that does not always service the needs of its users, and constant underfunding.

Whereas at one time, teaching was a profession for life, many teachers now leave after five years, finding the job simply too stressful, and then schools have to rely on agency staff. Many schools experience difficulty in recruiting a new headteacher, especially in challenging inner city areas, because the demands of the job can be so intense. School inspections are feared. Children today, even very young ones, are far more demanding, sometimes very difficult to cope with in a classroom situation, and many have additional needs, requiring a classroom assistant to work alongside them for much of the week.

So what can be done?

I have spent my entire life in education. I knew it was the career I wanted from the age of six, when my father made a blackboard and easel for me in the early fifties and I played schools in the holidays with the other children in my street. I became a teacher, then a deputy headteacher and finally a headteacher for thirty years, in a very challenging area of London. For sixteen of those years, I was also the 'back page columnist' on the weekly *Times Educational Supplement* newspaper, which gave me a unique insight into the views, problems and experiences of teachers and school leaders all over the country.

This book, then, reflects those years. It looks at every aspect of schooling, the successes and failures of various secretaries of state, the massive changes that have taken place over the years, the changing needs of children, and hopefully comes up with some answers to the difficulties teachers and schools continue to struggle with today.

It is not, however, intended to be a dry and tedious polemic. Humour is a splendid and essential piece of equipment in the teacher's toolkit, and hopefully the reader will find much of it in this book. As I did, in the many enjoyable years I spent with young children.

And some quite remarkable teachers.

2

FOLLOW MY LEADER

But What Makes A Good School Leader?

Headship. Such an important word. But in many ways, no less important than 'Newly Qualified Teacher.' So, in this chapter, we'll take a look at both ends of the spectrum, see why things can easily go wrong and look at how both might be improved.

Thirty years ago in London, if you wanted to be a primary school headteacher you'd already have been an extremely good class teacher who'd made it to deputy headship. You would have had a strong academic record, although not necessarily a degree, been passionate about education, and each year attended a selection of useful courses to increase your skills. You'd have become well known to your local inspectors and they'd have noticed your qualities, eventually recommending that you applied for further promotion. Then you'd apply for a school you liked the look of, and six candidates would have been shortlisted and interviewed by the school's governing body. Three would have been further shortlisted for interviewing by an experienced education committee, and the lucky candidate chosen. The system seemed to work well.

Then everything gradually became far more complex. In 2000, a 'National College of School Leadership' arrived, and if you wanted to become a headteacher, you had to get yourself on one of their accredited training schedules. Just filling in the on-line application forms was a task that discouraged many. Government wisdom had suggested that leadership could be learned by 'going on a course', albeit an intricate and very extended one. After enrolling with the NCfL you'd spend hours on the internet solving hypothetical situations. You'd write essays and spend time with other prospective leaders, discussing budget management, the curriculum, staffing issues. And you'd have plenty of lectures from consultants, many of whom charged a pretty penny but might not have been near a classroom for years. For part of the route to headship, some schools were selected as training schools. Mine was one, and during the course of a year we accepted up to six people, so that hopefully I could show them, day by day, what headship was all about in an extremely practical fashion. This part of the essential 'hands on' training lasted for a mere fortnight.

Vast amounts of money were invested in creating this massive new training organisation, the worthy aim being to turn out higher quality leaders. But stories I constantly heard made me question whether schools were really getting better headteachers than they had all those years ago.

Andrew, for example, was a newly qualified class teacher appointed to a city comprehensive under a newly trained head. One morning, after being subjected to serious verbal abuse by one child, Andrew took the boy's arm and gently tried to lead him back to his seat. The boy grumbled, but complied. The next morning Andrew was summoned to the headteacher's room, where he found the boy, his parents, the headteacher, and a deputy head. The boy had complained that he'd been physically assaulted, and Andrew was asked to explain himself, and then suggest better ways he could have handled the situation. All this in front of the child... who was obviously thoroughly enjoying himself. Appalled and very angry, Andrew left the school shortly afterwards, and found a different career.

David also taught in a comprehensive with a newly trained head, but in a pleasant London suburb. None of his classroom windows opened properly, and there was no air conditioning. One stifling summer afternoon, he managed to wedge one window slightly open. With the door open as well, a draft of air blew through, to everybody's relief. At that moment, the new headteacher happened to walk in, asking why the door was open. David explained how desperate they were for cool air. 'That's hardly the point,' said the headteacher briskly. 'The governors tell me that the policy of the school is to have doors closed. Children are very quick to spot an open door.' And out she went, closing the door firmly behind her.

Karen wondered how she managed to obtain a teaching post so easily at a modern primary in a nice part of town. She soon discovered that the new headteacher's intolerant, autocratic attitude had caused a number of staff to hand in their resignations. One teacher, who had worked for many years at the school, upset the head by refusing to take on yet another curriculum workload for no additional money. She decided to leave, and asked for a reference. Apart from writing 'Mrs Derbyshire has worked here for sixteen years. She is punctual, and rarely absent,' the head put nothing else on the paper at all, putting the teacher's chances of finding another job in jeopardy. Karen appealed to the chair of governors… an ineffectual lady.. who simply said she'd have a word with the head, but there wasn't really much else she could do.

If asked who are the most important people in a school, most people would probably say 'the children'. But they aren't. The most important people are the staff, teaching *and* non-teaching. Because if they're not highly motivated and happy, then the children certainly won't be. And the quality of the headteacher and senior management is absolutely central to that motivation. Worryingly, we seemed to be entering the era of the Stepford leader… the automaton senior manager who adhered strictly to policy and procedure, the assumption being that by sticking to the 'rules' you won't get anything wrong.

As a new broom at my first staff meeting, I was challenged on much that I said by one staff member. It was dispiriting, and it would have been so easy just to pull rank. Instead, I smiled and said 'Look, we hardly know each other. You'll just have to give me a chance to prove myself.' In the event, the teacher proved to be a loyal, dedicated and indispensable member of staff. He was just very wary of the new headteacher coming in and messing everything up. Had I not been cautious at that first meeting… and shown a little humility…we could have been at war from the start.

And for a headteacher, being a people person is paramount. I'd thought I was, but I soon learned that it was very easy to make mistakes. Although I'd been appointed to the headship of a primary school, I had little knowledge of nursery, reception or infant children. All my experience had been with Key Stage 2 children, so I was grateful for the support I received from a highly capable teacher in the infant department. When she went into hospital for a minor operation, I decided to surprise her by ordering some modern storage furniture for her classroom. She was horrified when she came back to school, demanding to know who'd taken her beautiful old oak cupboards and table. I ate humble pie and she forgave me… but it made me realise how important it is to fully understand the personalities on your staff. Barging in and making lots of ill-considered changes to the running of the school is a quick route to raising universal resentment.

Anybody can pull rank and coerce, but that isn't leadership. Respect and trust must be earned. You have to prove that you can inspire your team of intelligent, professional people, and it is absolutely right that you should need to. Experience is the route to achieving this, not 'fast tracking' into leadership, or assuming that managing people means ordering them about.

There's nothing worse than aggressive headteachers who bulldoze their way through people's feelings in their never ending crusade to 'drive up standards.' During my career as a young class teacher, I met several headteachers who were arrogant, quite a few who seemed mildly incompetent and several who were more than a little eccentric. I worked for a couple of the latter variety. One of them came to school in jodhpurs on fine days and went off in the afternoon to ride his horse on Hampstead Heath. The second dealt with lost property by chucking some of it out of his office window, where it landed on the branches of a sturdy chestnut in the playground. The bits of clothing were removed on Fridays by the premises officer with a long window pole.

Although standards of leadership are generally higher today, at least these headteachers were relatively harmless, very odd though they were. They didn't run around frightening the staff, or make them sweat until the midnight hours compiling endless and often useless lists of tracking data. That seems to be what often happens today though, and an increasing number of teachers seem unhappy and disillusioned about it all, because they're not doing what they were employed to do… teach the children effectively.

I have never understood why so many headteachers feel that a bullying and over-assertive nature is required to get the best out of a teaching staff. Hierarchy seems to be everything… the headteachers lean on their deputies, who usually no longer teach, and they in turn lean on the school's middle managers. Middle managers lean on the poor bloody infantry, evaluating, scrutinising and monitoring everything they do. No wonder the annual turnover of teachers in some schools is so high, and so many suffer from burn out or leave the profession. They never get a chance to show what they can do without somebody looking over their shoulder every five minutes.

A while back at a conference, I watched with interest an extremely large lady who was obviously an aspiring school leader rapidly moving up the ranks and she wanted everybody to know it. 'Yes, I've got five people under me now,' she announced in a loud voice to the people around her during a coffee break. 'Wow,' said one of them, 'Five people under you? They must be bloody uncomfortable.'

In my thirty years of primary school headship, my senior leadership team consisted of me and my deputy. That was it. There were no other managers, just people responsible for aspects of the curriculum. When there were issues to discuss, develop or organise, we did it as a whole staff. The view of the newest newly qualified teacher was just as valid and important as the opinion of somebody who'd been at the school for twenty years. In this way, I reasoned, everybody would feel involved and valued, and the accent was on being positive about people, not battering them until their job became a miserable chore. Like me, my teachers thoroughly enjoyed coming to work, and standards didn't suffer in the slightest, because the staff were given the freedom to develop their individual styles and talents for helping the children achieve. How some aggressive headteachers can live with their consciences I've no idea, but I suppose there will always be people who get a kick out of bullying the people under them.

When the National College of School Leadership arrived, it was announced that the teaching force should consist of graduates with no less than a 2.2 degree. The finest teacher who taught me at secondary school and gave me a lifelong passion for books and literature had no degree at all. Both my wife and I struggled with maths at school and the struggle stood us in good stead when we became teachers, because we understood why children encountered difficulties with the subject. And I know a teaching assistant, who achieves excellent results with the children, without a single GCSE. So making sure every entrant into teaching had a top quality degree seemed a bit of a daft idea. But then, what initial criteria should you use when trying to decide who is suitable for teacher training, let alone headship, and who definitely isn't? Let's consider this for a moment.

There is, I think, something special about a person who is going to become a really effective teacher. There's an immediate charisma, a sense of humour, burning enthusiasm but a certain humility, a passion for learning, a love of being with young people. When I was considering a candidate for a teaching position at my school, I usually knew within ten minutes whether I was going to be interested. I rejected one candidate at the end of her interview, because when she was asked what her interests were outside work and what she could bring to the school, she replied 'Oh I don't really have any.'

During my headship, we took many students from a local university at our school for their first teaching practice, and I remember with pleasure one particular group. They were bright, alert, asked lots of relevant questions, and I probably sat talking to them for far too long. I felt they would all be very successful, but one stood out. She'd become disenchanted in another profession and felt that primary education might be her forte instead... and there was something about her that made me feel we might have found a gem. After a blindingly successful teaching practice, I told her I'd be phoning her in three years' time to offer her a job, never thinking that she'd still be available. But she was, and she stayed with me until I retired. She was one of the finest teachers I've ever worked with.

But although we had many first class students, we also had our share of those who should never have chosen teaching as a possible career. The poor lady who was terrified of talking to a class, the boring young man with no humour whatsoever and who was only doing the course because his parents had been teachers and he couldn't think of anything else to do, the woman who thought it was okay to plan her lessons on a scrap of paper the night before, the student who kept turning up just before the start of school because she had difficulty getting out of bed... and the rather unsavoury character who, when he found out I was a film buff, thought it was a good idea to offer me rip-off DVDs of recent movies.

Ultimately, though, you can't make a blanket rule and expect it to work all the time. As a young teaching deputy head, I remember being given a very timid student who was thinking of giving up and doing something else. Then I found out she'd had a dreadful previous experience at a chaotic school and once I'd bolstered her confidence she had a stunning practice and ultimately became a highly successful headteacher. Which proves it's all about far more than a few paper qualifications.

Just as climbing the ladder to headship became increasingly involved, so did the route to becoming a class teacher. In the distant days of the Beatles and Bobby Moore, I was pitched into a Year 3 class in Islington, north London, and the only advice I received had come from vague training college tutorials, where ancient lecturers gave us questionable advice, such as suggesting we kept our blackboard writing straight so that the children's heads didn't lean permanently over and give them neck ache. I survived, of course. I lived for the job and loved it, and I can still remember the names of the children in my first class.

Undoubtedly new teachers do need helpful advice and mentor support, but how ridiculous things suddenly became. One September, I was required to attend a day's course with my local education authority as there were new guidelines for working with newly qualified teachers. I assumed it would be a day of basic common sense. After all, I thought, if I'd just started my teaching career, I'd only need four things. I'd want the school to be very welcoming. I'd want the headteacher and senior managers to be accessible, I'd want a kindly experienced mentor who'd support me, encourage me, and offer a shoulder I could lean on if I needed it. And, most importantly, I'd want to be given the chance to get on with the job without spending hours recording data on the children that wasn't useful.

Because teachers didn't tend to leave our school, I hadn't realised that a sizeable industry had grown up around induction, composed mainly of paper. At the meeting, we were given huge folders, each one containing 170 pages. There were forms to fill in, lesson record sheets, action plan templates, review meeting records, tick charts, planning sheets, boxes for recording discussions with mentors… everything except guidance on what to do when Tommy says you're a miserable old bat and he ain't doin' no more writin'.

It seemed to me that you wouldn't have much time left for teaching if you tried to comply with every nutty rule and regulation. And, even if you did, there would be scores of people breathing down your neck with clipboards because, apparently, you had to be monitored by your mentor, senior managers and subject co-ordinators. Aghast, I asked the course leader how much of this folder was actually mandatory. Not much, it appeared. I had to send a short report to the induction co-ordinator every term, and if all was well then the NQT would be designated a real teacher. So why the 170 pages? Ah, well, what if the NQT was in danger of failing? He or she could appeal, and then you'd have to back up your case with mountains of evidence.

But surely, I said, if the NQT was walking on quicksand, wouldn't you want to assess your support over an extra probationary term? Nope. It seemed they either sank or swam in their first year, and if they sank they drowned. They couldn't get another teaching job in a state school. Ever. (But interestingly, they could apply for a job in a private school.)

Following the meeting, I sat down with my NQTs and the teachers who were going to look after them, and asked them what they wanted. They chose the four essentials I listed above, and they looked relieved that they weren't going to be asked to justify every move they made and write a dissertation on it. When I popped in on one of the teachers the following week, she was busy, happy, stress free and totally involved with the children. Which was fine, because that's exactly how it should have been. Shortly after that, I spoke to four new young teachers, all from different schools. All were developing into good classroom practitioners, but all felt under stress. I wouldn't have wanted any of them to leave the profession… they seemed too enthusiastic about their job… but if these people were feeling intense pressure, I wondered what must it be like for probationer teachers who were even less sure of themselves?

This thought returned when I read a newspaper feature about teachers and headteachers who become so emotionally broken they have a complete breakdown and have even, in the most distressing cases, taken their own lives. It made terrifying reading. That anybody in the profession should be so unhappy they commit suicide is frightening enough, but the article made us realise this is probably the extreme tip of the iceberg. Beneath that, hundreds of teachers struggle daily to keep their heads above water and cope with the increasingly difficult demands of the job.

Good senior management, therefore, is utterly crucial to the ethos, atmosphere and well-being of a school. As a headteacher, most of my administrative work was done at home and I always worked several hours in the evenings and much of Sundays. It wasn't great for family relationships, but my hours in school simply had to be reserved for the people working in it. Access to me, or my deputy, was always easy. Often, a teacher would want to discuss an idea, or a lesson, or a child, or a way of doing something that needed my full attention and enthusiasm. But just as often, a teacher or a teaching assistant, or perhaps somebody on the administrative staff, would want to share something in their lives they were finding upsetting or difficult to cope with. And this wouldn't necessarily be related to work. A school, after all, is really a society in miniature, and just like everybody else teachers go through difficult relationships, have money problems, experience trouble with their own children, and have illness and death in their families.

As I became increasingly experienced as a headteacher, I realised that although my principle job was to lead and inspire, my position also involved being a councillor, a friend, a confidante and a support for anybody who needed it. I gave as much of my time as was needed, but I was rewarded richly. People loved coming to work, and of course the children were the ones who benefited enormously. But I also remember experiencing the signs of stress myself, early in my headship, when I was working long hours and struggling with the many things that needed to be done to put the school on a steadily upward curve. I began to feel a vague sense of unease and a faint dizziness every day when I got to work, as if I was experiencing everything at a distance. I even went to the doctor, who checked everything and pronounced me well, but warned about the dangers of working too hard. I thought it impossible that I could suffer from stress… I loved the job too much…. but from that moment on I became a little more cautious.

For the class teacher today, the demands of the job can be overwhelming if not managed carefully. The threat of an impending Ofsted, ridiculous paperwork demands from senior management, constant meetings before and after school, intensive monitoring and an ever-changing curriculum all add their toll. And that's without mentioning the children… who can be more challenging and demanding than ever, so I feel much anxiety for today's teachers. I believe they are better than ever, but many are working under conditions that can easily burn them out. It's so important to recognise the signs… and act on them.

And it's amazing how rapidly perceived 'wisdom' for teaching changes so quickly. Rather like newspapers telling us that if we drink too much coffee it could give us cancer. Then we're told that no, it won't give us cancer and we can drink as much as we like, but if we're older, more than a couple of cups could give our bladders a bit of extra work. Another 'health' article told pregnant women they shouldn't drink much wine during pregnancy. Then they're suddenly told it's okay in moderation; in fact, it'll probably do them good. Every week there seems to be new 'research' telling us to do, or not do, something… only for it to be disproved some months later. I can even remember the advertisements that told us a packet of 'Craven A' cigarettes would be extremely good for sore throats and when vaping was introduced, well, we'd be okay, because vaping was quite different from smoking a cigarette…. advice which is now rapidly changing direction.

Education, of course, has always been a prime target for whacky philosophising. How many ways of teaching children to read can you recall? Look at phonics. In the eighties you didn't dare mention the word phonics if you wanted promotion. If you just surrounded children with 'real books' they'd learn to read. Then, a few years later, phonics was a word you didn't dare leave out in an interview for a job. Then it was out again. In out, in out. It was a sort of hokey cokey policy.

There are always plenty of 'experts' with theories about the way children learn. Which is no bad thing, of course, as we wouldn't make progress otherwise, but it's so important to sort the wheat from the chaff. As these people move further away from the classroom, it is easy for reality to become increasingly blurred. Nevertheless, when these people are on television it makes fascinating viewing, as in the programme I watched where a professor of education spent some time in a Hertfordshire secondary school, trying out some of his theories.

Our education system isn't working well enough, he started by saying, and that was fair comment, although the things he thought weren't working weren't necessarily those the average teacher would pick out. Firstly, since asking children to put their hands up if they know the answer to a question apparently favours the able, sets of lolly sticks were issued to the classes involved with the experiment. The teachers had to write the children's names on them, and then pick out sticks at random. This meant that shy Charlene, sitting quietly in the corner, could be pounced upon for the answer, or to discuss her work. God, I've have hated that at secondary school. Naturally, the children who did know the answers were miffed, because they often didn't get the chance to say anything at all. Teenagers being what they are, it wasn't too long before they were mucking around with the sticks… removing some, and even swapping others between classes.

Next up were coloured cardboard cones, and the idea was to use these to indicate whether or not you were understanding the lesson. This saved the undoubtedly arduous task of raising your hand. Put a green cone next to your maths book and you signalled to the teacher that you had no problems with your quadratic equations. Put out an orange cone and you understood some of the task but not all. A red one told the teacher you hadn't a clue. Bear in mind that at the start of the programme, the children were extremely well behaved and articulate, and the school was in a well-heeled borough. I know a teacher in a local secondary school who tried the cone approach. Some of the children put elastic on them and used them to create false red noses, and one boy put a green one down the front of his trousers, to the great amusement of everybody around him.

Feeling sure I'd seen this professor before, I hunted through some old files… and sure enough he'd done some work with teachers in our own education authority on assessment for learning. Conclusions were interesting. It seems that teachers should first establish where learners are in their learning, then establish where they are going, and then work out how they should get there. I might have missed it, but I wondered if his emporium of erudition was offering a Masters in the bleedin' obvious.

Sometimes, heads of Ofsted can make quite extraordinary comments about class teaching and headship. One of them continually captured headlines with his outspoken comments and I assumed his political masters must have been well pleased at the hounding he gave the teaching profession. On one occasion, he'd said that 5,000 headteachers were hopeless. So where did he get the evidence for this? From Ofsted statistics, of course And we all know how reliable they are.

It would be interesting, I thought, to know the ages of these hopeless headteachers. Were they all ancient and decrepit, avoiding children like the plague and gagging for early retirement? Were they appointed even before the National College of School Leadership was created at enormous expense to ensure the nation's children would be nurtured by leaders who'd been 'grown' by seminars, lectures and lots and lots of paperwork? (Interestingly, all the future leaders who spent time at my school as part of their course didn't have many kind words for the NCSL. They felt everything they needed to know could easily be gained from shadowing good experienced headteachers running successful schools, which fortunately is what seems to be happening now.) And what did that leader of Ofsted mean by a 'good' headteacher? Judging by other comments he made, I assumed he meant somebody who 'gets results'.. in the form of a full complement of Level 4 passes at primary school, and the right GCSEs at secondary. In terms of what education should really be all about these days, this seemed a bit short-sighted to me.

When my first grandchild was about to be born, I wanted him to come home from his early days at school and run up to his parents filled with excitement and anticipation. As he moved through primary school, I hoped that he'd be introduced to an extremely rich range of experiences. He'd paint, craft, read, write, explore, experiment, act, socialise, learn to swim and play music, as well as relishing the excitement of rapidly changing technology. Above all, I hoped he'd become a happy, well-rounded young person who quickly cultivated a life-long love of learning and friendship. If he did all those things, I reasoned, he would have been led into learning by happy, strongly motivated teachers who enjoyed each other's company, wanted the very best for their children, and who were able to deliver exciting and interesting lessons, because they were lively and interesting people themselves.

The best headteachers aren't merely efficient managers who jump children and teachers through hoops. They are people who are fascinated by the process of education and they've grown through practical experience in the profession, leading them to really understand what young people are about and how they can be richly motivated. Of course, it was Ofsted inspectors who gave their leader those damning statistics about headteachers. Which should, I felt, have been taken with a large pinch of salt, because of the twenty three Ofsted inspectors who spent time in my school over the years, only two would have made the short list for teaching in my school.

Nevertheless, I'm always surprised by primary headteachers who choose not to teach any more. After all, they must have started in the classroom, and if they disliked the job, presumably they'd have left to become chartered accountants or something. It's as if, having reached the elevated position of headship, they never feel the urge to teach again. The less they teach, the less they want to, until the point is reached where any excuse is trotted out to avoid contact with children. I even spoke to a headteacher at a conference who maintained it wasn't really necessary to have been a teacher at all, because the job was now exactly the same as managing and running a business.

There are always a number of common excuses, such as 'Sorry, I'm snowed under with paperwork.' Of course, the pile of mail each morning can be large, but much of it can go in that finest filing cabinet of all, the waste paper recycling bin, especially the stuff addressed to 'the managing director' or 'the chief buyer', from firms who don't seem to understand what a school actually is and are just chancing their luck. Other mail will be from the Department for Education, or the local authority, often a questionnaire thought up by some bright spark with a couple of hours to kill before popping out for his lunch, or a demand for the latest ethnic codes on the computerised pupil returns, now running to a total of 8,243 and could you input them all by Friday please. A shrewd head can whizz through the post in minutes. Or give it to the office staff.

Another favourite is 'Sorry, I've got to rush off to an important meeting today.' These heads are rarely in school. In fact, their schools are often falling apart while they're attending meetings about driving up standards. They attend every possible cluster meeting, working party or steering committee, and have a great deal to say because they are practised at Parkinson's Law tactics…. making sure nothing is resolved because the meeting can then spawn further meetings. Courses are even better, particularly if it's a three-day jaunt at a seaside hotel, paid for out of a professional development fund, to listen to an obscure expert expounding on balancing perspectives in the divergent curriculum. When they return to school, any chaos can be blamed on the deputy and other senior managers. After all, they've got to practise for headship, haven't they?

Or there'll be 'Sorry, I have to finish the behaviour policy. The school governors are demanding it ASAP.' This is the typist head. The one who sits at his or her computer all day producing endless documentation for staff to read. It's all written at great length and, yes, I'd love to see a child but I simply haven't time. You can't get in to see this head. Parents have to book appointments many days ahead. I've even known a typist head who had a light outside her room which would change from green to red. If you knocked when it was red, you'd had it as far as promotion was concerned, and it only went green at 10.45am, when it was time for a helper to wheel in coffee and a jammy dodger or two.

'Sorry, I've got important visitors,' is a well-worn excuse. Schools often have visitors, ranging from the attendance officer or prospective parent, to a school governor or a local authority inspector. Local authority inspectors are particularly useful visitors because you can keep them chatting for ages and no one will come anywhere near you.

It seems to me that headteachers who retreat from the chalkface are missing out on the real pleasure of the job. Throughout my headship, I always considered my contact with children essential, and I wouldn't have missed my poetry session with Year 6, my jazz guitar group, my summer play production or Thursdays with the choir for anything. And I still managed to get the important administration stuff done on time.

I was browsing the adverts for primary school headships recently, simply because it's interesting to see what schools ask for in their leaders these days. My eye was drawn to one advertisement in particular, because I happened to know the school was in trouble. The governors had done a good job selling its positive attributes, although reading between the lines it was obvious there was a lot of work to be done. Rather like writing a reference, what you leave out is just as important as what you put in. But then I looked at the list of documents that made up the application pack, and one title intrigued me so much I couldn't resist downloading it.

If anything was guaranteed to put a prospective applicant off, this, surely, was it. Twenty pages long, it was a plan for raising standards at the school, and had obviously been compiled by some sort of audit team who presumably thought it might be a helpful way to attract candidates. Every page was a tedious mass of data, percentages and targets, all wrapped in the eduspeak jargon that these strange people thrive on and which drives saner headteachers absolutely nuts.

I tried to fathom the wealth of acronyms. EYFS... yep, that's Early Years Foundation Stage, and I was fine on KS1 and KS2... which mean Infants and Juniors, but CLL, ARE, PSRN and PSED? Perhaps, I thought, it was just a form of text speak, and my fault for not keeping up. But what on earth was a RAP... unless it was one across the knuckles for whoever wrote the stuff. Delving further, I learned that it was a 'Raising Attainment Plan.'

Did the person who compiled this RAP document work for SMERSH, I wondered, because the more I tried to decipher, the more I realised I might need Rosa Klebb's Lektor to translate all twenty pages. Maybe trainee headteachers have riveting lectures that teach them how to handle this foreign language when they're on the route to headship? Or, God forbid, perhaps some of them actually enjoy it.

If you were taking over a school in difficulties, I wondered, would you really need to know all this? Wouldn't you want to get the staff together and offer strong, friendly and above all supportive leadership? Wouldn't you want to enthuse, excite, and bring out the very best in them? Wouldn't you want to get the parents together and tell them that things were changing but you'd be depending on their help and support too? And having got the staff on-side, wouldn't you want to make your classrooms into environments children were excited to experience... because all young children love learning and it really isn't that hard to fire their enthusiasm and passion. And none of that involves saying to a teacher 'Sorry Mrs Jenkins, your percentiles are all over the place and 0.45 down on your last predicted quadrant percentages, so pull your socks up because every level 4 not achieved is a blot on my CV and you'll be up for a raising attainment review.'

As I came close to retiring, my school began the process of finding a new headteacher. We had to advertise several times, because in today's climate headship is ever more demanding and test driven, and people who can't cope are swiftly made aware they should think of moving on. Simply winning a headship today demands the successful navigation of a variety of tasks and courses. And then, when you've found a school you like, you'll need to negotiate and pass the tasks set by the governing body... usually once the incumbent head and staff have subjected you to a grilling after innocently inviting you for coffee, cucumber and cress sandwiches, a bit of cake and then a guided tour of the school.

In our case, the governors set the shortlisted candidates some rigorous tasks. Firstly, three written questions, where a computer couldn't be used, so no chance of a grammar or spellcheck flagging up mistakes. One question was very testing... imagine a classroom ceiling is being repaired by a tradesman who turns out to be unapproved and some plasterwork falls down and badly bruises a child's head. The parents want to know what's going on, the LEA is breathing heavily down on you, and the press has just been alerted. Write a letter to the parents allaying their fears...

Next, the candidates had to organise and present a morning assembly for an audience of classes from both key stages. Although there was comfort in the fact that they could choose any theme, maintaining the interest of different age groups was the tricky bit. Then, the candidates had to teach an hour's lesson to a Year 5 class, following up their assembly theme. Very few schools now saw this as part of their appointing procedure, because headship was seen solely as a management role, with no teaching involved. But if you're not a first class teacher yourself, how can you possibly lead a staff effectively, or gain their respect, without an intimate knowledge of what the job entails? Then, the final hurdle... the interview with a hand-picked selection of governors, prefaced by a presentation from the candidate about their vision for the school; what did they feel primary education was all about? What could they bring to the school? How could they build on an already very successful primary school and what would it look like in a year's time...

Although I played no part in the interviewing or task-setting process, my role was crucial. I invited every applicant to spend a morning with us. I took them around the school, answered their questions, visited every classroom and introduced them to lots of children. Interestingly, it was easy to spot the people I guessed wouldn't make the short list; the person who didn't smile at all, the lady who rattled off all the things she had done in her career and barely seemed to look at the school, the one who told me how he'd moved a school from mediocre to outstanding by 'moving on' lots of teachers...

And then, finally, we were down to two, both of whom stayed the course and both highly capable. I've no idea what swung the interview, but, asked about his vision for the school, it could have been the photo one candidate showed the panel. Of a baby, and some bathwater....

3

IS CHARLIE JUST BEING... NAUGHTY?

Children's Behaviour In School

Perhaps it's just my age, but it seems you can't watch an adult film these days, on television or at the cinema, without everybody saying fuck every ten seconds.

I remember the first time I heard it in a film and, yes, it was 18 rated ('X' certificate in those days). It was used only once, which is why it had particular force, but the audience sat up in astonishment, and then laughed nervously because we all realised another boundary had just been crossed. I also remember when Kenneth Tynan, a theatre critic with a highly regarded opinion of himself, first used the word 'fuck' on black and white television. It was during a late night interview on a programme with a relatively small audience, but the next day the newspapers had a field day. Tynan's point was that it was a word. Just a word. And quite a forceful one in the right context, so why get upset about it? The thing is, people *did* get upset about it, and it isn't a particularly pleasant word anyway.

Nowadays, a certificate 18 film isn't a proper 18 unless it's peppered with fucks, and I pine for the days when you could watch a strong adult drama without much of the dialogue being given over to one word. Was the strength of the dialogue years ago diminished because nobody said fuck? Of course it wasn't. I don't recall Beckett, Pinter, Sillitoe, Albee, Tennessee Williams et al, or even Jimmy

Porter in his wildest moments cursing about those church bells, using it.

Nevertheless, I suppose it's a gift for the screenwriter. After all, you only have to write half as much dialogue. The rest can be filled in with fucks. 'Where did I put my car keys?' simply becomes 'Where the fuck did I put my fucking car keys?' Taken to its logical conclusion, it shouldn't be long before Daddy Bear may well be asking who the fuck has been eating his fucking porridge. After all, we've already had books entitled *'Go The Fuck To Sleep'* and *'You Have To Fucking Eat'*.

When my eldest daughter was studying drama in the sixth form, I remember going to an evening show put on by the students. They'd taken a current news theme, and split into groups to dramatize situations around it. Part of it was scripted, the rest improvised. The fresh-faced youngster introducing the event said: 'I'm afraid we're likely to be using the f-word tonight.' There was a whisper of inevitable, resigned acceptance from the audience of parents. I wanted to shout out 'Why?', and I still wanted to shout it out after the performance.

Fortunately, my school playground was never a hotbed of profanity because the children knew how strongly we felt about it. But towards the end of my headship it was obvious things were changing. The early morning playground began to suffer from it, possibly because the children didn't think I'd arrived at school yet, or that sound didn't travel up to my window. The playground supervisors at lunchtime were subjected to most of it, particularly during a heated game of football, whereas the children did at least hesitate at morning playtime if a teacher was within earshot.

But then, can you blame them? Many of their parents swore a great deal, often at them. And just as the children watched their football idols spit on the grass, so they spat on the playground floor in emulation. Switch on the telly after the so called watershed and the language in most dramas is likely to have a fuck or two, or worse, somewhere along the line. It is accepted now as part and parcel of being 'adult drama' or humour. Watch a few *'Nights At The Apollo'* and you breathe a sigh of relief when a genuinely funny and inventive comedian comes on who doesn't resort to either insulting the audience or dipping into his barrel of bad language. And it's not only used by adults. Last night I watched a film where a very young child stood gazing around at the richness of an ornate room and said 'Wow! Fuck me!' It wasn't funny and it certainly wasn't necessary or appropriate.

These days, how many children are actually in bed by the watershed anyway? Most of them have TVs and other screens in their rooms and there are plenty of parents who couldn't care less what their children watch. I'm certainly not advocating our children exist on a diet of Sunnyside Farm... God forbid... and some of Pete and Dud's Derek and Clive dialogues amused me greatly. But sometimes when I settle into my cinema seat and a stream of invective hits the screen in the first two minutes, even one fuck seems a fuck too many.

But far worse, as I write this, the midday news tells of another teenager stabbed to death. Three this month already. It's what all parents dread and they do everything possible to shield their children. They drive them to school, ring their friends if they're later home than they'd promised, ensure they carry their mobiles, carefully concealed, so that they can locate them easily. Grandparents remember the freedom of their youth and wonder how we could possibly have come to this. In reality, we know. Feckless fathers siring youngsters and casually moving on; bored teenagers with little to occupy them seeking more extreme highs; parents and teachers unable to control poor behaviour, the disappearance of the extended family, children constantly aware of their 'rights', a materialistic and highly manipulative society, easy access to dubious media material, children questioning their sexuality, parents worried about whether their child has some sort of syndrome or special need... so many reasons, but you know them already.

And there are the buzzwords. Challenging. Difficult. Has anger management issues. Needs handling with patience. Finds it difficult to settle. Argumentative. Physically demanding. Words and phrases that schools use when talking about children who are a problem in the classroom. Notice they are never labelled as disobedient or badly behaved. There always has to be an explanatory reason.

Of course, some things have changed dramatically. Now, most teachers go out of their way to deliver exciting and stimulating lessons, but the behaviour and abuse they are subjected to from a minority of young people has to be seen to be believed. Watching documentary programmes set in school makes me wonder when we decided that teachers should be required to tolerate vile language, deliberate and aggressive classroom disruption, and occasionally serious physical abuse simply because a child has 'anger management issues'. School should be a place of harmony and safety, both for pupils and those who teach them.

A recent head of Ofsted said it was the job of a headteacher to provide strong leadership on disciplinary matters, and he was right. But far too many headteachers and senior managers deliberately squirrel themselves away in their offices. Low-level disruption needs to be dealt with firmly and quickly, and teachers need to know they have the support of their headteacher and their senior managers. I recently read a book by a teacher, a very brave soul, who gave up his comfy job at a grammar school because he wanted something more demanding. So he travelled the country, supply teaching in inner-city schools. Some of the behaviour he described was horrific, but one institution was a haven of calm. Why? Because the wise and experienced headteacher, much loved by staff and children and an inspirational teacher himself, was constantly visible and always accessible. Problems were addressed immediately and poor behaviour was rare. Headteacher: It seems to me that the clue is in the name.

Behaviour in schools is a very hot current topic. Steam comes out of my ears when I hear privately educated politicians talking nonsense about state education, children's behaviour and coarsening language. In a recent radio debate, a politician raised the topic of the Pisa (the Programme for International Student Assessment) tables yet again.

'We simply can't afford to stay low in the tables,' he said. 'Standards must be raised, and if other countries can do it, then so can we.' Fortunately, a university lecturer on the panel pointed out that some countries at the top of the tables had unacceptable levels of aggressive competition, causing them to have the highest child suicide rates. But what was not mentioned was the increasingly serious and challenging language and behaviour that teachers in this country's state schools face.

So I'm always pleased when good documentaries about schools appear on television and highlight this. On BBC Three's *Tough Young Teachers*, we followed a group of new teachers who had received their initial training and were now in secondary schools. They were committed and enthusiastic, their lessons carefully designed to engage their students. All of them said they worked incredibly long hours. 'I wouldn't have believed,' said one, 'just how long it takes to mark one book.' Then we watched, in agony, as a female trainee tried to keep order in her class. A chair was kicked around, missiles were fired from elastic bands, objects were hurled, and some children were rude and belligerent. 'I don't understand it,' says another trainee. 'They just seem to want confrontation with you. And it's so awful for the children who do want to work. They know we've just started our careers, but even so...' One child, returning to mainstream school from a pupil referral unit, is especially difficult. 'Your lessons are boring me, Man,' he says, obviously having trouble with a bit of gender recognition, 'I don't need school. I can get any job I want.'

And what solution is offered? The child is invited to sit down with the trainee in a one-to-one session, so that they can 'work out their differences.' Watching the programme, I wondered how we'd got to the point where a stroppy thirteen year old is considered the teacher's equal? In a brief interview with a trainee's parents, her father says: 'My daughter's heart was set on teaching, but I hate seeing her abused by these unruly children.' Teachers want to be able to teach, but without high quality, supportive leadership, what chance do they have? No wonder so many leave now, burned out, after just a few years in the profession. But at least some of the trainees were beginning to enjoy what they were doing, and showed a steely determination to get on top of their classes. Unlike Clare. So please draw your chairs closer to the fire because we're going to enter the realm of horror stories.

When I employed Clare she proved herself a talented, dedicated teacher. After three years she wanted to travel, but she was a teacher through and through, and I guessed it wouldn't be long before she was back in a classroom again. When she returned, I didn't have a vacancy for her, so she enlisted with a supply agency and her first assignment was a day with a Year 5 class in a leafy suburb. She was directed to a hut, cut off from the main school. Surprised to find she had to shout to be heard, the child assigned as 'behaviour monitor' told her that misbehaving children had to write their names in a box on the board. The child then had ten minutes to improve, whereupon their name would be removed. Unfortunately, she wasn't told what would happen if the behaviour didn't improve.

Warren, a large boy, began to fool about. Clare asked him to put his name in the box, and he refused. She asked again. He stood up, kicked his chair, and swaggered to the front, deliberately knocking books off a display. He stared at Clare, wandered into the cloakroom area, banged the door, and then made faces through the window.

Other children now began to show off, too. Clare scribbled a note to the headteacher, asking Andrea to take it quickly. She didn't even reach the door. Warren came in, leapt in front of her, and shoved her back. Unnerved, Clare ordered him to sit down. Still punching Andrea, Warren walked up to Clare and screamed 'No!' in her face. Then he turned and started fighting two other children, saying he would only sit down if Clare didn't send a message to the head. She told him she did not bargain, and was here to teach, not referee. Warren knew that Clare was a supply teacher and that she had no way of getting help. Again she tried. Immediately, Warren jumped on the child she tried to send. During the commotion, the classroom assistant was able to run to the office, but there was nobody of any seniority available.

Eventually, the regular class teacher arrived back for lunch from the course she was attending, and reluctantly told Clare she'd try to sort out the problem using some calming techniques she often used. She managed to lower the noise level, and asked the children to explore their anger and examine their feelings. Warren raised his hand and asked the class teacher if he could have a bag of pins, explaining that he wanted 'to stick 'em in the kids he didn't like'. The class teacher urged Clare to stay, so that she could return to her course, and after four children had been removed by a reluctant deputy head, Clare managed to stagger through the day. The experience haunted her for weeks, but some teachers now experience this on a daily basis. It is no longer exceptional. These children were 10-year-olds, and reaching the end of what should have been an enjoyable chunk of their education. It seems appalling that some children can be so uncontrollable at such a tender age. What chance has the secondary school receiving these children got? Precious little, I suppose, except to expel them. And that solves nothing at all.

Often, after the latest outburst of teenage public disorder, schools are targeted. They should do more to counter racism. Or bullying. Or sexism. Or aggressive behaviour. But we won't even have approached the heart of the matter, that we're often frightened to discipline our children. If we do, there's even the possibility of social workers calling.

As a headteacher, I had policy documents coming out of my ears. Schools have to write one for everything, because 'following procedure' avoids trouble from parents, newspapers, the media in general and the local education authority. Following procedure takes time… during which the child becomes more unruly. Eventually, when nothing has changed, everybody sighs with relief because the child is excluded, goes off to secondary school or the family relocates. It certainly can't be called problem solving.

Back in the last century, I grew up like most children. Usually well behaved. Occasionally naughty, a word we rarely use these days. I was also a challenging child for some of my teachers at secondary school, but at least I felt I had a legitimate excuse. Most of them were old and tired, they didn't seem to like children very much and very few bothered to create interesting lessons. The headteacher was hardly ever seen, and if he did enter your classroom, kitted out in mortar board and black gown, you were required to stand up instantly, presumably as a mark of respect for his position in the school hierarchy. Then he simply waved you back into your seat. Ridiculous. My French teacher sat on her desk filing her nails while she delivered lists of French verbs to us, my metalwork teacher got out his cane if you spoke in his lessons, my maths master ridiculed any child who couldn't keep up, and my geography teacher was so boring I went to sleep in his lesson one hot summer afternoon and fell off my chair. So I tended to muck about. Nothing major in those days, although my parents would have been furious at even the slightest hint of school naughtiness…but enough to let teachers know they were messing with the education I had an absolute right to.

This was back in the fifties, when parents in our street would often wallop their children with a stick and caning at school was an accepted fact of life, but I only remember my mother smacking me on two occasions. Both, such as the time I caused an elderly neighbour to jump out of her skin when I lit a firework behind her, or the time when my classmate Clive and I decided it might be a bit of fun to set light to the pile of empty wooden fruit crates at the back of Sainsbury's, were well deserved. I think I grew up to be a reasonably well-adjusted adult.

But these days, it's difficult to comprehend the lunatic lengths we go to when a child does something wrong. And even then, we often think there is no such thing as a child simply being naughty. There has to be a reason. The child has an awful home background. The child has some sort of syndrome. (the worst I heard was WSA…

workshy addiction) It's the teacher's fault. It's the school's fault. It's society's fault. Well, often it is, but the stark reality was brought home to me by a letter a colleague showed me recently. It was going to be sent to Kim's parents. Kim was just twelve years old, but she was just about to be permanently excluded from her secondary school.

The school had gone to extraordinary lengths to avoid this and had finally run out of ideas. Her primary school had been going through a very difficult patch with several changes of senior leadership, and there was no line in the sand over which you did not cross. Like several children, Kim quickly took full advantage of this. When she reached secondary school and found challenging her teachers a lot of fun, Kim had been placed on 'daily report', initially to her form tutor and then to the head of year. Later, several pastoral plans had been developed for her. They hadn't worked. Then, mentoring and counselling from an external clinical psychologist. That hadn't worked either, so a consultant had organised a special routine to help her when she encountered difficulties during lessons. One of these, incredibly, involved providing Kim with a cassette recorder, on which a bleep was recorded every ten minutes. When it sounded, Kim was supposed to check whether she was on task. The psychologist presumably walked away with his cheque without giving any guarantees, because Kim's behaviour simply worsened.

She spent some time in a special referral unit, and then the school tried to re-integrate her with the help of an independent behaviour advisor. Kim and her despairing parents signed a 'behaviour agreement'. No change, so the school devised a unique support plan, with a local education authority representative being called in to agree it. Unfortunately, none of these strategies were successful, and Kim continued to be insolent, defiant, and aggressive. In desperation one morning, a teacher asked Kim if she could simply go to her class and stop shouting in the corridor. Kim became even louder, calling to her mates to watch her. She took a large carton of orange juice from her bag and hurled it with extreme force at the opposite wall, causing the contents to shower over everybody. Then she threatened to beat up anybody who came near her.

Despite this appalling behaviour, 'procedure' had to be followed. A meeting with the governing body, and a checklist of criteria to be discussed before any action could be taken. Had there been appropriate early intervention? Was the child responding to provocation, bullying, racial or sexual harassment? Had achievements (dear God!) been rewarded? And on it went. If any of these criteria hadn't been followed, Kim's parents could have had a field day, although in fact all they wanted was for their daughter to behave in school. And then, of course, the child's rights. If, for example, the parents thought that the exclusion related to a disability Kim had, then they could consider whether 'disability discrimination' had taken place, and take appropriate action against the school. Consider the cost of all this. Not just in money, but in teacher hours, form filling, letter writing and stress for everybody concerned. It's a wonder there was any time left for the children who did want to learn.

And I've just read about a policeman who was trying to stop teenagers wrecking public property. When he received a torrent of verbal abuse from one of them he lost his temper and forcibly manhandled him. It was a moment of rashness that almost cost him his job. Teachers will sympathise and every teacher will have more than a few tales of children they struggled with. There must be many young teachers who look out of their classroom windows to see if Billy is on the way to school. He always is, because Billy is never away, and Billy demands a great deal of attention.

Even in a school where good behaviour is insisted upon and there are clear guidelines, occasionally a teacher will step over the line, and then the headteacher has to decide what to do about it. I remember a particularly difficult eight-year-old who had transferred to our school. His mother was a tall, intimidating lady, and the child's previous teachers had been very cautious about approaching her, so Curtis had got away with many things that other children wouldn't have. We weren't having any of that. One day, Curtis had spent much of the afternoon with me. Instead of going back to his classroom at home time, he wandered into the hall, where a play was being rehearsed. He began to fool about, interrupting the performance. The teacher put up with this for a while, and then in frustration guided him firmly into the corridor. Like a footballer falling to the ground from a mild challenge, the boy deliberately fell over, banged his shoulder against the wall, and feigned tears, pretending the teacher had punched him in the back.

Frightened because there had been no witnesses, the teacher assumed his career would shortly be in tatters. He informed me about the incident immediately after school and, true to form, mother appeared at my door, accompanied by Granny. The mother was livid. A teacher had assaulted her son and she was going to the police as soon as she had finished with me. What's more, she said, the law demanded that I suspend the teacher immediately, and she would accompany me to his classroom to witness me doing just that. It occurred to me that she was probably right, but I told her firmly that I had absolutely no intention of suspending the teacher, and that if her child wasn't such a thorough nuisance we wouldn't be in this predicament. For a moment, I thought both mother and Granny intended to attack me, but then they thought better of it and strode off down the corridor. I have no idea whether they talked to the police, but since the pair of them were well known to the lads in blue I suspect they hadn't dared. Nevertheless, the teacher spent the next fortnight in a state of nervous tension, fully expecting the law to turn up at any moment.

It's a sad fact of life that young teachers coming into the profession now *expect* to be frequently challenged, and, of course, respect has to be earned. If you're a boring person there's no way you'll become a good teacher, and nor should you be. It's also natural for young teachers to want to be friendly and liked. But there is a danger in that, because teachers need to be both liked and respected.

One young teacher who joined my school was creative and inspiring, and she wanted to start her career with a Year 6 class, because that was the year group she'd had with us on teaching practice, but she didn't fully understand the sheer skill of the class teacher she'd been placed with. And although she listened to my advice, she also wanted to be a friend to the children. She reasoned that if she chatted with the most challenging ones at playtime, she would 'win them over.' And then she couldn't understand why they weren't perfectly behaved when they were back with their mates after play. By her second year, however, she had learned from her mistakes. She knew what she wanted and her next class wasn't given a moment to waste. Gradually, she cultivated a class of lively, responsible young people. They knew and understood the boundaries… which all children need and want, and they had total respect for her. By year three she was stunning. She'd learned that it pays to say "Don't do that!" and really mean it.

There will always be constant dialogue with parents of challenging children; letters on file, telephone calls, sleepless nights for the teachers and plenty of 'experts' called in to suggest remedies for the various syndromes students may have. And in the end, in desperation, some schools have to resort to exclusion. But exclusion is no solution at all. In dealing with poor behaviour, we seem to have lurched from one extreme to the other over the years. And sometimes, I fear, actually solved very little.

Of course, troubled children and families require considerable support. Not just from schools, but from a range of agencies, and this can include social services, the police, the educational psychological service, behaviour advisors, and medical services. There will often be a 'team around the child' meeting, where everybody, parents included, sits round a table and discusses the difficulties the child is experiencing. Notes will be compared, each agency will be listened to, and then decisions will be taken about possible ways forward. It sounds promising. In reality, of course, some people won't be able to attend the meeting, others won't have received the notes from the previous meeting, a few will have forgotten to write their notes up, and the meeting itself will ramble round in circles because people don't have enough information to make effective decisions. A new date is made and the cycle repeats itself.

An innovation called the CAF, or Common Assessment Form, initially seemed a good idea, and most education authorities used a form of it. The CAF would be available, confidentially, to everyone involved with the case. They would be able to access the form on line, put their notes on it, get up to speed with everything everybody else had written, and be fully up to date by the time a team meeting was called. The original CAF was commendably brief, and didn't take long to complete. But whoever invented the form would have been quickly weeping into their beer. The CAF changed. And changed again. It grew longer every time, until it eventually reached...wait for it... version fifteen.

This version started with a page of notes telling you what the form was for, who could fill it in, and what it couldn't be used for. All fair enough. Then we got to page two, there were twenty boxes to be completed about the child *and* the unlucky soul having to fill it in, ranging from their immigration status to whether they've been checked by the Criminal Records Bureau. Next a page asking for family composition, with fifteen questions and a note asking whether an interpreter will be required, followed by a long section requesting details of all the agencies and services involved with the child and what they had done thus far.

By the time you'd hit page five and worked your way onwards you realised it was a good thing you'd achieved a decent GCSE in English because there were large blank boxes needing vast amounts of information. Then back to the tick boxes and the endless demands for personal information.... is the child a traveller of Gypsy, Roma or Irish heritage, are they white, black, white and black Caribbean, black and white African, black African and so on, through another twenty permutations.

When I'd reached page eighteen of my first CAF, version fifteen, I'd begun to wonder if this was all a plot. Make the form complicated enough, and nobody would bother to fill it in. If nobody filled it in children wouldn't be referred. If children weren't referred, everybody could pretend there wasn't a problem. At my school the Special Needs Co-ordinator, (SENCo) dutifully completed the CAFs, but when I talked to her about Version 15 she was scathing, saying it had grown out of all proportion and if she wasn't careful all her time could easily be used up just doing paperwork and never interacting with a child. And these days, it seems to be exactly what has happened. What a shame that such a initially sensible idea, like so many others, has ultimately reached the bureaucratic graveyard.

My long headship was spent in an exceptionally tough area of London, with huge social deprivation, but it was a happy, settled school. It took a while to achieve, we constantly worked hard at it, and we certainly had our hairy moments. But the children were constantly reminded of one simple rule: in a civilised, safe school there's room for lots of individuality, but not at the expense of others. If teachers experienced behavioural difficulty with children, my door was open and I was always available to help. I knew I wasn't seen as an ogre, but the buck had to stop with me, and good behaviour had to be insisted upon in the very earliest years.

We didn't spend hours listening to Damien explaining why he felt it necessary to thump Charlie, we didn't give good behaviour certificates, we didn't offer 'anger management' or make contracts with children. They were simply *expected* to behave... and like all children, they responded to a secure, highly enjoyable environment with lots of exciting things to do, exceptionally clear boundaries and dedicated, interesting teachers.

We wrote a behaviour policy, because we had to, but nobody ever read it. You could feel our policy when you walked into the school. Children and teachers smiled at you warmly. If students on teaching practice asked for my written discipline policy, I would tell them to come back in a week… because by then they'd be in no doubt what our policy was without needing to read a thing. And a child's primary school years are so important. We need children to become responsible social creatures right from the start, because the social aspect is increasingly the most vital aspect of being at school. And we have to insist that parents back us up, taking full responsibility for their children too. If we can't succeed before the child goes to secondary school, it'll already be too late.

Perhaps one of the most important steps is to train senior management to be 'hands-on' leaders, not people who hide in barricaded rooms under piles of paperwork. After watching a Channel 4 programme about badly behaved primary school children, I thought for quite a long time about the statistics it gave. They were certainly depressing; the programme makers had carried out a massive survey of primary teachers and a staggering 93% of them said they had experienced disruptive behaviour in their classrooms during the last eighteen months. And the programme became more jaw-dropping by the minute. We were taken to a primary school where three adults… yes three… were shown restraining a child and carrying him to a room where he could calm down. I'm amazed the school let the cameras in. The room, like a large prison cell, was devoid of furniture or equipment, in case children escorted there kicked it to bits. As the child was carried, he made the expected gestures of struggling to get away and telling his captors to fuck off. Then he stood kicking the door while being told it would be helpful if he made some 'sensible choices' about his behaviour. The programme concluded by stating that aggressive behaviour like this could be avoided if there was funding for nurture groups in schools.

When children are extremely disruptive, there is almost always a reason, and it is usually obvious with a little investigation. It may be a syndrome the child has which needs sympathetically addressing. One child, for example, had a mother with a serious drink problem. Another came from a chaotic home where various 'uncles' were visiting a single mum. And yet here were teachers asking a child who'd experienced little sense of normality to make 'sensible choices.' Watching the programme, it struck me that in every example we saw, the child was in charge. At no time did an adult challenge the poor behaviour, or try to get to the root of it. It was all about the child's options and 'choices'.

In my first term as a headteacher, the behaviour of my top juniors was grim and the class teacher really wasn't interested, usually arriving just as school was starting and leaving as quickly as she could. We weren't going to be able to work successfully together and fortunately she decided to take early retirement, but I needed to sort things out quickly. Younger children look up to the older ones, so I spent every Tuesday teaching Year 6. They had individual wooden desks in those days, and on the first Tuesday they deliberately banged their desk lids every time they lifted them to gauge my reaction. I'd been expecting something like this… so I put on a theatrical display of losing my temper. They certainly sat up and took notice. From that moment on, I didn't give them an inch. And fairly quickly, they discovered that I cared about their progress, and that my lessons might actually be worth listening to.

At my school, the biggest difficulties occurred with children who transferred to us from schools that tolerated poor levels of behaviour, excusing it with a fancy psychological label, or not doing anything about it until it became a real problem. It's only a small step from there to the behaviour shown in the programme I watched. The vision of three adults carting a small child off down the corridor stayed with me for a long time.

Good behaviour starts in the very earliest years. I was always firm with small children who misbehaved. However young, they, too, are testing the water to see what you'll accept. If teachers, or parents, don't try to get things right when children are very small, they won't have much of a chance later on. There's a wonderful line in the film *Aliens*, where futuristic soldiers are up against deadly acid-bloodied creatures and they are told to be cautious with their firepower. 'What exactly are we supposed to use, then?' asks one, 'harsh language?'

I was reminded of this when teenage stabbings began to become more frequent, and the front page of a daily newspaper suggested that police knife searches in school should become routine. Some months before that, the same newspaper told us about a primary school headteacher called in front of the General Teaching Council's disciplinary panel because, among other things, she had removed the shoes of children who repeatedly kicked other children. These pieces of news were obviously quite separate from each other, but it struck me that they are actually inextricably linked.

Although during its tenure the GTC did very little for the teaching profession apart from gather mandatory subscriptions from teachers, the function of its disciplinary council was very clear indeed, even if for the life of me I could never understand why disciplinary matters couldn't be dealt with at local level by a school, its governors, or the local education authority. In this particular case, there was a witness who said the boys whose shoes had been removed were 'very embarrassed.' Then the chair of the committee said, incredibly, that removing the shoes was a practice that 'could lead to children being demeaned.' I could hardly believe what I was reading. Wasn't that the purpose of removing the shoes? Weren't the children *supposed* to be embarrassed? Wasn't the idea to deter them from doing it again? And how did the children who had been kicked feel? Weren't they… and their parents… entitled to feel that something had been done?

Of course, the headteacher had a number of options. She could indeed have used harsh language. Or asked the miscreants to sign behaviour contracts, or called in a behaviour therapist. She could have summoned the parents and spoken to them, although it's often the children of parents who can't control their unruly offspring at home who behave particularly badly in school. Probably, she'd done some of these things already, before resorting to shoe removal. Too often, though, nothing at all is done, or at least nothing that is effective, and misbehaving children start to realise they can get away with almost anything. We'd rather bring in the educational psychologists, or make excuses for badly behaved children, or give the children a label, rather than tell them off or 'embarrass' them. Which is why we've reached the point where a newspaper suggests that knife searches in secondary schools should become routine.

Another statistic. Last weekend, I read that police had investigated a four year old for disorder and vandalism, that the child is among ten children aged around five years old being investigated for crimes, and that more than 6,000 offences have been committed by children under 10 in the last three years. Heaven only knows what is going on in their homes. But if the parents can't handle it, the primary schools certainly have to. And maybe taking the shoes from children who are kicking is a start.

Back in David Cameron's reign, the government considered offering a hundred pound voucher for adults with young children to have parenting classes if they needed it. A hundred pounds wouldn't have gone very far, but it was an interesting idea, because becoming a parent is, and always has been, exceptionally intensive and demanding and until you have been there, you have no understanding of how hard it is. There is certainly a case to be made for older children to be given a variety of life skill lessons, whether it's changing a tap washer, learning to cook simple but healthy meals, or understanding that a child's very early years can be highly stressful for parents, often leading to arguments, aggression, extreme tiredness and the breakdown of relationships. Often, these days, there's no extended family to help or offer support. Many parents have to work hard simply to get by and afford their weekly shopping or energy use, and they don't spend enough time with their children, with meal times rarely shared as a family. They're afraid to let their children play outside, so they spend hours cooped up in tiny bedrooms with televisions, tablets and computer games as the only stimulant. In my last two years of headship, I watched the quality of incoming nursery children plummet; a few had no social skills whatsoever and were almost feral. In one home my nursery teacher visited, there was no furniture in the lounge at all, just some paper plates and a massive widescreen telly.

So could parenting classes help, and could primary schools play a part? I think the answer is a definite yes, but it would need to be done with sensitivity. It is so easy for teachers in a challenging area to feel they are social workers rather than educators, and a good, caring relationship with parents has to be built up gradually. But it is perfectly possible to build social group activities that parents will want to attend, especially in the early years, and once their reputation has grown parents will be very receptive to discussing their problems… which invariably turn out to be universal.. with group leaders and visiting speakers, as well as each other.

When I consider my own childhood, we were, by and large, fairly well behaved. At primary school, you knew where you stood. Muck about in class and you got a severe telling off, a slap, or at worst, a stroke of the cane from the headteacher. If the school told your parents you'd been a nuisance, your parents would usually give you considerable grief as well. You were respectful to the police, the clergy, most grown-ups, and if you assumed you had any rights you were quickly taught otherwise. But it certainly wasn't an ideal world. Maths, for example, was ruined for me by a sadistic secondary school teacher who considered the key to understanding algebra was sarcasm and an occasional caning. None of this, thank heaven, could possibly happen now. Most public services and institutions are under scrutiny as never before and in the main I think this is a good thing. My mother, for example, a devout and committed Church of England Christian, thought that all priests had been more or less hand-picked by God, and they could do no wrong. I was never able to tell her about the time my scout troop chaplain had made a determined effort to sexually abuse me. Even as a young teenager, you quickly learned never to be alone with an adult you had the slightest doubt about.

When I was a young boy scout, Brian, previously a senior scout who'd now joined the police force, came along one evening to talk to us. During a refreshment break, I heard him chatting with a few of the older scouts, telling them how he and another young policeman had dealt with somebody they'd had trouble with at Paddington station. 'He was resisting arrest,' said Brian casually, 'and then we suddenly found he'd fallen down three flights of stairs. Funny, that.' Even at the tender age of thirteen, I was inwardly horrified. These days, with CCTV everywhere, body cameras, and with people using mobile phones to instantly record any breech of law and order, the police are now constantly under surveillance for their attitudes and behaviour towards the public. I can understand why this is important, because although I have had very few dealings with the police, other than visits to my school where they always seemed polite and helpful, several personal incidents have made me think 'If they are treating me, an older white indigenous male, in this manner, how are they treating the less well behaved members of the public?

The first incident occurred when I was driving my deputy head home after the annual staff Christmas meal. Ahead, I noticed a police car stopping some of the traffic. Great, I thought, they're actually out catching people who don't have an MOT, a licence or road tax. I was pulled up, and asked to get out of my car. The officer looked me up and down, and then he looked the sky up and down, then he looked behind the car, and then he said 'Hmm. Funny, isn't it, I just can't see any.'

Mystified, all I could say was 'I'm sorry, I don't understand.'

'And can you see the stars on this nice clear night?'

'Yes, I can.' I still didn't understand.

'There's no fog then?'

'Not as far as I can see, no.'

'Good. I don't see any fog either,' he said in a sarcastic manner. 'I think we can agree that neither of us can see any fog.'

'There isn't any,' I said. 'So that's good, isn't it?'

'It is,' he said. 'So why, on a lovely clear, starry night like this, do you consider it important to have your fog lights on?'

Because I'd only had the car a few days, and was unfamiliar with every switch, I'd had no idea the fog lights were on. But instead of the nasty and unfunny sarcasm, all he'd had to say was 'Did you know your fog lights are on? They're distracting for other drivers. Turn them off please.'

But far worse was a visitation I had at home from two female officers one winter Sunday afternoon. Although we were just about to eat, they demanded to be let in, and one of them, obviously the senior of the two, said they were here because I'd been writing highly offensive emails to Paddy Power. Since I have never entered a betting shop in my life, I assumed Paddy Power was a person, and I said that not only did I not write offensive emails to people, I had no knowledge of anybody called Paddy Power. My wife and I were questioned for a good half hour, the less officious officer looking more uncomfortable by the moment, and I was told I needed to sign a document stating that I wouldn't send offensive emails. I said that I wasn't signing anything. They hesitated, thought for a worrying few minutes about it, and then left without the slightest apology. I could only assume that things must have been a bit quiet down at the nick that Sunday, so the leading officer thought it might be an idea to add an easy notch to her belt. Fortunately, their senior at the station was receptive to my written complaint, and a month later we had a letter saying that the complaint against the senior officer had been upheld.

I appreciate that policing, like teaching, is often a very tough job these days, and I'm not sure I'd want children of my own going down that career path. Which is a shame, because of course there are hundreds of good, dedicated coppers who try to serve the public well, and I found a recent documentary, *To Catch A Copper*, almost impossible to watch. The programme took a look inside the Avon and Somerset's Professional Standards Department, including its Counter-

Corruption Unit (CCU), shining a light on an area of policing which acts as a guardian of the high standards expected of officers who vow to serve and protect. In one episode a highly abusive woman on a bus who'd argued aggressively with the driver and refused to leave the vehicle was equally abusive and aggressive towards two officers who were trying to be perfectly reasonable with her. They asked her to leave the bus, but she refused, continually telling the officers she couldn't breathe and thrusting her child in harm's way. Eventually, another half dozen officers arrived to try to get her off the bus, while she telephoned friends saying she was battling with a large group of troublesome Feds. It was a dreadful spectacle, and in this instance the first officers on the scene had been perfectly reasonable. Even worse, the PSD had invited community leaders to view the footage and offer their opinions, and, of course, the usual accusations about bullying and racism were trotted out.

The trouble is, things have definitely slipped a bit too far the other way. In schools problems quickly occur if nobody is firmly steering the ship because headteachers are buried in their offices or always out at meetings, deputies show no interest in dealing with the problems, and staff morale is low.... which children sense immediately. I was reminded of this when the quickest way to cock up a school was clearly demonstrated to me by Janice, a young teacher from a neighbouring school. She'd been talking to one of my teachers on a course they were both attending, and my teacher had suggested I might be able to help.

When she phoned, I suggested that it might be an idea to chat with her senior managers first. After all, what worked in our school wouldn't necessarily be suitable for hers. No, she said, her senior managers were unhelpful, and since she knew our school by reputation and lived very close, she'd be really grateful if she could drop in for an hour. I arranged to talk to her after school the next day, with two of my key curriculum leaders.

Janice arrived with a bundle of papers and we spread them over the floor, since my desk was covered with the day's ephemera and two pairs of Oliver's glasses, which I was currently mending on a daily basis. I asked Janice to describe her role in the school, and the conversation left me in no doubt where the problems lay.

'I'm the co-ordinator for history and geography, and I have to plan these subjects across the school.'

'Then you've a lot on your plate. It's unusual for a young teacher to be given two subjects to look after.'

'Oh, that's not all. I've got PHSC and Citizenship as well. There are problems with the budget, so I don't get paid for those.'

I asked her why she had to take on so much.

'Because so many staff leave,' she said. 'We have lots of supply teachers and newly qualified teachers, and the children are very difficult. Some of the behaviour is awful. The morale in the school is low, so it's difficult to plan for consistency.'

She showed me a piece of paper covered with topic headings.

'This is what I have to start from,' she said. 'The deputy head worked out the topics we have to follow. She has time, because she never teaches.'

'So the curriculum plan is worked out in discussion with the staff?'

'Oh no, it's not discussed. I just have to integrate all my subjects into it, and then she has to approve it. I'm desperate for good text books. We don't have much equipment, either. The children break it.'

'But you have a budget?'

'No. If I want something I have to ask the headteacher, but she's always out at meetings. We had three visits from our local inspector recently, though.'

'And you explained your difficulties...'

'Well no.. she terrified everybody. She's also an OFSTED inspector and she said if we get an OFSTED soon we'll go into special measures. Then she told us we need to get tracking and targeting in place, but she didn't really explain what she meant.'

So, a chaotic curriculum, badly behaved children who were probably bored stiff, rapid staff turnover for the same reasons, disillusioned co-ordinators, a deputy who doesn't go near children... and an inspector who thinks the answer is a fashionable bit of tracking! If I was writing a recipe for educational disaster, I thought, I couldn't improve on this.

If the inspector had any common sense, she'd have told the headteacher to stay in her school, spend her time with staff and children, and start getting the place organised properly.. including trusting her co-ordinators with a budget. If teachers are happy and motivated... and they see senior management rolling their sleeves up and getting stuck in.. morale will rise rapidly. The children will catch the change in atmosphere, and behaviour will improve.. as it must if progress is to be made. At least I felt we had given Janice some help, even if it was only hot coffee and sympathy. But as a young teacher, even though she clearly recognised some of the fundamental changes that needed to be made, she isn't in a position to make them and she'll probably leave.

Proving once again how essential strong, competent, and, yes, sympathetic and friendly leadership is. I certainly think there ought to be more guidance for teachers who are bullied by their managers, because I have heard some worrying stories recently. Sadly, I'm sure much of it has to do with the aggressive society we live in. Switch on the television and if you coast around the channels it will only be moments before you see people being unpleasant to each other... on an extreme quiz show, for example, or *Big Brother*, or *Love Island*, or *Naked Attraction*, where participators and the viewers can examine each other's genitalia, the series where people actually marry other people they've never met, or that dreadful programme where people earn a colossal amount of money by eating an animal's entrails in the jungle somewhere. It's all part of the 'fun', not dissimilar to visiting a mental asylum in Victorian times for a Sunday afternoon of amusement and entertainment. Interesting that the jungle get-together is popular with a few politicians, too, although the remuneration presumably makes it worthwhile for them, even if hopefully it doesn't go down too well with their constituents.

A previous head of the Ofsted machine once said that if morale wasn't low in your school and the teachers weren't afraid of you, then you were doing something wrong. What an astonishing thing to say. It almost amounted to a licence for bullying, and over the last few years I have met an increasing number of teachers who have experienced unpleasantness from somebody in a leadership or management role. The tormentor might be a head of department, a curriculum leader, a middle manager, or any of the other grand leadership titles that education has invented for itself during the past decade.

Indeed, I sometimes wonder if the idea these days is to get promoted as quickly as possible to a position where you can avoid coming into contact with children. Then you can lean on other people, setting their targets, monitoring their lesson plans, criticising their work and raising their anxiety level. The meaning of managing in teaching has changed out of all recognition. A manager now 'drives up' standards, 'roots out' failure, 'moderates' target setting, or sits in the corner of a classroom with a clipboard, critically observing the person who is doing their best to create an absorbing lesson for children who don't necessarily want to listen. If you're the kind of teacher who can hold your own and deal with this so-called leadership, then fine, but what about the many who can't?

Worryingly, it seems that every educational initiative gives managers a bit more licence. When whole school 'managed learning environments' were introduced as IT and computers became ever more sophisticated, teachers and children could be in touch about their work from anywhere, at any time. 'It's great,' one headteacher said to me at a meeting. 'It will mean that I'll have constant access to staff for checking their planning, even at weekends.' And, sadly, she wasn't joking.

Doctors, crime fighters and lawyers have always been popular subjects for British television programmes; teachers less so. But for a while there was plenty to watch if education was your thing: Programmes such as *Educating Yorkshire* were fascinating. So was a programme whereby a celebrity had tried a unique experiment and asked leading famous specialists in the major curriculum subjects to come and teach a class of teenagers, to see what would happen. The idea was that if you had a famous chef teaching cookery, a historian teaching history, an actor teaching drama and an Olympic champion the children couldn't fail to respond. Frankly, I knew what would happen and, I suspect, did most of the teachers who stopped marking books for an hour and watched it. Apart from the Olympic athlete, who had charisma and an engaging personality full of bubbly humour, they were all a failure. Well, they would be, wouldn't they? Few people seem to realise that having letters after your name and a string of academic qualifications doesn't automatically make you an effective teacher of young people.

Then there are the school 'sitcoms' like *Waterloo Road*, or the truly excellent *Grange Hill* years ago, which cleverly created characters and situations that youngsters could easily identify with, and raised problems which many might be experiencing. And then there were the absolute disasters. I remember the BBC trumpeting a sitcom called *Big School*, set in a secondary school, and never able to resist watching anything to do with education I decided to give it a look.

Right from the opening scene, I was staggered by how awful it was. Perhaps, like the delightful St Trinian's films of years ago, it simply wasn't meant to bear the slightest resemblance to life in a real school. And I could have accepted that, if it had at least made me laugh. Perhaps the thought of bringing together stars such as David Walliams, Catherine Tate and Frances de la Tour (so good in Alan Bennett's *The History Boys*) stopped anyone from noticing just how bad the script was. Let me describe what happened in *Big School*. See if you find it amusing.

Walliams plays Mr Church, a science teacher. He is an arrogant, petulant twit with a silly haircut but at least he prepares his lessons well; each episode starts with a spectacular experiment that should have students riveted. But the kids look bored rigid and the bell often rings at the most exciting part of the experiment, causing Mr Church to be splashed with liquid that is wiped enthusiastically from his groin by an unattractive lab assistant. Then we meet Miss Postern, the new French teacher played by Tate. The Neanderthal games teacher informs us that he would like to 'slip her a length', which is apparently what he's done with most of the female staff. Except the lesbian, of course. From this point on, Mr Church spends every available moment in hot pursuit of Miss Postern. He even asks the mandatory 'boffin' student how he can set up a Facebook page because it's so funny, isn't it, that children know much more about computers than their silly old teachers. On asking the advice of a boy in detention (arrogant, streetwise and with his baseball cap on backwards, natch), Mr Church is told that if he really wants to make out with Miss Postern, he should 'text her a picture of his nob'. In assembly, Mr Church is forced to describe what another teacher has allegedly been doing to a sheep. Meanwhile, the headteacher confiscates alcohol brought into school by children and necks it herself... when she isn't puffing on a spliff the size of the 'Camberwell Carrot' from '*Withnail And I*' and proclaiming it to be 'good shit'. And, just for good measure, an elderly teacher who suffers from dementia always turns up for the wrong lessons at the wrong time. Mercifully, we don't see how the students treat him. I didn't watch the remainder of the series. I couldn't stand it.

But at least we don't have to look far to find celluloid gems about school life that are genuinely hilarious or insightful. To cheer myself up, I watched the football scene from Ken Loach's wonderful film *Kes*, a ten minute depiction of a secondary school games lesson, which always reminds me of my own cold, wet, interminable sessions on the football field as a teenager.

Its brilliance utterly eclipsed anything on *Big School*.

4

CAN WE HAVE A DECISION, PLEASE?

Schools And Their Governing Bodies

Apart from the few occasions when I was being interviewed for promotion, I had very little to do with school governing bodies until I became a headteacher, although as a deputy head in a school in London's Bermondsey there was an occasion when I managed to infuriate the chair of governors, and in my innocence I didn't really understand why. A Cambridge college had asked my headteacher to give a talk to prospective teachers on the huge changes that were taking place in primary education following the Plowden Report, and how schools like ours, in buildings built for educating Victorian children, were managing to cope with them.

Since I was an avid cine fan at the time, I suggested that I should make a half hour documentary film about the school, which could then be used as a strong basis for discussion with the college students. The filming went well, and I decided to open my film with scenes of two children walking through the streets near their high-rise flats towards school, chatting excitedly to each other about what the day might hold. As they walked, the camera revealed a background of poorly maintained housing, rubbish strewn roads, a burst water main, a rough sleeper still on a bench and a distinct lack of grass, trees, or places for children to play. The aim was to contrast the environment the children lived in, with the pleasure of learning at our school, and the abundance of activities we offered them.

My headteacher loved the film, and suggested that before we went off for our day at Cambridge we should organise an evening showing for the school governors. Most of them came along, and at the end of the showing when the lights went up, the chairman shot to his feet before anybody else could say a word. Yes, he said angrily, the film might be very professionally made, but the opening scenes should be immediately lopped off. They were a highly biased slur on the work done by the borough council, of which he was a prominent member, to improve the environment, and he certainly didn't take kindly to what had been shown, never mind how good the school was when the two children actually got there.

Since he was an extremely forceful character, and viewed with considerable distaste by my headteacher, everybody else sat quietly with their hands in their laps, even though it was obvious many of them disagreed, because they had clapped enthusiastically as the film had ended. Calmly, I said my camera hadn't lied and if councillors thought the area around the school was improving it might be an idea if they actually came and took a closer look at it. Not wanting things to become too heated, my headteacher quickly suggested that everybody should repair to the staffroom for a nice cup of coffee and a chocolate biscuit or two. Fortunately, the chairman said that he had a meeting to go to and hurried off. The remaining governors told me how much they had enjoyed the film and thanked us for everything we were doing for the children. I didn't remove the opening scenes… indeed, I thought they were crucial to the film, and I rather suspected my headteacher had enjoyed irritating the chairman.

Twelve years later my next encounter with school governors was for headship, and I was about to discover the vagaries of a school governing body. I arrived for my evening interview, a little nervous, knowing that for three quarters of an hour I would be receiving a grilling from an assorted collection of people. I had a streaming cold and felt very unwell, but I'd liked the school when I visited, and I knew this was the only chance I'd get of leading it. A dozen people sat at trestle tables arranged in three sides of a square, and a chair had been placed for me in the middle. It was somewhat intimidating, but I just wanted to get it over with and go home to a warm fire, a hot lemon drink and bed.

As I smiled and strode purposefully into the room some people smiled back at me, and some didn't. The man at the centre of the table opposite me pushed his fierce black spectacles to the end of his nose and looked cautiously over them. 'Good evening, Mr Kent. Thank you for coming. These are the school governors, I'm the chairman and I'll be asking you some questions first. Then the other governors will introduce themselves and everyone will ask you a question in turn. So, tell us why you would like to be the headteacher of our school.'

That, naturally, was an expected question and one I'd prepared thoroughly for. I talked about the achievements in my career so far, the pleasure I'd had from my deputy headship, and the reasons why I now felt ready for the ultimate challenge. For a fleeting moment I considered raising a smile by mentioning my hefty mortgage and then immediately dismissed the idea. If they didn't laugh I'd have wrecked my chances from the start. The chairman seemed satisfied with what I'd said and he turned to the elderly gentleman sitting on his left, whose arm was in plaster. He saw me glance at it.

'I fell off my bike,' he said. 'Getting too old for it, I suppose. Roads are getting more dangerous every day. Far too many cars in my view. Would you have far to come to get here?' This didn't seem particularly relevant to primary education, but I explained that I only lived twenty five minutes away by car, so the journey would be very straightforward.

'Important for the headmaster to be in before everybody else,' he said. 'Traffic can be terrible. Ever thought about getting a bike? Keeps me fit and trim. How old do you think I am?'

I hadn't the slightest idea. This seemed to be a strange way of conducting an interview, but I felt it best to go with the flow and prudently err on the side of flattery.

'Not a day over thirty, I'd say.' There was a ripple of amusement
'No. Try again.'
'Um.. Fifty eight? Or thereabouts?'
'Seventy three. Would have come here on my bike tonight if I hadn't fallen off it.'

I suddenly felt much more relaxed. I realised that I knew infinitely more about primary education than the people in front of me and answering their questions suddenly became very enjoyable. I think they had sympathy for the fact that I had a dreadful cold, too. It was all practical sensible stuff, with several rich moments of humour thrown in, one by a whiskered gentleman with a face like thunder who'd been frowning at me throughout the whole interview.

'Discipline, Mr Kent, discipline,' he said, when the chairman indicated that it was time for him to hurl a question at me. 'What are your thoughts on that hot little topic?'

I explained that it would be impossible to have effective learning without it. It sounded a little trite.

'Well, obviously', he replied bluntly, with a ferocity that surprised me. 'The thing is, what are you going to do about it? It's all very well saying you need it, but you've got to have a plan. What's your *plan*?'

'Of course. It's something I'd want to sort out at my first staff meeting. It's essential that each teacher has the same expectation of good behaviour, and. ..'

He waved his arm. 'Yes, yes, yes, they might have the same expectations, but some teachers can do it, some can't, and some make a total cock-up of it. And half our intake come from homes which are a shambles. The premises officer tells me the toilets have been flooded yet again. If they carry on like this you won't be teaching 'em maths, you'll all be gathering wood to build a bloody ark!'

My voice rose a little as I explained firmly that it didn't have to be like that. I said there were lots of techniques for cultivating good behaviour in children and I'd happily expound my theories if he wanted me to, but it seemed the chairman didn't, explaining that he was happy enough to know that I'd been very successful as a deputy head. The frowning gent was still looking angry as the chairman pointed to an elderly lady at one end of a trestle table. She inspected me quizzically.

'Mr Kent,' she said, 'When I was a little girl at primary school we all sat in rows doing the same thing at the same time. Lady Plowden certainly turned that on its head in the sixties, didn't she? It gave schools far more freedom with the curriculum, wouldn't you agree?'

'Far too much in my view,' interrupted the aggressive governor with the bushy eyebrows. 'If you've got thirty kids, all wandering round doing a painting whenever they feel like it, you've got a recipe for chaos. Be like a bloody wet playtime all day.' It seemed that the two governors might quickly get into a heated debate and forget about me entirely, but the chairman quickly called them back to order.

It was a view I was familiar with, anyway. Primary schools across the country were still coming to terms with the massive changes in education and the new ways their classrooms were being organised, and many teachers were struggling with them. I explained that children can only learn when they're interested and enthused, a view I held passionately throughout my career. A classroom should be organised for their benefit, I explained, not the teacher's.

'Still sounds like a recipe for chaos to me,' he said. 'I'd be interested to see you make it work.'

'Hopefully you'll be giving me the chance to,' I countered as enthusiastically as I could. Despite the head cold, I was enjoying myself, especially as the questions became more probing. By the time I'd been asked how I would deal with a difficult staff member, what provisions I'd make for children with additional needs (although hardly any were recognised then), and how I'd handle an emergency such as a broken boiler in the middle of winter, the chairman thanked me for turning up on such a rainy night, wished my cold better and said the interview had come to an end. I felt the governors had had their money's worth, and I drove home wondering whether I'd answered the questions sensibly, or merely irritated people. Several weeks later, after I'd had a second interview with members of the education committee and the inspectorate at London's County Hall, I learned that I'd got the job. From now on, I was going to have regular contact with a school governing body.

These days, apparently, it's becoming increasingly hard to recruit school governors. I'm not surprised. I'm not even sure what makes people want to do the job. A little power, maybe? A political leg-up? Or perhaps some spare time to offer and a heart full of good intentions. Who can become one? Well, anybody really, although there are strict rules for the make-up of a school governing body. A primary school's governing body might consist of about fifteen members. Some would be elected parents of children at the school, others lay people with, hopefully, an interest in education and a desire to see a successful school, usually a couple of teachers from the staff, perhaps a local dignitary or two aspiring to a political career, a knowledgeable clerk who keeps the documentation in order and takes minutes, plus the headteacher. One of their number is elected annually by the whole governing body to be the chairperson… often the same person year after year because it's not a position many people covet. The chairperson often has to control strong personalities with entrenched, often political, views and sometimes referee effectively a heated meeting. Attracting lay people who have the right kind of knowledge can therefore be a difficult task, especially in socially deprived inner city areas, where people often feel, wrongly, that they need to be academically inclined to make a worthwhile contribution. Working with school governors can also be time consuming and difficult for a headteacher.

These days, school governors have awesome responsibilities over the curriculum, health and safety, the school budget, and teacher's salaries, and they are expected to attend many meetings and training sessions, although surprisingly these are not mandatory. I sat in on an evening lecture arranged for our governors on how to interpret data in the same manner as an Ofsted inspector and the only governor who understood any of it was a chap who just happened to be an accountant… and even he struggled. Furthermore, all this has to be done on a voluntary basis, because no governor ever receives any money for their work. Since school governors are elected for four years, they need real commitment to stay the whole course, and only the most dedicated do.

It wasn't always so. When I began headship, governors had a minimal workload. They were simply required to turn up for one evening meeting a term, to make sure the headteacher hadn't run off with the school funds. Visiting the school wasn't a requirement, so many didn't bother. Some were helpful, others were not. Some gained full marks for eccentricity and used meetings to air their own prejudices, often political, and gave dubious advice at considerable length. For a headteacher who'd already had a long and hard day at school, this could be extremely frustrating. Some governors would join as many as four different governing bodies, and often get decisions made for one school mixed up with another. I suspected they may have been rather lonely people looking for something to do in the evenings.

In my early years, I'd arrive at the termly meetings laden with documents and a long written essay on the progress the school was making, and then find myself listening to earnest but pointless discussions. Invariably, a resolution would be made for the headteacher to present more documentation and I'd work for the next few evenings producing it. Then a more experienced colleague let me in on the secret. 'Show what a co-operative chap you are by smiling and agreeing to absolutely everything, and then only do what's important,' he advised. 'And the only important things are those which directly affect the children or the teachers.'

It was good advice. At the next meeting, an elderly governor demanded to know why our school was no longer allowing visits from home beat police officers. I was astonished. We'd done nothing of the sort and I said so. He merely repeated the accusation, thumping his fist on the table until a hearing aid shot out of his ear and I realised he had a hearing defect. He was also on three other local governing bodies and often got us hopelessly mixed up. While he hunted under the seat for his hearing aid, the chairman moved the meeting rapidly on.

Back then, most governing bodies had elderly members like Miss Johnson and Mr Eldridge, whose hearts were in the right place but whose minds meandered alarmingly, and there were always amusing moments to help with the tedious business of trawling through authority documents. Although petite, Miss Johnson had a ravenous appetite, marking her place at the table with sandwiches cut to a thickness that suggested they only came three to a loaf. She'd wait for what she considered a tedious agenda item, and then tuck in. Assorted fruit and veg would fall softly to the table. Once, she forgot her sandwiches altogether. She'd been for a day at the seaside and came to the meeting armed with a collection of shells she thought the children might find interesting. Becoming bored halfway through the meeting, she took a magnifying glass from her bag and spent the next agenda item closely studying a family of periwinkles.

Mr Eldridge did his bit for the community by coaching the local youth in football skills, although his enthusiasm vastly outweighed his ability. He had a tendency to slip on the grass and appeared at meetings with appendages bandaged or covered in sticking plasters. Around the third agenda item he'd often place finger and thumb on a furrowed brow and dip his head with intense concentration. It took me several meetings to realise he'd fallen asleep.

One hot summer evening, we'd got through about half the agenda when I was suddenly aware of an appalling smell drifting across the room. Almost as soon as I'd noticed it, so had the other governors sitting on my side of the table. We'd had some trouble with the drains and I assumed they must have become blocked, or were overflowing again, and I made a mental note to ask the premises officer to have a look at them before school in the morning. And then my deputy, sitting next to me, pointed to the end of our table. One of our older governors, no doubt trying to make himself more comfortable, had taken off his shoes....

Like juries, school governing bodies have always contained a fair cross section of society. Juries are composed of twelve people, in the hope that having a reasonably large number they'll make a sensible group decision. A similar reasoning applies to school governing bodies, but this throws up anomalies from time to time. When we co-opted a retired headteacher from a small, respected academy for young ladies, she was never to reach a real understanding of life at a tough London primary. Offering to do a regular slot on Tuesday afternoons reading to a class of infant children, she said plummily: 'I've decided on Beatrix Pottah. All the younger children at my school adored Beatrix Pottah.'

She stuck it out for a full half-hour, only losing her patience when a child sitting at her feet scrawled, in felt-tipped pen, on one of her suede shoes. 'What on earth are you doing?' she snapped. 'Drawing Peter Rabbit,' said the child innocently. For the next few months she spent her volunteer time digging our small school garden instead.

Times change, though, and governors with them. To cope with the massive workload, a prospective governor today needs an enthusiasm bordering on insanity. Nevertheless, new governors do often have this sort of zeal. The morning after appointing two new parent governors, I found one pounding the playground beat, handing out questionnaires about school dinners, while making sure no parents parked on the zig-zags or dared to light a cigarette under the playground shed, and generally letting parents know that if there was a complaint about the school, she'd be more than happy to take the matter up with the headteacher, which didn't fill me with pleasure.

There's no denying that a governor's workload and responsibilities, if they apply themselves to it with due diligence, are awesome. They are required to hire and fire, oversee the curriculum, listen to complaints from parents, and have a good knowledge of quickly changing trends in education. They are also expected to turn up for all school concerts and functions. Not that they always do. After I'd produced my first school musical, I put reserved stickers on seats at the front, expecting all of my governors to turn up and applaud enthusiastically. Only three governors came, which particularly irritated some of the parents who'd wanted more than a couple of tickets to watch their offspring tread the boards. I never reserved seats again.

A few always attended our annual Poetry Week and brought along a poem to read, although this was never completely without incident. Poetry Week was a time for the whole school to enjoy a wealth of poems, some read by parents, some written by the children, some chosen by the staff of the school and others performed in costume by the classes, who'd always learned them by heart. Since I knew it was possible that our children would grow up and never read poetry again, I felt that by exposing them to the delights and enjoyment of verse, it was always possible that they might.

I recall the year three governors came along, each slightly misjudging the occasion. Miss Brierley, presumably thinking it might be an idea to throw a bit of ancient culture at the children, chose a rendering of Sir Patrick Spens, a tedious and lengthy poem I hadn't heard since secondary school. When it was the chairman's turn to read a poem, he announced that many poems moved him to tears, and this was one of them. Sure enough, half way through his reading, tears were running down his cheeks. Now, I've been known to be made tearful by some of my favourite films, pieces of music and poems, but I felt he might have chosen a little more wisely, because the children were totally bemused by the sight of a grown-up reading a poem with tears rolling down his cheeks. And governor Anthony had misjudged things altogether. He'd chosen a poem, for some reason only known to himself, called 'Shoes', but with his pronounced lisp, this became 'thoose'. Perhaps he wasn't aware of his lisp, but since the poem contained multiple repetitions of the word (black thoose, brown thoose, everybody likes to wear thoose) it wasn't long before the youngsters at the front of the hall were staring, open mouthed, and Year 6 children (and a fair sprinkling of staff) were having quite a job trying to suppress their mirth.

Governors are also required to approve how the school arranges its annual budget and spends its money. Any major decisions must be approved by them. Early on, when I asked the children to design a new school uniform, one parent governor was furious that the whole governing body hadn't been consulted, because there would be many costs involved for parents. He calmed down a bit when I explained that children whose parents couldn't afford to send their children to school in reasonably fashionable clothing tended to be side-lined by the ones who could, and I hated the possibility of any kind of bullying. Also, the uniform was going to be attractive and inexpensive, and give the children a strong sense of belonging to a school that was rapidly becoming very popular in the locality.

Governors nowadays must also form themselves into committees, to discuss and evaluate every aspect of school life. Which is fine when a school is running like a well-oiled machine, but what happens when it isn't? Well, amazingly, they can simply walk away. They're unpaid volunteers, after all. What an eccentric system it all seems. In that respect, it's not very much different from my very first teaching post at a primary school in London's Islington. I had a very happy three years there and shortly after I'd left the headteacher moved on to a much bigger school. The authority found it difficult to recruit a new head and within a few years the school had completely fallen apart, with the governors and authorities unable to do anything about it, except keep away and pretend it wasn't happening. A huge public enquiry, costing many thousands of pounds, eventually followed.

For sheer paper mongering with precious little result, your average governing body can't be beaten. Swamped with documents from every level of educational bureaucracy, these worthy volunteers struggle to create effective committees and working parties against massive odds. At my governors' meetings, we rarely discussed day-to-day school reality. Instead, we stared at papers on educational matters that had little bearing on our own school, some of them only understood by our highly capable clerk, who I felt could probably explain the theory of relativity in a couple of easy lessons. Two of my best governors, expecting simply to deal with matters that only affected our school, eventually resigned in annoyance at the rambling and remote discussions. Others left almost as soon as they joined, because they'd expected meetings simply to be about our own school, not educational philosophy or government educational policies.

Some governors, like Hilda, I was delighted to see the back of. A rigid religious fanatic with time on her hands and no humour whatsoever, she spent a great deal of time examining the school's religious education policy in excruciating detail and visiting classrooms to make sure it was being adhered to. On one occasion she was accompanied by the newest addition to the family, and when she was sitting in a class watching a lesson she wasn't averse to popping an ample breast out for the baby, while the teacher was in full flow. The class teacher said she'd never see the children's mouths drop open like that, and had simply thought she must have been delivering a riveting RE lesson. And sometimes, a governor that you'd worked well with could suddenly show another, darker, side of her personality. When one of our classroom assistants, a dedicated and popular lady with enormous classroom skills, died from cancer at a young age, I decided to close the school, so that the staff could attend her funeral. All the governors were agreeable to this, apart from one. 'It's not my concern that somebody has died,' she said. 'I have a job to do, I have to work at home, and I can't have my two children running around and pestering me all day.'

Anthony, the empty vessel with the pronounced lisp who made a great deal of noise at meetings, never seemed to be available when there was work to be done or a committee to be attended. I'm certain there is at least one Anthony on every governing body. He would regularly turn up fifteen minutes late for meetings, apologise to the clerk, hunt around for a spare chair, and then want to know in detail what had happened about an agenda item we'd discussed ten minutes earlier. When he came up with a request that was going to cause me or my teaching stuff a great deal of work, I quickly found the best solution was to give him responsibility for the task. When he suggested that we should be giving our children far more homework, I said that we worked the children hard enough during the day, and I had no intention of sending them home to do a lot more. He persisted with his demands, so I asked him to contact four neighbouring primary schools to find out what their arrangements for homework were, and whether they found it worthwhile. He could then report back to us at the next meeting. He agreed, and promised that he would. Of course, he never did, and the matter was never raised again.

My tolerance of Anthony came to a head when my current secretary was moving away from London and we needed to appoint a new one. Fortunately we had the ideal person to hand. Sandra was a teaching support assistant, adept with any age group. She had the right qualifications, excellent relationships with everyone and was efficient with parents and paperwork. She also had a delightful sense of humour and was very keen to do the job. What more could you ask? At the next governors' meeting, I suggested we wouldn't find a better person, and that we should appoint her. Since Anthony was on the personnel committee, he said it was important that we followed the rules by advertising and interviewing. Other governors nodded, so we discussed dates for the personnel committee to meet.

Unfortunately, Anthony couldn't make any of them, but he said it was fine for us to go ahead without him. I phoned the local newspaper, discussed the wording for an advertisement, and said I'd like to book it for two weeks. Horrified at the price I was given, I hastily reduced it to one insertion, which was fortunate, because the phone didn't stop ringing for several weeks after it had appeared. I asked Anthony if he'd like to help me draw up a job description, but unfortunately he was busy that day.

By the end of the week I'd printed, packaged, posted or e-mailed a large pile of application forms and detailed job descriptions. It took a great deal of time to go through the applications and give them the attention they deserved. I'd asked Anthony to help, but unfortunately he was busy, so I divided them between the remaining three of us on the personnel committee.

Some candidates were weeded out quickly; two years as a swimming pool attendant was not quite the experience I was looking for, and a spell as a bookie's assistant didn't really light my fire. But eventually I shortlisted half a dozen from my pile. Then it was back to the other committee members to see what they'd come up with. I didn't get much school work done that week.

Ten applicants (more postage, stamps, phone calls) were invited in to look around the school. It's always fascinating to compare the reality with what's written on an application form. I hadn't bargained for Caroline turning up in what looked suspiciously like carpet slippers, and Deirdre may have been nervous, but after half an hour of being unable to get word in edgeways I felt I'd been verbally ravaged. By the time I'd shown the last person round the school I'd forgotten what the first one looked like, but after another long evening with the personnel committee we managed to whittle the number of applicants down to five people. Plus Sandra.

On to the interview and by now my wife was getting used to the idea of eating alone. I'd hoped Anthony would be available for the interviewing panel, but unfortunately he was very busy that week. On a rainy evening all the candidates turned up in their Sunday best, ready to convince us that salary was the last thing on their minds, because they all knew how cash-strapped schools were. All six smiled a great deal and said how wonderful they thought children were. Particularly Sandra. By 10.30 that night, it was all over. What did the committee decide? We appointed Sandra. I didn't even bother telling Anthony.

Sometimes, governors would come to meetings with ridiculous demands, seemingly totally unaware that I'd just worked through a very long day and would be going home to a few hours more in the evening. One governor turned up to a meeting with five books on social and ethnic integration and he asked me to read all of them before the next meeting.

But even though every school has a few tiresome and demanding people, there's always a deeply committed and enthusiastic soul, even though there can be a little naiveté about the realities of school life. Eleanor was a newly appointed parent governor who, understandably, wasn't a great fan of our playground toilets. They may be Victorian, she said, but couldn't we put decent paper, in decent holders, on the cubicle walls, just like we have on the inside ones? Couldn't the children have soap, and paper towels? We explained that the playground helpers carried all these things in a bag, as we'd had lots of problems when they'd been put in the toilets. 'But the children are so well behaved here,' she persisted. 'Couldn't we try it again?' We did, and I waited with bated breath.

By Thursday, it looked as if it had been snowing. A visiting after-school group had decided there was a lot of fun to be had from decorating the small school garden with Tesco's best. Then, on Friday, things took a turn for the worse in the shape of a large forehead lump, a swollen eye and a cut lip. Infants Billy, Rashid and Thomas had been playing 'Pirates of the Caribbean', using the paper towels to fashion pirates' hats and the little bars of soap as missiles. Billy had dodged the missiles by hiding under a sink, but then cracked his head on it when he stood up. Following a further week of incidents, the governor agreed it might be best if we went back to the old system, whereby the materials were freely available from the duty helper's bag, but you had to ask first.

Of course, governors can often agree to an event without anticipating the problems it might cause. Which is why I was in two minds when our local MP, Harriet Harman, asked if Gordon

Brown could visit and chat to the parents, hopefully fired by the current election fever, outside the school gate. I had a lot of time for Harriet, as she knew our school well and had visited with interest on a number of occasions. Our chair of governors seemed to think it was a worthwhile idea, so everything was green lit, especially as we'd been talking to the children about elections and how they work.

Harriet asked if I'd mention the Chancellor's visit to parents, and since I was finishing a parents' newsletter at the time, I suggested I put it in that. 'Good idea,' she said. Within three minutes she was back on the phone saying that, actually, it wasn't such a great idea after all. Half the neighbourhood might descend, and there would be all kinds of security problems. Then a call came from Labour Central Office, asking for a resume of the school by e-mail so that Gordon could be fully briefed before arriving. I hurriedly typed a detailed note, saying what an utterly wonderful school we were, doing all sorts of things on a very meagre budget.

By 8.00am on the big day photographers had commandeered the road outside the school gates. Labour party aides arrived soon afterwards, several asking if they could pop into the school powder room. I agreed, warning them that our powder room might not meet the powder room health and safety standards they were presumably accustomed to at party headquarters.

Then, as parents and children and a few of our governors began to gather inquisitively around the school gates, boxes of leaflets and stickers were unpacked by Gordon's team, and bright red balloons distributed. My little group of 'challenging' mothers, always ready to grumble about anything to do with school, perched themselves as usual on the low wall opposite, inspecting the scene suspiciously. 'If you want all them balloons blown up,' advised one of their husbands, nodding towards the group, 'pass 'em over there. They've got enough hot air to fill a gasometer.'

Children were arriving, asking what was going on and whether the Queen was visiting. A few of them soon spotted the stickers, and the children quickly realised the aides weren't sure who'd been given one and who hadn't. By hiding stickers under their coats they could keep going back, saying they hadn't had one. Ten minutes later, many of them looked like walking sticker banks.

Meanwhile, Mr Brown had arrived in his chauffeured motor, and was already shaking hands with a growing crowd of people. Harriet took me out to meet Gordon and he shook my hand enthusiastically. 'It's a great little school you have here, Mike,' he said, obviously having been successfully briefed but not remembering enough to elaborate. 'Make sure you keep up the good work!'

I had to admire his conversational skill with the crowd, and he was completely unfazed by one of our parents helpfully suggesting that, in his opinion, the current prime minister was a fucking liar. Then, it was time for the whistle, and the road show moved on. The governors who had attended the brief session thought it all seemed to have gone well, and that it could only help the rising reputation of our school, which was probably true.

I am in no doubt that schools need to be held to account, but I'm not convinced that the current method of appointing a random group of people, most of whom simply won't understand the pressures heads and their teachers now have to contend with, is the appropriate way to do it. Nothing, absolutely nothing about my school would have changed if we'd had no governors at all. Although they are responsible for appointing most teaching or managerial staff, they have to rely totally on a headteacher's knowledge and advice, because it is only the headteacher who will have met them and spent a useful amount of time with them.

I encountered this problem when my first deputy head retired a year after I'd joined the school. The governors interviewed the shortlisted six, and most of the governors wanted to appoint the candidate who'd interviewed the best. I didn't. I wanted to appoint the person whose wonderful classroom I'd seen when I'd visited her school, whose personality delighted me, and who I believed would really bond well with the staff. She had simply been very nervous in her interview. I persisted and wouldn't budge, saying that I was the person who had to work with the appointed candidate, not them. I got my way, and my deputy was with me almost until I retired.

I thought of governing bodies and committees when I watched a television programme last week, where two juries listened to a murder trial. The trial was a replication of a real one, but neither jury knew of the existence of the other one, since they were both carefully concealed from each other. Because it's currently the best and only system we have, we watched their analysis of the evidence, their deliberations, and the way decisions were made and some jurors opinions changed by the others. Unsurprisingly, one jury came up with a murder verdict, the other with a manslaughter verdict. When both juries were told that there had been another twelve people doing the same thing, they were aghast, and neither jury could understand how the other had come up with a completely different decision. Summing up, the programme suggested there might be quite a strong argument for some professionally trained juries to travel the country as a full time job. It seemed an option well worth considering.

There needs to be similar thinking around school governing bodies too. Yes, it may currently be the best system we have, and unlike yesteryear there are plenty of courses available to governors if they have the time and the dedication, but each year when I watched my governors struggling and attempting to understand the school budget I'd worked on for a whole week each Easter holiday, or the intricacies of the national curriculum, it did make me think there has to be a more efficient way of looking after a school's welfare.

Perhaps I should give the last word on this to Marjorie, an older, somewhat disillusioned member of the governing body, 'We seem to be weighed down with paper and sometimes I don't think we support you well enough,' she said, after a particularly strenuous and drawn out meeting. 'Some of us are just grateful you seem to know the right direction the school should move in.'

'Well,' I said, 'You have to understand that I love the job and I'm here for the long haul. Right direction or not, it's down to me to grab the wheel and try to steer a path through the murk. Remember, if things get sticky, you can resign at any time. I'm the one who has to take the real responsibility....'

5

ELF N' SAFETY

Avoiding Harm In School

My parents knew Bill, who worked for the railways. Bill was fastidious about time. Every day, as he parked his car in the garage at the end of his garden, he pulled a string which ran the length of the garden. The other end was attached to a bell in the house. This was a signal for his wife to put his dinner on the table. If it wasn't there dead on time, and hot, he wouldn't eat it. God knows what he must have been like to live with. I was often reminded of Bill as I encountered the various Jobsworths who entered my school every year. They either parked themselves in my office expecting me to spend two hours answering their inane questions, or wandered around the school, clipboard and pencil in hand, sucking their teeth at each perceived safety indiscretion before delivering a doom-laden verdict at the end of the morning.

So different from the start of my career. When I was a sprightly young class teacher working in Islington, I used to organise and run a school journey to the Isle of Wight each year for the oldest children. I considered school journey to be a very important part of the school year, both socially and educationally. Most of my children hadn't ventured far outside London, and they certainly didn't go on extended holidays, if they actually went on holiday at all. At least half a dozen of them had never seen the sea. A subsidised school journey meant that the two week experience was valuable socially too. The children were away from their parents for fourteen days and nights, and they learned to value each other in a setting outside school or home. There was also the opportunity to have a great deal of pleasure on the beaches, and in the woods, the parks and the fields. Throughout my teaching career, I organised a school journey to a countryside setting every year, and would never have wanted to miss it.

But in those days, teachers didn't have to worry about risk assessments, crates of medicines, and an adult to every one and a half children. It was all so much easier. As a headteacher, when my imagination ran riot and I considered all the things that could go wrong, I'm surprised my teachers even agreed to go on a school journey. But they always did, common sense while looking after the children was always to the fore, everybody had a thoroughly enjoyable time, and accidents and incidents were minimal.

But shortly into my headship, things were quickly changing and health and safety took on a much stronger role. Before taking a class on a simple day trip to a museum, the seaside, or a visit to the Tower of London, a risk assessment had to be undertaken. This seemed a relatively sensible idea at first, until eventually risk assessments had to be submitted to the local education authority. They became more complex year by year, until one spring morning I was faced with the new *'Policy And Procedures For Off Site Visits document, Edition One.'* After reading it, I'd have been hesitant about taking children to the end of the road, let alone to such a hazard laden place as the local park, or… heaven forbid… on an underground train, where children could have been chewed up in the escalator, fallen off the platform, or had their hearing severely impaired by the noise of a train emerging from the tunnel.

The document started by stating how much the authority valued the LOtC agenda. Yep, I didn't have a clue, either, but it was the acronym for 'Learning Outside the Classroom'. The local authority had even set up an online notification system called EVOLVE, to ensure that visits were planned in a methodical way for a 'safe experience.' Apparently, it wouldn't have been sensible to charge parents for an Isle of Wight school journey unless you'd actually organised somewhere on the Isle of Wight for the party to stay. And it would be sensible if the place wasn't on the edge of a cliff, because that would be classed as hazardous.

The document had forty two packed pages. Page four offered a helpful acronym guide, so if you weren't quite sure what an ESRA was, all was explained. It's an Event Specific Risk Assessment. And just in case you thought ALF was the name of the bloke leading the expedition, it wasn't. It was an Activity Leader Form.

A list of important rules for the EVC (Educational Visits Co-ordinator) followed, because every school was supposed to appoint one. The rules offered many surprises: the person must be competent to organise and lead a visit. Naturally, that came as quite a revelation to me. No good putting my Auntie Jean in charge, then. As well as the other twenty one things they'd have to be good at, they'd also be required to keep lots of records, so they'd better be good at form filling. But then, since teachers spent so much time filling in forms anyway, that was more or less a given.

No document of this type is complete without a flow chart, and this one was no exception. You started at the box that said, 'Are you planning an Off Site Visit?' Yes, you said nodding enthusiastically, indeed I am. That's why I'm reading this form. So on you go to Box 2, asking if an external provider of the activities will be used. And so on through a dozen boxes of the obvious. Answer the questions correctly, and you're told, 'The Visit May Proceed. Please forward this form to your Authority'.

And that's before you reached the risk assessment itself. Incredibly, there were multiple types of risk assessment, all with silly names. Generic, event specific and on-going dynamic. Naturally, there was much additional guidance for all this on the Department for Education's website, but it would take you so long to read through it all that you'd never actually get to the Isle of Wight. I'd have loved to climb into the minds of the people who write this stuff to see what made them tick. On the other hand, perhaps not. I'd have needed a comprehensive risk assessment before going there.

As time went on, health and safety bureaucracy for schools increased almost annually, and every season seemed to bring a new piece of advice, legislation, booklet or form to complete. Common sense, like a weary stranger, began to hobble into the background, and I even started to anticipate the material that would arrive in the post. I began to think like a bureaucrat. What would the particular dangers this month be?

Snow. Now there's a real hazard. When I started my headship, if we'd had a heavy snowfall in the night, the children would wake up extremely excited, because they'd be able to create a super slide in the playground, have a snowman competition and as likely as not, have a snowball fight with the teachers.

'Thousands of schools haven't bothered to open,' shouted the media one very snowy morning. On the radio, elderly people told us how, as children, they walked two hundred miles through fifteen foot snow drifts carrying school books, sandwiches, a snow shovel and their little sister on their backs... and still managed to arrive an hour before the whistle blew. What wimps we are, said the commentators. No moral fibre. No get up and go. If teachers can't be bothered to get to school, what kind of example are they setting for the children? They're all going to grow up work shy...

What they overlooked, of course, was that teachers lived much closer to their schools in those days. People didn't travel very far. And health and safety regulations were unheard of. Imagine that now. If little Charlie got a direct hit in the ear from Sir's snowball his mother would be digging a pathway through the snow to the local litigation office. A playground ice slide? What if Maisie slips and sprains her ankle, or topples over and ruins the new coat her mother shouldn't have sent her to school in? But on one occasion, when the snow drifts were really deep, my school was closed too. I live on a steep hill, and though I tried, I couldn't move the car. If I'd put on my boots and walked through the drifts, I'd have arrived just in time to start walking home again. All but two of my teachers were in the same position. Buses had stopped running and there were no trains. Closing was the only option. Even if a few teachers had been able to keep the school open, they could have done little except park the children in front of a television or play a few games.

But teachers always feel guilty if they're forced to stay at home on a school day. My wife's school was closed too, so she settled down to laminate pictures for a classroom display, and I planned assemblies for the next fortnight. Unsurprisingly, children all over the country stayed at home, had a wonderful time playing in the snow, and probably learned twice as much as they would have done at school. Looking out of the window that day, I watched a neighbour play with his children. He was still playing with them late in the afternoon. He doesn't have time to do that very often. Next door, the children built a massive snowman in the garden. All sorts of learning took place as they struggled to give his head the right proportions to balance on his body. And on the evening news, there was much footage of families in the parks, simply enjoying themselves tobogganing and making snow angels with the snow.

Two days later, everything was returning to normal. There was still some snow around, and my teachers seized the opportunities… did the children know how snow was formed? That no two snowflakes were identical? That snowflakes had six points… and here's how to create a beautiful symmetrical snowflake using a piece of carefully folded white paper and a pair of scissors. Even the playground became an area of unusual interest. 'How does the snow stick so neatly on the branches?' asked Hannah. 'Look at the patterns in this slice of ice,' said Oliver. And Sam, rolling a massive snowball and staggering out of the gate with it, announced that he intended keeping it in his bedroom. I bet his mother was thrilled with that.

Or consider rain. When it rains, it is possible that pupils may suffer from wetness at playtime. There are, however, factors governing this. If the rain is very light, then the level of wetness would be low. A headteacher, or designated body, should determine whether the rain could be categorised as light by performing an action known as 'looking out of the window'. If raindrops cannot be clearly seen, it is likely the children will not be affected by wetness. If, however, the rain can be *heard*, there would be two clear ways to proceed. The children could go out to play, but put on waterproof clothing. If the rain became heavier while they are playing, they could take refuge. This would be known as 'sheltering under the playground shed'. Of course, if the rain became torrential, it would be preferable for the children not to go out to play, otherwise the teachers would waste much valuable time drying out clothing on the classroom radiators.

During the winter it can occasionally rain for the best part of an entire week. When I started my teaching career, it was all so easy. If it was raining, hailing, snowing or a force 9 gale was sweeping across the playground, the children still went outside, and they loved it. They were always told to dress appropriately, and some of them, of course, didn't. This meant they got wet and they sat uncomfortably through the next couple of lessons while their clothes dried out. If they had the luxury of sitting near the radiator, they dried out rather more speedily. I remember a child placing his socks on the radiator after a particularly heavy downpour, to the great consternation of those around him, since he wasn't renowned for changing them with any great frequency. The whole thing was an effective learning experience though. If the weather threatened inclemency, you brought your raincoat and your wellies to school. If it was raining at playtime, you wore them. If you didn't, you became wet and miserable. Which taught you to put them on next time the weather was grim.

By the time I'd done ten years in the classroom, things were changing. A few parents regularly complained if their offspring went into the playground under a threatening sky, and letters would be received if the teacher hadn't made sure everybody's coats were tightly buttoned, hoods pulled carefully around cheeks, and appropriate footwear done up tightly.

These days, of course, you daren't send children out to play in the rain. It probably contravenes every health and safety rule in the book. They must stay tucked up inside, in the warm. Which poses a problem. Teachers are entitled to a tea break, and somebody must look after the children while they have one. Earlier in my career, primary schools usually had a maximum of three teaching assistants, known merely as 'helpers'. They were people who mixed paint, cut card and made tea, but were rarely entrusted with anything more ambitious. Nevertheless, during wet playtimes they were charged with moving around the classrooms trying to make sure the children behaved themselves. Since their monitoring was necessarily spread thinly, the children took the opportunity to muck about as soon as the helper had moved to the next classroom, and the teacher could return from tea break to a scene of devastation.

Forewarned, I solved the problem at a stroke during my first year of headship. At that time, the school had just 147 children. If it rained, the infants took a favourite reading book into one hall, the juniors into the other, and they spread themselves comfortably on the floor to read quietly for fifteen minutes. I supervised the older children, my deputy supervised the infants, and the teachers had their break. On other occasions, we read to the children, or played simple activity games with them.

By the time I retired, my school had nearly 400 children... but technology had come to the rescue of wet playtimes. The children came into the hall, where I'd set up a DVD projector for them to enjoy the adventures of Spider-Man splashed on a ten foot wide screen with surround sound. Wet lunchtimes no longer seemed interminable. In fact, I often sat with the children and, like them, became absorbed enough to miss my own lunch.

And what about leaves? My bureaucratic mind meandered again. Leaves fall off the trees in November, and they can be very dangerous, especially when combined with wetness. Children can slip on them. So could the older members of staff. It would be good practice, therefore, to suggest that eyes should be trained downwards in Autumn, to avoid foot slippage. Of course, the children could gather the leaves for collage work, but everybody should wash their hands thoroughly after handling them. You never knew where they'd been once they'd left the tree.

It will be obvious that I quickly became conditioned to expect seasonal health and safety directives telling me how to proceed. The summer term, for example, had brought documentation about the inherent dangers from a bit of sunshine.

Firstly, a leaflet telling me how public services could be affected in the heat. There would be an increased demand for water, the implication being, I guess, that we should go easy filling the staff room kettles. There could be staff shortages... presumably if teachers had been silly enough to lie naked in their deckchairs all weekend. With global warming, there could be sudden changes in the weather, or flash flooding, or an increase in fires.

Accompanying this was an NHS booklet about looking after myself (and presumably my staff and children) in the hot weather. On the front there were pictures of the sun, an older bloke sensibly putting his straw hat on, and a tree, because that would be a jolly good thing to sit under when it's hot. Inside the booklet there was more helpful advice, telling me that looser clothes would help me to keep cool, and that if I came across someone suffering from the heat, it would be sensible to move them to a cooler place. Drinking, it said, is a really good idea too, water being the ideal beverage. Best to keep Year 6 off the lager, then.

I wondered how we'd managed in the past? Had we suddenly become so stupid that blindingly obvious procedures needed constantly stating in words and illustrations that would insult a ten year old? And what was it all costing? Then I was reminded that several fast food restaurants, ever wary of litigation, were issuing customers with notices telling them to take care when drinking coffee because when the liquid is first served, it tends to be hot, and somebody had sued.

It wasn't just the material that arrived in the post, either. Each education authority began to appoint a team of health and safety advisers, and their brief was to visit schools regularly, talk to the teachers at a staff meeting, and make sure that everyone fully understood the current rules and regulations that were now integral to all public bodies, and particularly to schools and classrooms.

Philip, you want to perform a simple experiment to show how much oxygen there is in air? It involves placing a jam jar over a lighted candle? You'd definitely need to have a full written risk assessment for that lesson. What if the candle fell over and set fire to something? You say you'd embed it in a lump of plasticine so it wouldn't? Well, that's a good idea, but you could still accidentally knock it over. You could move the entire class to the back of the room, of course. They wouldn't see the experiment if you did that? Well, better just not do it, then. Tell them about it instead, or let them watch it on line. After all, you don't want Mrs Brown rubbing her hands at the prospect of compensation. Maria, you want your class to construct miniature balsa wood Tudor houses? I think I'd hold off using the craft knives and hot glue guns if I were you… A farm visit, Katie? Great idea! I'm certain your Reception class would love it, but you'll need to consider the food poisoning organisms present in farm animals? Campylobacter, salmonella, cryptosporidium, listeria monocytogens, that sort of thing.

What about the suitability of places the children can eat at the farm? Timber benches? There could be a real danger of splinters. What about their footwear, the risk of infection from animal bedding, the dangers of foodstuff and animal faeces, the importance of remembering to dress cuts and grazes appropriately and ensure little hands are washed? And since small children have a tendency to kiss the animals, better warn them about that too… And Katie, there's now an important debate about whether children should visit farms at all. As I listened to all this from a health and safety adviser at a staff meeting, I recalled always spending a day on a farm with my Year 6's on school journey to the Isle of Wight. Perhaps I shouldn't have let the friendly farmer allow the children a drive of his tractor….

There's certainly no shortage of health and safety 'specialists' eager to tell you what you're doing wrong, at a price. Every now and then schools are alerted to a new health issue. When an urgent directive was issued to premises officers telling them to remove cabin hooks from the doors along school corridors and at entrances to halls, it seemed the thinkers and planners had decided that if a fire broke out and the doors were hooked back, the flames would spread more rapidly. I refused to remove them, and I had my reasons carefully prepared when the fire officer arrived.

I explained that in forty years of teaching in buildings like mine, I had never seen a fire, and that if there was no adult in sight, children would sprint through the doors on their way out to play Spider-Man (health and safety unapproved version) because children were children. Then I stood an infant in front of a door, showing how, if it slapped back, the doorknob would effectively remove all his teeth. In my view, the danger of a fire was therefore considerably lower than the likelihood of a door-knobbed face. The officer nodded gravely, jotted down a note or two, and left. I didn't hear from him again.

During a school year, a headteacher endures a variety of 'audits'. Officials arrive with briefcases, jotter pads, pens and serious faces. They peruse your documentation, make tutting noises, and then send you a report saying you're not fully complying with current legislation, usually designed by suits who change it every year because they've nothing better to do. There will be a financial audit, to make sure money isn't being siphoned into your personal Barbados holiday fund, a health and safety inspection to check that children aren't playing dangerous games like conkers, and a fire safety inspection to make sure the fire alarm Darren keeps setting off, because the fire department insisted on putting the new alarm buttons at a height that a child could easily reach, is still working properly.

But the one that always got to me was known as the Human Resources Audit. Four areas are checked; performance management, policies and procedure, safer recruitment and personnel files. Each area is scrutinised, boxes are ticked or crossed, and a rating from outstanding to inadequate given. Could I see the school's whistleblowing policy, I'm asked. I try humour, explaining it isn't needed because I've run an after-school workshop on blowing a whistle and my teachers have mastered it. Humour doesn't work, so I turn to my computer, and triumphantly screen the approved local education authority policy. I'm told it won't do, because that is last year's and it's been amended. I hunt through my electronic file of policies and… hurrah… I have the up to date policy. I'm asked when the school governing body adopted it and I can't remember. So, no tick in the box for that bit, then.

I'm asked about performance management of my teachers to check that they're all working their socks off, and please show me the documentation to prove it. I explain, at length, why I think performance management is patronising, unnecessary, unacceptable and a potential recipe for senior management to bully those lower down in the pile. The auditor doesn't expound a view of her own, simply pointing out that it's statutory now. Never one to break the law, I show the auditor how I comply with it by getting my staff to fill in a simple form. It seems the teachers find my way of managing their performance more than acceptable, but giving out a simple form is not the accepted way of doing things, so I'm afraid I fail on that one too.

Throughout the afternoon, I question the sense of what I'm asked to do. When a teacher returns to work after illness, I'm supposed to hold a 'Return to Work Interview'. If they've returned to work, I ask, why do I need to interview them? If they've been ill and they've now returned to school, I'm working under the assumption that they're no longer ill. It's good practice, I'm told. I explain that I don't ask my teachers to waste hours on unnecessary paper-filling exercises. They're free to enjoy teaching.. And because they enjoy it, they're rarely away. If they do happen to be ill, I want to welcome them back, not conduct an interview. Unfortunately, my view is frowned upon. Oh dear, another unticked box bites the dust.

We're not even safe when we turn the staffroom tap on. Have I had the water tested, because there's always a risk of Legionnaire's Disease? I explain that I wouldn't let a diseased legionnaire within a mile of my school, but that doesn't even summon a smile. I also explain that the loft tanks have just been replaced, that we don't have air conditioning, and that water doesn't have a chance to stagnate. But I'm told it would still be a good idea to have it checked. Just in case. Better safe than sorry. It'll only cost £1,500 to check. And I'm afraid, yes, it would have to come out of the school budget.

These officials constantly remind me we live in a litigious society. I know, I say, a society where policemen refuse to jump into a lake to save a drowning child, flower baskets are removed from lampposts lest they drop on people's heads, a game of conkers becomes a dangerous playground activity, and Ofsted inspectors (of all people!) tell policewomen they're not allowed to childmind each other's children.

Then I'm told that when writing my 'person specification' for a job, I should mention that the applicant needs to be 'motivated to work with children'. Surely, I say, this can probably be taken for granted? If I was advertising for a zoo keeper, would I need to say that a motivation to work with animals was desirable? If I were advertising for a dentist to work in my practice, would I need to say that an interest in teeth would be an advantage? By three o'clock my patience, and that of my auditor, is wearing thin. I'm given a rating of totally inadequate.

Two weeks later, I attend a one day obligatory course with the Human Resources department on 'safer recruitment'. At the end of the day we're given a written test of our knowledge, and we are promised certificates if we pass. I passed, but I never received my certificate. Naturally, I immediately wrote to HR and told them this was totally inadequate.

I often wondered what the government thought being a headteacher was all about. It wasn't about cutting bureaucracy, certainly. Single day compulsory courses for headteachers blossomed, and I often returned to school wondering what I had learned and how useful that day had actually been, apart from the chance to eat expensive three-tiered sandwiches and some quality biscuits with the coffee. When I eventually managed to compile and gather all the policies that were deemed statutory, I realised I had sixty seven of them. Whatever it was, you could be pretty certain I had a policy on it. The biggest problem was trying to keep them all up to date.

And still the authorities wanted more. One Monday, I was visited by a nice man from Educational Welfare, who wanted to talk about child protection. It had rightly assumed increased importance due to something called the 'Every Child Matters' initiative. He needed an hour and a half of my time, he said, and he came with a large cardboard box filled with fat booklets, pamphlets, checklists and the new child protection policy for us to evaluate and discuss. I pointed out that it looked virtually the same as last year's child protection policy, but I was told it had changed in 'significant detail'. What detail? He wasn't sure, as it was a big document and he hadn't had time to read it fully yet. At that moment, a child was sick in the corridor, so it was a good moment to cancel the interview and rush off for the premises officer.

The following day, I received a letter saying I hadn't forwarded the certificate for my annual fire risk inspection. Oh dear, I'd forgotten that one. The inspection has to be carried out by a qualified inspector, naturally, and I knew jolly well that I'd end up having a row with him, because last time he told me I shouldn't have all those 'decorative paper hazards' covering the classroom, hall and corridor walls. He was referring to the explosion of colourful children's art and craft which, amazingly, happens to be such an important a feature of the things we call primary schools, especially mine, and which visitors to the school so admired.

The end of the week brought a bill for £2,500. This was for an asbestos inspection, arranged by the local education authority, and which I'd no idea I'd have to stump up for. Since we'd had an asbestos inspection several years ago, when just two tiny non-dangerous segments had been found in the boiler room, common sense told me the LEA would have looked up its previous report and not bothered to re-inspect the building. But no, life isn't that simple, and I'm left arguing the toss about a huge bill I have no intention of paying.

And then my Premises Officer asked me what he should do about PAT this year. No, PAT wasn't a troublesome cleaner. It's an acronym for Portable Appliance Testing. To ensure children and staff don't disappear in a puff of smoke, we should have every electrical item in the school checked annually by an accredited electrical firm. Even though we've got hundreds of electrical items in this age of technology, all with proper, tamperproof moulded plugs on, they have to be tested annually. Every item costs £3.50 to test. We could buy an awful lot of reading books with that.

I could have understood the testing if we were in the situation a couple of decades ago, when teachers could bring in any old piece of electrical equipment to use as a visual or aural aid in their classroom, most of which they'd attached plugs to themselves. But we're not. And much as attaching a thirteen amp plug to a bit of kit might seem a relatively simple task, it isn't. Most premises officers could do it properly, but if a teacher brought something electrical in I always insisted on looking at the plug, and I sometimes found plugs where the earth wire hadn't been fixed, or the wrong fuse had been fitted, or the wires inside the plug had frayed, or the wire clamp wasn't clamping. These days, of course, every electrical item you buy, from a dishwasher to an electric toothbrush, has a properly wired fuse and plug attached to it, so spending a couple of grand on checking all the plugs now seems an incredible waste of money.

When the *Guardian* newspaper published a little booklet of things children should do before they're eleven I read it with fascination in the light of today's limitations, because I remembered the halcyon days of my own childhood. I had parks to play in... one with a huge pond for sailing boats on, a wood close by for damming a stream and playing Robin Hood (occasionally with Maid Marion if Margaret from three doors away was up for it), a grassy common with a hill for racing our home made go-carts on, allotments for the occasional spot of scrumping, and streets that weren't full of cars, so marbles could be played in the road. Summer holidays seemed endless and idyllic.

The Guardian recommended that children should have walked along a fallen tree trunk, played conkers, eaten an apple from a tree, built a den, rolled down a hill, and buried someone in the sand. All simple activities I'd undertaken as a child. But I could imagine the health and safety advisers throwing up their hands in horror.

Walking along a fallen tree trunk? A highly dangerous activity. The upper surface of the tree trunk would need to be levelled, because a child could easily slip from the slope of the trunk. At the very least, it would need an approved safety surface placed at both sides of the trunk, with the child wearing a hard hat and safety jacket suitably inflated. Inappropriately trimmed branch stubs could prove a trip hazard, so stout boots should be a mandatory item on the risk assessment.

Conkers? A primitive game long outlawed in sensible playgrounds for its inherent dangers. Unless approved cord is used, there is a danger of the string snapping and a conker striking one of the players in an exposed bodily region, with bruising and possible laceration. An approved face mask would need to be worn. If unavailable at the time of playing, an improvised helmet, suitably fastened, may be deemed suitable, provided it conformed to health and safety standard BS31BBCITV.

An apple from a tree? Appropriate fruit recognition would need to be made, and the child would need to be given a short visual test before undertaking this activity to confirm familiarity with the appearance of a safe apple. Tests would need to be done to ensure the apple is ripe, and of a variety suitable for eating. Otherwise there could be a danger of stomach ache, cramps, or at the worst, an irritated bowel, especially if the child is not conversant with the principle of eating fruit in appropriate quantities. The apple should also be cleansed before consumption, and a visual check made for maggots and other unpalatable fauna.

Build a den? A very worrying proposition. Advice would need to be given about materials to be used for this activity, and from where they should be gathered. A child should therefore undertake this activity only after obtaining written consent from a parent, guardian, or other appropriate adult. The adult would then assume direct responsibility in the event of any accidents or incidents. On no account should children sleep overnight in their dens, due to close proximity with creepy crawlies and the trauma that could result from direct contact with them. A test should be made to ensure the den covering is watertight, as contact with inclement weather may cause wetness and discomfort. Changes of clothing should be stored in a large waterproof container.

Roll down a hill? Not recommended, as this could cause dizziness, nausea, and a great deal of silly laughter. It is also possible that the child may swerve out of control and cause injury to other rollers. If this activity is undertaken, the gradient should be measured with standardised approved equipment, and be within the recommended slopeage.

Burying someone in the sand? A dangerous suggestion. If this is undertaken, only plastic digging implements should be used, and the child should dig no further than waist height, as there is a danger of the trench sides collapsing and therefore possible suffocation. During all excavation activity, the child should wear suitable apparatus to avoid breathing problems in case of sand slide. If unavailable, a simple breathing device fashioned from hollow tubes and masking tape may suffice. It should be stressed that all outdoor activities should be approached with caution. It is far safer for children to sit in the warm with their play stations.

When I was a Boy Scout, a favourite game at our Monday night meetings was a little divertissement known as 'Fight For The Chalk'. Two rectangles were drawn on the floor, one at each end of the room, and a circle was drawn in the centre. A lump of chalk was placed in the circle. The boys were divided into two teams and they sat facing each other, stretched out between the rectangles. The boys in the teams were given corresponding numbers, and you sat cross legged waiting for your turn to play.

If your number was called, you leapt to your feet, grabbed the chalk, and ran to make a mark inside your team's designated rectangle, thereby scoring a point. The only problem was your opposite number. He'd be trying to do the same, so you had to fight extremely hard for chalk possession. This meant grappling energetically with your opponent until you'd got his head firmly jammed between your legs. Then you squeezed, while trying to prise his fingers open... a process that could take a good ten minutes, with much egging on being done by your mates. If you weren't too keen on the tussling element of the game, the tactic was to sit still for a fraction of a second too long, let your opponent score, and then pretend you hadn't heard your number called. It was an accepted way of saving face.

We all thought it was tremendous fun, and I don't remember anybody being carted off to hospital. But how times change. Recently, I read about a group of Scouts who erected an aerial runway on a camping trip. The Scout leader had fully equipped the boys with hard hats and harnesses when two louts gate-crashed their enjoyment and climbed on the runway. One fell off and injured himself, whereupon his mother successfully sued. Unbelievably, the Scout leader was told he should have forced the louts to wear protection.

Obviously, the judge had never played 'Fight For The Chalk.'

6

THERE'LL BE ANOTHER ONE ALONG IN FIVE MINUTES

Fads, Fashions and Failings In Educational Policy

You stand waiting for ages, and then three come along at once. That old adage applies to buses. Fads and fashions in education come along even faster. Headteachers and class teachers try to keep up, governors continually struggle and often give up, and many of the initiatives designed to improve the quality of education the children are receiving are often unworkable, impossibly demanding, or, on so many occasions, simply ridiculous. They are often instigated by politicians whose knowledge and experience of schools, especially in areas like the ones I spent my entire career in, is virtually nil. I recall a book for sale on Amazon recently, advertised as 'a great gift for teachers' and entitled 'What Our Current Education Minister Knows About Education.' The entire book was blank.

My local authority played its part too and I sometimes felt it treated me like a fluffy-brained youth. Especially when I received circulars such as the one announcing 'The council's vision for success is PRIDE in its education services.' Well okay, I thought, I'm proud of my school and so are the headteachers of quite a few other primary schools around me. I hope the council is too. But then the word PRIDE is repeated, and printed *vertically*, in large letters, down the length of the page. 'P', it says, stands for 'promoting learning', 'R' for 'raising achievement', 'I' for 'instilling confidence', 'D' for 'developing competence', and 'E', would you believe, for 'empowering communities'. Frankly, I wondered if the idea had been given to a fresh-faced council junior to work on, although I knew that acronyms were all the rage that month. My chair of governors, who worked at the Home Office, was very fond of SMART targets (specific, measurable, achievable, relevant, time-bound), but I found the whole notion ridiculous and obvious.

Or, horror, had it been put together by a *team*? I could just imagine WPFACS (Working Party For Acrostics And Catchy Slogans) getting together to dream up this stuff...

'Gottit! What about EDUCATION? After all, that's the game we're in.'

'How do you spell EDUCATION?'

'OK then, something simpler. What about SOARING TO SUCCESS? 'S' for Selebrate...'

'Too many S's. It needs to be catchy. What about ACCESS FOR ALL?'

'No, they'll think you're flogging a credit card. How about ACHIEVING EXCELLENCE?'

'Does the i come before the e? No, wait, there's a c in there, so wouldn't the e come before the i...'

'Simon, we haven't got all day. Let's go for a one-worder. PRIDE?'

'Wow, yes. Nice one Nigel. That'll give us Promoting, Raising, Instilling, Developing. What about the E? Education's too obvious. Energetic, Effective?'

'What about Empowering?'

'Empowering! Lovely word. Empowering what?'

'Children?'

'No no, broader, bigger!'

'Communities?'

'Super! What does it mean, empowering communities?'

'Nothing, really. Sounds *great* though. Five thousand copies before noon, Doris. Oh look, it's 10.30am already. Coffee break.'

And on it goes. Piles of paper. Mountains of nonsense. Money wasted that is needed in schools. All headteachers will tell you that nowadays a policy is mandatory for everything, because it keeps local officialdom, and inspectors in particular, very happy. It doesn't mean you have to do anything, you just need a policy. You don't even have to think one up, because several astute firms out there produce policies online covering everything from personal health For Year 6 to citizenship for the under-fives. Just load 'em in the computer and put your school's name where it leaves a space. Half an hour's work and job done. And you've no idea how much it'll impress your governing body. Meantime, when I drive to work, the streets are in poor repair and full of rubbish, although I bet there's a policy for cleaning them up somewhere.

Then there are the fashionable words and phrases. When David Miliband was minister of state for schools he made a great deal of 'tailor made learning' and 'personalised learning'. Neat buzz words, yes, but he never seemed able to say exactly what they meant or how they could be applied to the everyday classroom. He'd reported that he'd visited a north London comprehensive and it was undertaking 'tailor-made learning'. He told us that Ofsted says it works incredibly well, although they'd seen it in hardly any schools. If it hadn't been explained clearly to the rest of us, that was hardly surprising. He went on to say that whatever it was, it would give us 'a powerful new analysis of pupil achievement with data based on 'value-added''. Then he added a bit about prior attainment, poverty and gender, and 'key aspects for a reform agenda'. 'Every pupil needs a curriculum that is inspiring and interesting,' he said. Well, I certainly wasn't one to disagree with that. The trouble is, a curriculum like that needed money, and at the time he was writing, the government was busily making cuts.

As I read further, the buzz words and jargon came thick and fast. He stated that 'embracing' ICT was essential, because it would 'make a reality of personal learning paced to meet individual needs'. What did this really mean? Screen-staring, button-pushing youngsters with numbingly boring individualised learning programmes? These ICT programmes have their uses, of course, but there are dangers. Prior to the days of technology we had learning systems like the SRA reading laboratory. I knew one primary school which had given the whole of its mornings over to SRA, which was essential a box of colour coded cards with literacy tasks on. Once the child had completed the tasks, he could mark his own work by returning to the box and taking out the answer card. Naturally, with the entire class doing this and while the teacher was bent over a desk helping somebody else, it was extremely easy to cheat and have a look at the answer card before writing your answers. And the system emanated from the United States, so at the time I watched it demonstrated by a proud headteacher, it was full of sentences like 'Charlie Brown went down to the drug store to buy some candy and cookies.' Rather than asking the teacher to help with working out an answer, the child usually needed to ask what a drug store was. There were a number of similar systems for learning maths, none of them lasting very long.

And then Mr Miliband's piece ran away with itself. 'Individual pupils need individual attention,' it said, hence the government intended to deliver an extra 50,000 classroom assistants. (Remember, pre Brexit, the bus that said £350 million a week would be going to the NHS?) It seemed obvious to me that a lack of funding meant a lack of classroom assistants. Then, summing up, we were told that we 'needed to make secondary school children a new offer, delivering quality and equity wherever they are from and wherever they might live.' Since the purpose of education is to let people cut an informed path through the life's chances, I couldn't imagine any teacher believing that kind of simplistic politicking unless they were going to be told, in detail, exactly how it was to be done.

Sometimes, I simply couldn't believe what I was reading. When I opened my *Times Educational Supplement* newspaper one Friday morning, an article suggested that secondary school teachers often appeared stuffy and out of touch to the youngsters they were teaching and that they should get more up to date with what was happening in their lives and the street language they used, possibly putting some of it into the delivery of a lesson. The article didn't exactly say that Shakespeare should be abandoned, but it was hinted that his plays should be made far more accessible.

Well, fine... I remembered how, at my own secondary school, well-worn ancient copies of Macbeth were thrown at us one afternoon to introduce us to the Bard, and not having a clue about the language used. It would obviously have helped enormously if we'd been taken to see the play or watched a film of it before we studied it. With the addition of a good dollop of 'street', I could just imagine how Macbeth might be presented to a bunch of twelve year olds these days…

Yo Doods, lissen up.
I is readin' in dat Time Educashun Supplimint about how some of you is havin' problems with yo learnin' 'cos we teachers ain't speakin' in de language wot you understan'.

Now I don't want you failin' yo tests or de govermint will be leanin' heavily on me shoulder, know wot I'm sayin'? So I hope you is appreciatin' that I has spent my weeken' on a corse run by de local educashun honchos to learn us teechers a bit o' street, innit. Now, where wos we in our learnin' last week? We was talkin' bout that well-good playright Willyum Shakespears and I was extollin' his virtues. Yo! Wot dat man cood do wiv a feather an' a tub of ink, eh?

Now, we is studyin' Macbeff an' I know some o' you doods is havin' a bit o' trobble unnerstandin' wot this guy Shakespears is on about, but patience man, you gotta give him some respeck. OK, he ain't no Ediff Blighton, but that don't mean he ain't got a tale worth tellin'. I is gonna sum up dis tale for you 'cos I know you is anxious to get outside and do some twiddlin' on yo mobiles.

This honcho Macbeff is a cool dood. He is well in wiv de King, and people was well feared of him and Bro' Banquo, wot was also a mean fighter. Anyway, they is returnin' from battle and crossin' this blasted heaf. That ain't Shakespears doin' a bit o' swearin'. You gotta 'ppreciate that this dood lived in the sixteenf sentry, before you is even born. So Macbeff ain't sayin' 'I hate this blasted heaf, 'tis a bleedin' nuisance', he is sayin' de heaf ain't got much plant growin' on it.

Anyways, they is crossin' de heaf when they is confronted by these three bitches, man, and they is well mingin'. They has warts on their noses and hairy chins and stuff like dat. They is tellin' Macbeff he will be main man o' Scotland before much time is pass.

Well, when Macbeff's Mrs hears dis, she ain't waitin' 'round till de king die, so she get her husbind to waste him instead, when they is comin' for tea an' cake one day at their castle. It ain't too long before he is murderin' dat Banquo too.

Nat'rally, Macbeff don't sleep too easy. His missus is up all nite tryin' to wash blood off her hands wot ain't there and sayin' 'Is this a shank I see before me?' And then Banquo come back as a ghost right when Macbeff is eatin' his dinner, scarin' de shit outa him.

Macbeff thinks he better talk wiv them heath bitches again and they tells him 'Beware, man, specially of a dood called McDuffer.' But Macbeff thinks they probly bin on the weed 'cos wot they say don't make a lotta sense, specially when they tell him he can't be wasted by man born o' woman. They tell him to stay cool, man, less he sees Burn 'em Wood come to Duncesname.

So Macbeff don't do no serious frettin', but then McDuffer gets this army o' bruvvers together and they dress up as trees, man, and they come and attack the castle, innit. Macbeff says 'You can't waste me, man, 'cos you is born o' woman'. But dat's the catch, 'cos McDuffer was born in a Caesar Section, so Macbeff is wasted and Malcum de King son get to be main man after all.

Next week, we is doin' Chorcer. Meantimes, text me an essay. Yo!

I don't think anybody took the idea too seriously, and perhaps it was written with a tongue firmly in the cheek. Not so the arrival of the 'Gifted and Talented' agenda, however.

In the late 1990s the Department for Education introduced the term 'gifted and talented' or 'G&T' to describe children who were attaining a high level at school. At that time, G&T referred to children whose attainments put them in the top five per cent of their year group. Later, this was changed to the top ten per cent. It was an utterly ridiculous idea that disappeared almost as quickly as it arrived.

Let me tell you, for example, about Christopher and Natasha. Natasha had a real talent for the violin and was the best violinist we'd ever had. We made special provision for her and she achieved a very high standard. She could, I felt, go on to play professionally. Christopher was clever, too, and he was a pupil in my Year 6 class when I was a deputy head. He showed a real aptitude for woodwork. Since I've always loved DIY and woodwork in particular, I designed many special projects for him and he finished Year 6 by making a beautiful bathroom cabinet, all fitted together with carefully crafted dovetail joints. It wasn't hard to make these special arrangements. I didn't write copious notes or have a co-ordinating team to check everything. Catering for the differing needs of children is part of a teacher's professional responsibility and, because I didn't have to write reams about it, all my energy went into gathering the materials and ensuring it was actually done.

But when G&T arrived in earnest, I received a large, glossy folder from the government telling me how I should address the needs of the gifted and talented children in my school. I groaned inwardly as I opened it, because I knew what was coming: a fat wad of paper that would say much and mean little. Page one told me how to recognise a G and T. Had I any children with intrapersonal intelligence (no, I hadn't a clue what that meant either) or bodily-kinaesthetic potential? (Stop that bodily-kinaesthetic behaviour, boy, or you'll spend the morning with your nose on the wall.) Then I was told that the diverse range of abilities in children should be nurtured. Fancy, I thought, I hadn't realised that.

Then I had to... well, of course, write a policy. Nothing can be done in schools these days unless a policy has been written for it. My school had 43 written policies; Anything you could name, we had a policy written for it. Spider-Man cards and bubble gum packets? In the bin with them. You know they're not allowed in school. It says so in our Spider-Man cards and bubble gum policy.

Then I was told I needed to have a named person for co-ordinating 'all the issues relating to the education of G and Ts'. No doubt, I thought, the co-ordinator would need a working party and a steering committee. Probably lots of time out of class, too. You can't co-ordinate when you're teaching. Then came a page of 'school responsibilities' where those familiar words 'monitor and evaluate' popped up repeatedly. And there was plenty of edujargon too; the school should 'respond flexibly', 'celebrate diversity' and 'use a wide range of identification methods'. The booklet didn't, however, tell me what these methods might be. Which was just as well, because on it went, for 85 pages.

When one of my teachers was told that her son, at secondary school, had been deemed 'gifted and talented', she wasn't told at what, exactly. Simply that she'd hear more soon, because they'd formed an initial working party. She never heard from the school again. The co-ordinator was having trouble finding a date when the members of the working party were available. Which made my teacher fancy a G and T herself. A strong one...

During one of my Ofsted inspections, G&T was fashionable and high on the agenda. I explained that a number of children in my school had particular talents and I talked about every one; Ellen whose art work was stunning, Kwaku who was already a writer, Hamed who played the clarinet in the hall at lunchtime rather than go out to play... I knew them all. But, I said, I refuse to write anything down, have a policy, or a steering committee or any of the other rubbish these 'initiatives' seemed to demand. We didn't need them. We were more than able to nurture talent.

Sometimes, when a circular arrived from the local education authority, you checked the diary to see if it was April 1st, you scratched your head in amazement... and then you thought 'Really, you simply couldn't make this stuff up.' Such as the circular detailing the school holiday dates for the following year. On the list of public holidays at the bottom of the letter, we were informed that Christmas Day would be on December 26th, Boxing Day would be December 27th, and New Year's Day would be January 2nd. Fascinated, I emailed the LEA asking them if they'd alerted Christians to this important change of Christmas date. Of course, the dates on the letter were incorrect, and there were apologies all round, but nobody had bothered to check the letter before sending it out to every school. Which amazed me, because even if I was sending a letter to a parent, I would check it several times.

A minor incident like that doesn't cause any disruption, of course. It was merely a moment of amusement that lightened our afternoon and caused slight embarrassment to the authority. But local and government educational bureaucracy can sometimes reach mind numbing levels of asininity. A friend of mine is headteacher of a small school in the countryside, and he was recently told by his LEA that all its schools had to produce a travel plan for the children. Two people had been employed by the authority specifically to visit every establishment and explain exactly how it should be done. As in all schools, town or country, the idea was to promote walking, cycling, or the use of public transport... and no teacher would have a problem with that.

However, with this school, there was one major and important limiting factor... just seven pupils live in the village, relatively close to the school, and the rest travel considerable distances. There is no public transport, and they are therefore forced to travel by car.

This fact cut no ice with the LEA. The head was instructed to form a Travel Plan Working Party, consult widely, and then compile a series of targets with a time scale. Astonished, he completed the LEA's proforma with wisely worded nonsense, was thanked for his submittance, and told somebody would be in touch if the Department of Education felt that anything had been left out.

Early in the dawn of the ICT age, another colleague received an email informing his independent school that information could be sent to parents by electronic means, and that he might not be aware of that. Almost immediately, the email was recalled. Then the same email was sent to him again, with minor adjustments. An hour later, this too was recalled. The same thing was sent again. And again. And again. The head sent an irate note, asking if the DfE would be kind enough not to waste his time. Back came a reply, apologising for the fact that it had taken seven e-mails, but it was 'a genuine attempt to determine whether measures put in place by the DfE to reduce bureaucracy were being successful.'

Daniel, a headteacher in Oxfordshire, had to submit a staff absence return to the DfE, but their computer rejected his results. They were too low, and, astonishingly, he was asked to increase his staff absence numbers so that the return could run. Naturally, he went straight to his hard working staff and told them to be ill a lot more often..

And then there are the 'buzz' words. Throughout my headship, I was always wondering what the next buzz word would be. It wasn't so long ago that every teacher's lesson, every school governor's agenda item, or every group discussion had to have a 'focus'. If you were a student teacher in school on your teaching practice and you missed the word focus out of your lesson plans, you were in very deep water when your tutor visited.

And then 'share' became the fashionable word. If the inspector called to look round your school (in the days before they came in bundles and were labelled Ofsted), he or she offered to 'share' some thoughts with you. He actually meant that he intended to run through your school's good bits and bad bits, just like he'd always done.

And what about 'mission statement'? A truly stupid phrase that caused me amusement initially, and then annoyance. I associate the word 'mission' with the armed forces, NASA, and Tom Cruise's impossible ones, but not with education. Once, presumably at the whim of a government suit, every school in the land was required to write a 'mission statement'. No longer could your prospectus simply tell parents about the exciting things going on at your school, nor could you make the assumption that a parent with even half a brain could work out from reading it what your aims were. No, you had to start with a mission statement, and you invariably opened with: 'We aim to develop every child's ability and potential to the full.'

Throughout the UK, every school mission statement was virtually identical. After all, you'd hardly say you that *weren't* trying to develop each child's ability to the full, would you? I remember visiting a school which had its lengthy mission statement blazoned in huge letters along the entrance walls. Further along the corridor, I could see four older boys beating up a first year…

And targets, well, they're something else. For starters, governors in primary schools were required to predict what the children would achieve by the time they were eleven. Masses of computerised school data would have been collected to help them, but governors are voluntary workers and it was always down to the headteachers to do the real spadework, taking their valuable time away from doing something more useful, like expanding the school's musical curriculum.

Since we were dealing with children, and not sales graphs of potatoes, results were, and are, often difficult to predict, especially for the required two or three years hence. In my neck of the woods, families tended to move in and out of the area constantly, and once, when I sent our targets to the education authority, I was told I'd set them too low. I pointed out that I was actually making an accurate prediction because the cohort wasn't especially able, and was quite likely to change during the year anyway. Immaterial, I was told. The government had demanded a minimum level from the local authority. I couldn't help wondering if a looming election had something to do with that.

Even so, some of the advice emanating from government circles convinced me the writers hadn't been near a classroom since their own childhood, if they actually had one. Silliness had segued into high art. We were advised, for example, to set different kinds of 'target *zone*': historic, challenge, unlikely or comfort. I had no idea what they were. The only person who really applauded all this was my chair of governors. His work at the home office presumably meant he spent a fair amount of time inventing this kind of stuff.

Alongside the litany of odd phrases, buzz words and meaningless targets, the demand for lesson planning in extraordinary detail arrived, supported and advocated of course by the Ofsted inspection system. A neighbour of mine is a head of department in a secondary school. He is experienced, dedicated, an excellent teacher. Religious education isn't the easiest of subjects to teach, but children look forward to his lessons because he entertains them, and he continually seeks out new ways of capturing their interest and involving them. When he tells me about a lesson he's taught, I often think how much more enjoyable my own secondary school education would have been if I'd had a few teachers like him.

But now a new broom is sweeping his academic corridors, and he's no longer a happy man. Before he teaches he has to fill in three sides of A4 paper. Not once a week, or even once a day. Before each and every lesson. I wondered why I hadn't seen him in his garden, and it seems he's kissed goodbye to evenings and weekends. The depth of planning he has to undertake is ludicrous, and virtually impossible to achieve without working every evening. The lesson planning sheets are complex and detailed. On page one you fill in your name (get the tough ones over with first), the day, the date, the time of day, the room you're teaching the lesson in, the class being taught and the topic you're teaching. I was surprised you didn't have to say what you'd had for breakfast.

Then, there's a space for your desirable outcomes. To remain upright throughout the day, presumably? Next, a slot for equipment requirements. (I shall need an overhead projector. I must remember to write down 'overhead projector' in case I forget. Oh, and some overhead transparencies. And pencils. And paper.) Next, a section for 'key words', presumably important words and phrases you're trying to emphasise in the lesson. ('Andrew, would you kindly stop firing screwed-up wet tissues at the ceiling' springs to mind.)

Now 'context' must be considered. There's quite a large space for that, whatever it is. Then we need to show how the lesson incorporates key skills, literacy, numeracy, ICT, citizenship and SMSC (sado-masochism for stressed colleagues?), all of which must be related to the lesson in hand and explained in a sentence or two.

Close behind are children with additional needs, English as an additional language, hearing impairments and, of course, gifted and talented. Naturally, we need a full explanation of what these groups will be doing. Then, differentiated homework plans, and finally a risk assessment, just in case somebody is going to inadvertently connect the Bunsen burner to a water tap and soak the ceiling, or put a staple through their finger while trying to put their work on the classroom display board. As far as I can see, the greatest risk is that the teacher will go nuts and try to chew his own leg off.

But that not it, yet. Not by a long chalk. Take a deep breath, because here comes page two! Now you have to sketch out your entire lesson structure for the three main elements: introduction, development and plenary. Not only the teacher's activity, mind, but a full explanation of what the children will be doing as well. Then there's a space for 'assessment opportunities', 'lesson comments' and 'next week'. Presumably the latter is like a cinema trailer to whet the children's appetite for the next episode. ('Wow, I can hardly wait for next week! The chance to complete another photocopied worksheet because the poor bloody teacher's too busy to talk to us!)

And even now we haven't finished. Onwards, to the final page, where we find a 'class information sheet.' This time, we fill in the number on register, the number present, the very able students, the classroom seating plan, the group ability, and the higher, middle, and lower ability students in the group.

Finally.. do stay with it, we're almost there.. we have a space for any additional comments or suggestions. Having read the whole of this, both of us could think of a few. My suggestion would be that whoever wrote the form should roll it up very tightly and.... but there, don't tempt me.

To keep up with the spiralling demands on schools, most local education authorities, including mine, offered what they hoped would be useful and helpful meetings, although when local management of schools came along... whereby schools had to manage their own budgets, do all their own accounting, and send off monthly reports to the audit department of the council, my authority gave its schools some accounting computer software to make things easier, although computers in school offices were still relatively new then.

Unfortunately, it had been designed 'in house', and although it was accepted by the council's education department, it wasn't good enough for the council's auditors. Another bit of software was designed and linked into the first programme, complicating things even further. I struggled and worried about it continuously, because people's wages depended on me getting it right, and in the end I drove over to the council's education department to seek out help. 'Frankly, we haven't a clue, either,' said the first auditor I spoke to. 'The whole thing's a mess.' Fortunately, computer software development being what it is, several astute firms saw an open market, and I had little option but to buy expensively into one of them, but at least it saved me a great deal of grief.

Attending meetings was never my favourite activity, which is why I always kept staff meetings relatively short and efficient. Everybody needs a chance to contribute their point of view, but it's amazing how even the simplest aspects of school life can go round and round and risk not being resolved. Like why the washing up rota doesn't work, and how David refuses to go on the rota anyway because he doesn't drink tea or coffee or any other hot beverage and doesn't dirty a plate because he eats his tuna sandwich and banana from a paper bag.

But the meetings organised by the local authority could be much worse and I usually avoided them unless there was a life or death issue to be discussed, like boycotting SATs or striking about pensions. And headteachers usually have strong opinions about educational matters. A few… the professional meeting attenders… can cause meetings to drag on for ages. They're easy to spot; they're never in their schools and can be seen at every meeting you go to.

Meetings where the LEA instructed you on something or other could be quite frightening, such as a one-day course one of my governors and I attended on teacher recruitment. The rules had changed and it was important for heads and governors to know them, in case a job applicant 'grieved' and we were hauled to an industrial relations tribunal. Until then, I'd thought finding a new classroom teacher for September was relatively simple. Either you offered the job to a particularly good student on final teaching practice, or if you didn't have any outstanding students, you ran your eye over the LEA pool of newly qualifieds, chose a handful, invited them to look at your school and then did a quick interview, usually knowing exactly which one of them you wanted.

In fact, we discovered that the correct procedure had become incredibly detailed, time consuming, and… surprise… paper driven. Well over twenty separate stages, all of which had to be carefully recorded and filed. And following this procedure rigorously still wouldn't guarantee you got the best person for the job. If anything, it made things more complex for everybody concerned.

Another unnerving type of one-day course would always be the one that made you feel guilty because you weren't keeping abreast of current educational developments, which is hard anyway, because they changed at a moment's notice. Usually this would be run by somebody who had long since left the reality of the classroom. There's a PowerPoint presentation, and just in case anybody falls asleep, the same presentation is also handed to everybody on a sheaf of paper. I remember the furore around the Literacy Hour, a Labour initiative in which all primary schools were given big boxfuls of teaching materials and masses of instructions which even included what the teachers had to say. Schools were subtly persuaded it was statutory, and told Ofsted would have your head in a noose if you didn't do it. In fact, it never was.

After attending one on huge changes about to descend on Key Stage 1 children, my deputy head came back to school looking gaunt and worried. The agenda had been packed... reading surveys and league tables, raised achievement floor targets, changes in phonics teaching, new children with additional needs regulations, and revised Ofsted inspections before which, apparently, headteachers would be required to have an extended conversation on the telephone with the lead inspector. In answer to my deputy's question 'How on earth are we going to cope with it all?' I gave the usual response. 'The same way we usually do. Half of it won't happen, so let's just carry on doing what we're good at. Teaching children superbly.'

These days, the staff of a school is categorised. If you're a very important person, such as the head or deputy, you're in the leadership class. If you're not quite so important, you're probably a member of something called a senior management team. If you lead a curriculum area – surprise, surprise – you're a curriculum leader. But if you're a classroom teacher, well, even though you concentrate on the most important job of all, teaching the children, I'm afraid you don't count too much in the greater scheme of things.

The route to leadership has gone through many changes, but these days, it's easy to forget that schools are about people and, although some of the skills of headship can be taught, there is no substitute for experience and a feel for what makes people work well. Just as there are definable qualities about an outstanding class teacher, so it is with deputy headteachers and headteachers.

During my long career in education, I met and liked many headteachers. The best I knew had much in common. They were interesting people to talk to, very amusing, had a passion for education and their schools, enjoyed their job and, above all, had a certain humility about their own abilities. Undoubtedly, most consultant agencies would be willing to do an expensive four-month study and come up with the ingredients of a good leader in several fat volumes, (in fact, a Labour government did a very similar thing. A survey costing several millions was commissioned on what makes an effective teacher. I don't think teachers ever read it. They were too busy.) but I wonder if their shortlist for a successful headteacher would include what I consider to be the eight basic essentials.

1. Have a teaching timetable, however minimal, and keep to it. It gives you an enormous amount of staffroom 'street cred.'
2. Value everybody working in your school and make each one of them feel that what they have to say or contribute is important. If you make much of their good qualities, it's easier to change the things you're less happy with and if the teachers enjoy school, so will the children.
3. Visit classrooms often. The staff will feel you're interested, the children will welcome you, and you can tune in to any problems.
4. Don't become exasperated with the deluge of glossy DfE and LEA booklets, and the unlimited form-filling demands.

After all, the DfE is only trying to get rid of all that wretched taxpayers' money. Put them in the staffroom. They'll disappear quickly... not because they've been read, but because they're ideal for collage work. Or wait until somebody rings up demanding your reason for not having sent a form back and then question the relevance of the form in a mildly hysterical voice. You'll get bothered a lot less because the rumour will circulate that you're on the verge of a breakdown.... and headteachers are getting much harder to find these days.

5. Always have lots of time for children and the work they want to show you. It'll help with monitoring classroom standards too, and since the children invariably tell their parents they've been to see you, there will be a general view that you're still upright, interested and in touch with what's going on.

6. Give teaching and non-teaching staff the freedom to show what they can do. (I discovered by chance that one of my classroom assistants spent her spare time designing and building doll's houses, complete with furniture and accessories. She gave three fascinating assemblies on how she built them and the materials she used.) Trust them. Regard targets (and all similar buzz words) with healthy cynicism. Targets and graphs are for businesses. We're dealing with youngsters and we need to remind ourselves they aren't commodities on a sales chart. Every good teacher has targets, but their professional judgment used to be trusted and they weren't required to write them down every five minutes. If you know what is happening with progression and continuity in your school, and you can justify it, targets are irrelevant.

7. Don't take much notice of inspectors. You'll spend time reorganising your curriculum to incorporate fashionable ideas that will quickly go out of fashion. I speak from what we used to call 'first-hand experience'. I was criticised for recommending group reading, phonics and the teaching

of grammar. The inspector who criticised me became the leading light in the government's Literacy Strategy and then recommended group reading, phonics and the teaching of grammar.
8. And, finally, it's common to hear laughter in the staffroom at 4pm on Fridays, but if you hear it at five to nine on a rainy Monday morning you don't have too much to worry about. Your school is working well.

Then there was the 'whacky ideas' branch of education. One education authority spent £90,000 on two reflexologists to massage the feet of disruptive children. Teachers in the borough were fed up with bad behaviour. Children as young as three were swearing at adults, hurting other children, breaking the equipment. The authority was naturally worried because replacing equipment is expensive, so it gathered a working party to look into the matter and suggest some remedies. I could just imagine being a fly on the wall at the first meeting…

'Morning everyone. Thank you for attending today. I'm the Senior Education Officer, so I need to get you people devising a solution as soon as possible.'

'How bad is this behaviour, Barry?'

'Well, as SEO I don't actually go into any schools, of course. That sort of thing is way down the hierarchical ladder. But I can tell you we've sent our schools lots of documentation about getting children on board… personalised learning, deep drilling down, targeting and tracking, hourly assessments for incomes and outcomes, the pupil as stakeholder…'

'Isn't this the problem Barry? Schools are swamped with this stuff. They don't have time…'

'Well, let me stop you there, Deidre. Valuable though your opinion as a class teacher might be, we do have some important thinkers in the room. Anthony, you're an educational psychologist. What's your view?'

Thank you Barry. I think we've all heard of Gumbert's Rings and their relevance to patterns of behavioural decline? In my view, intensive training courses for teachers on observation of partitional nodes in first category incidence would lead to improvement at base level.'

'Thank you Anthony. That certainly gives us something to think about.'

'Sorry to interrupt Barry, but I do have some personal experience…'

'Everybody in this room does, Deidre, but as a class teacher you are a mere practitioner. We need to think outside the box. Run ideas up the flagpole and see who salutes them… see which ideas the cat licks up when we put them in the saucer, do some deep drilling down to see what comes up. Anthea, you're a practising school nurse… any ideas?'

'Couldn't each school be issued with a weekly Mogodon voucher?'

'Great thinking, Anthea. Have to means test it, of course. A school with swearers would receive less than a school with multiple chair throwers. Swearers are more cost effective in terms of broken equipment. The rate payers would like that. William, you specialise in behaviour therapy. How do you deal with these children?'

'I don't deal with the actual child, Barry. The LEA employs me to visit classrooms and observe. I make lots of notes, and then advise on ways forward. Unfortunately I've been off sick because a child threw a shoe at me. Would anybody be interested in my book of behavioural strategies? I wrote it on sick leave. I've got copies with me…'

'Later, William. Time's getting on and we haven't come up with much. Now, I had an ankle problem last week and the doctor recommended a first class chap who massaged it and cured it completely. Calmed me down, too. I wondered...'

'Massage! Splendid idea, Barry. That'll calm them down! Could we give it a trial first? I've got an ache in my thigh... could we get Daniel Craig...'

'Remember the ratepayer Anthea.... Deidre, as an infant teacher, what's your take on this?'

You don't need it Barry. You see, I've discovered something that works. I told a naughty child off yesterday. Firmly. He was quite taken aback. It costs nothing. This could be the way forward...'

'Oh that's dreadfully old fashioned, Deidre. The ratepayers like to see councils moving forward. Let's go down the reflexologist route. In fact, let's employ two of 'em...'

And then, 'Pupil Voice'. As a child at primary school, I walked home for lunch. During that hour, my mother sat and talked to me. We'd read books together... particularly, I recall, the Arthur Mee children's encyclopaedias... and she taught me the fascination of acquiring knowledge. I remember her as supportive, kind and loving. Except when I'd done something naughty, damaged property, or hurt somebody, and then she could be severe. On a tiny handful of occasions, she smacked me.

I was reminded of her influence when I read that a poll of two thousand teachers had shown that almost half felt 'Pupil Voice'... the fashionable term meaning giving children, however young, the chance to voice their opinions about everything... was hugely important. I'm afraid I sided with the other half.

But let me qualify that view. From the start, I wanted my school to be an exciting and interesting place, where children felt safe, valued, and happy. I wanted to enjoy conversation with children... and I did, because many came to see me throughout a school day, to show work or to chat to me. I had a teaching timetable. And I always believed that children had an entitlement to the highest quality of teaching.

But I never pretended that children are miniature adults, with similar reasoning skills. They aren't, and nor should they try to be. They inhabit a wide-eyed world of their own, one they don't fully understand, and they want… and need… rules, consistency, and boundaries…. even though most will test them occasionally. They want to feel that the adults around them are knowledgeable and wise… and worth taking notice of. They don't want a questionnaire thrust in front of them every five minutes.

Pupil Voice started in an insignificant way. I began to notice it in written reports accompanying children transferring to my school, because there was a space for 'the child's view'. What was written ranged from the mildly sensible… 'Andrew thinks science is interesting' to the paper-wasting 'Darren says he enjoys McDonalds and chips', 'Charlie likes staying at his Nan's' and 'David likes playing Batman games with his friends'. None of the comments were ever the slightest use to us. What worried me more was the insistence from social services or educational psychologists that the child's view is included on referral forms. One of my Year 2 infants had suffered an horrendous family situation, but her thoughts were still demanded. In reality this tiny, distressed child ached for somebody to make a few sensible decisions for her.

And there was a sinister dimension too. When Pupil Voice arrived, Ofsted seemed keen to train older children to monitor and assess their teachers. I've no idea why we should assume Ofsted knows much about the coalface, but teachers seem to be increasingly compliant to this disturbing notion, constantly questioning their every move. I even knew a school where classrooms had seats at the back for parents… who could come in whenever they liked, make notes on the teaching, and openly criticise it afterwards by dropping their comments in a box. Everybody seems entitled to have a 'voice' apart from the teachers. Who were the professionals supposed to be, I wondered?

On the occasions when we needed supply teachers, I was always delighted when they told me how pleasant and well behaved our children were, and how refreshingly different our school was from many they encountered. I heard from them of schools where five year olds swore at adults, where classrooms were chaotic, where teacher turnover was so great some children had six teachers in a year. Even a school where children were escorted at hometime by policeman on horseback. End products of a bit too much pupil voice, perhaps. Somehow, I think my mother got the balance about right.

So, it can't be denied that education has been littered with failed fads and fashions. Sir Jim Rose was a much-liked figure whose pioneering work on dyslexia training for teachers and the primary school curriculum improved the lives of countless young people, who will never know of him but can be supremely grateful for what he did. He made an immeasurable impact in the whole field of education and specifically dyslexia. But he certainly wasn't a fan of an initiative known as 'Circle Time.' It was intended as a classroom forum for children to share views, anxieties and concerns, but, like Sir Jim, I never thought it offered the benefits its disciples liked to claim.

All sorts of successes were claimed for Circle Time in building 'the balanced child', and teaching practice students coming into my school sometimes incorporated it into their weekly routine. The children sit in a circle performing various activities, such as saying three nice things about the person on your left, or listening to Tommy explaining why he felt it necessary to give Susan a thump at breaktime, or talking about how everyone feels because somebody has written 'bum' on a display in the maths corner.

Now this was all well and good, but why was it necessary to invent Circle Time for it? Surely, one of the qualities of capable class teachers is the trusting empathy they should be able to achieve with their children? Within a short time they should know them all thoroughly... and the children should feel safe, interested and comfortable in the environment provided for them. The children should also know that their teacher will find time to help them, encourage them, laugh with them, and chat with them individually outside lesson time when there is a need for it. They are her family. They should feel a real sense of belonging and identity, and want to share her values because a good teacher is still the very strongest of role models.

And call me cynical if you like, but I became a little suspicious when educational writers who knew a profitable thing when they saw one were offering books on every shade and variation of Circle Time. I found four while rummaging through the education section of my local bookshop, and I was fascinated by the warm-up activities one of them described. 'Start today's Circle Time by holding hands, and passing a 'squeeze' round the circle,' it said. Frankly, that would rate quite highly on my scale of pointless classroom activities. Consultants, of course, also latched on to the potential goldmine. 'Solve your classroom behaviour problems,' said a leaflet that arrived on my desk. 'Attend our course on Bubble Time, an advanced version of Circle Time.' I wondered whether you had to take along your own flannel and soap.

I've even seen a Circle Time training video, in which a lunchtime supervisor was summoned to the school council circle and required to sit cross-legged on the carpet while she explained how she felt about the rudeness she was experiencing from the children. The poor lady looked extremely distressed and the headteacher simply looked embarrassed. Perhaps if she'd had a firmer grip on the school the children wouldn't have been rude in the first place.

Even those ideas which have had relevance to primary education have often been misinterpreted. The 'real books' fiasco of the eighties, for example, started out as a worthwhile idea. A talented class teacher, disenchanted with the turgid text of many reading schemes, designed one of her own.. using only good quality children's books. She spent hours grading them to ensure children would progress at their own pace, but absorb worthwhile literature at the same time. Her children made such rapid progress the method was hailed as a reading panacea, and inspectors instructed schools to throw out their reading schemes and buy 'real books' instead, failing to appreciate that simply exposing children to decent books wouldn't guarantee reading success. It became known as 'reading by osmosis'. And failed.

Sometimes, organisational ideas which are intended simply to make the teacher's day a little easier, and introduced with the best intentions, can prove extremely difficult to organise in practice. When I was a newly qualified class teacher, I didn't have planning, preparation and assessment (PPA) time. I arrived early for school, taught my class of thirty and had at least one day a week when I did two playground duties without anyone assisting me. I also had a lunchtime duty, after-school club supervision and no non-contact time at all. I planned and marked at home, and I can't say that I suffered. I remember only enjoyment from the job. I expect I sound like your elderly relative telling you how he was caned mercilessly at school and it never did him any harm, or how in his day you could take a girl to the pictures, have a couple of pints afterwards, buy a packet of Woodbines and still have change from half a crown for the bus fare home.

So I'll probably get shot down for heresy but I do wonder if PPA was such a good idea, especially after talking to a couple of headteachers who are having awful problems with it. When it was introduced it seemed like a victory for the unions and a positive help for teachers. Every full-time class teacher would receive half a day away from the classroom, giving them freedom to catch up on marking, lesson planning, data recording or the preparation of lesson materials. Newly qualified teachers would receive a whole day away from the classroom, as they were already entitled to half a day during their first year.

But many schools found PPA timetabling nightmarish. Cover had to be found for all these half days, which was fine if your budget was strong and you could find good supply teachers who wanted short-term work and a range of age groups. Even better if there were part-time teachers on your staff who were willing to divert to PPA cover, because they were a known quantity and could be allocated appropriately, although the fly in that particular ointment was an entitlement to a percentage of PPA time themselves, so you had to find cover teachers for your cover teachers. And since school mornings are usually longer than the afternoons, people who had afternoon PPA tended to lose out. Not by much, admittedly, but I've known people to grumble about it.

And where do you put your teachers on PPA? Space was always tight at my school and a teacher could wander around for half an hour trying to find somewhere peaceful to work. Then there is the discipline issue. Nobody would deny that children are more challenging these days, and I haven't met a supply teacher yet who doesn't have a stock of hair-raising tales. A good class teacher establishes a strong and trusting relationship with a class, but many children are quick to take advantage when a stranger takes them for half a day each week. I've spoken to many teachers who have returned from PPA to find their classrooms in a mess.

And consider things from the children's viewpoint, too. If they have an NQT teaching them, and that teacher is also out for a couple of days on a course, they could be taught by somebody else for two days a week over an extended period. Which doesn't help class stability and continuity. If teachers weren't under so much pressure these days, with constant and sometimes unreasonable demands from senior managers right up to government bureaucrats, perhaps PPA wouldn't even be necessary, and they could achieve a much better work-life balance.

And still have change for the bus fare home.

7

HOW'S HE GETTING ON, MR BROWN?

The Curriculum, Children's Achievement and Monitoring It

I wouldn't want to be a politician. Criticised from every quarter, and subjected to all sorts of abuse and denigration on social media, it must be almost impossible to get things right and make a real difference. A few manage to do it... Rory Stewart, for example, possibly the most able prime minster we never had, and an excellent constituency MP, managed to achieve some important changes with our prisons, but as so often happens, just as he was getting to grips with things he was moved on. The important thing, however, was that he spent a great deal of time actually talking to the people at the coalface, people who knew the job... and its problems... inside out, and who were obviously best placed to know what was needed to improve things. Money, of course, is always needed, and there is never enough, but with a good knowledge of their brief and hands-on experience, it is possible for a politician to make effective changes. Some politicians simply don't bother to consult people in the know, almost as if it was beneath them. Chris Grayling, for example, who as justice secretary made a mess of the probation system. He seemed unable to make any of his briefs work, and quickly became known as Failing Grayling, running up billions of expenditure.

Unfortunately, this happens all too frequently… and especially in education. Since I've been involved with education all my life, I've seen a huge number of politicians come and go, and I've watched so many education ministers of state make a hash of things, sometimes through the best intentions but with little knowledge of schools or classroom realism, sometimes because they think quick, big changes are needed, and sometimes through sheer incompetence. But most of all because they hardly ever talk to the people who are actually at the coalface. The teachers. Michael Gove famously referred to thinkers, educational philosophers and educationalists as 'The Blob.' (There was some justification for this, because occasionally the thinkers are as bad as the politicians.) For some reason Mr Gove even sent a copy of the King James bible to every school in the country with a little introduction by him. How whacky is that? What were the schools supposed to do with it? The cost of that little wheeze ran into many thousands… money that could have been spent in far better ways.

Margaret Thatcher's time in the education department is mostly remembered for the removal of school milk for children over seven, which had been provided since 1906, because it was recognised as something that was good for helping children with poor nutrition, and getting nourishment from eating and drinking is absolutely essential for effective learning. It was something she apparently didn't want to do, but prime minister Ted Heath was determined to make cuts everywhere he could, and free milk had to go. Mrs T was vilified for this and quickly became known as Maggie Thatcher, milk snatcher. When I took up headship, daily milk in third of a pint bottles was still provided from other LEA budgets, but I felt that most children didn't really need it. Much was left over and curdled, especially in the summer, and few children enjoyed it. I was much happier when a daily piece of fruit or crunchy vegetable was eventually provided, although the crates containing it had to be quickly shifted from the bottom corridor in my school because parents tended to help themselves after they'd delivered their children to the early years classes!

One of the ministers who made the most changes was Kenneth Baker, the most important being the introduction of a national curriculum. I began teaching in what became known as the Plowden Era, when strict timetables became a thing of the past, 'project and topic' based learning was the fashion, and the mantra was that the child should be 'the agent of his own learning.' It seems extraordinary now, but straight out of training college I was handed a set of classroom keys, given a class to teach for a year, and whatever I taught during that year was more or less entirely up to me. Since film has been a lifetime passion for me, I remember undertaking a topic on the cinema, after teaching several lessons to my Year 6 class about the influence of the media, which was very primitive compared with what we experience now. We'd been concerned about the amount of litter in the school grounds, and since the school had a movie camera and a sound projector, I decided we should make a short film about it. The plan was also to encompass a whole range of curriculum subjects.

The children produced story outlines, one was chosen, and a storyboard designed. A creature arrives from Planet Tidy, is horrified to see children dropping litter, and uses its amazing powers to make the litter jump back on to the children who dropped it. A simple idea, but making the twenty minute film involved several weeks of intensive work: acting, writing, directing, science, art, special effects, scripting, sound, and a great deal of problem-solving. We also had to design and build a creature that could be animated convincingly. One morning, a parent stopped me as I was lining my class up at the start of the day. 'I don't know what you're doing, exactly,' she said, 'But my David can't wait to get to school these days. He loves it.'

Eventually, the film was finished and ready for its premiere. We advertised, (lots to be learned here, too!) each class was shown the film, and a screening was also held for the parents. It was a great success, and other classes were encouraged to write reviews and articles, and to take up the theme of keeping the school tidy. These days, I'm always delighted when I see capable young teachers finding inventive ways of tackling the national curriculum. Nevertheless, when I peer through my rose-tinted spectacles, I tend to think that children in the less prescriptive days often had the best of it.

Of course, schools naturally recognised that children needed to read, write and add up, but other than that the sheer freedom was extraordinary and very exciting for teachers who were good at their job. But reality soon intervened. All this was fine in the leafy shires, where children usually came from homes where there were good books, interesting conversation, weekend trips to places of interest, and where parents took an active interest in their children's education, but in inner city schools young children were being left behind. If teachers didn't feel like teaching maths or, as was often the case, weren't actually very competent at maths themselves, they simply avoided doing much of it. The Inner London Education Authority, for whom I worked as a teacher, became increasingly political and strongly at odds with the conservative government. Mrs Thatcher, as prime minister, had suddenly had enough. Her education minister, Kenneth Baker, was therefore asked to design and initiate a national curriculum. The advantages, the government insisted, would be many. Since children across the land would all be working to the same curriculum, the children of a family moving to a new area could simply pick up where they'd left off at the previous school. And there would be genuine progression, because what was to be learned each year would be set in stone.

Of course, things didn't work out quite like that. They never do. Kenneth Baker's team of experts couldn't agree on what should go into the curriculum, and creating it dragged on and on. When it did eventually arrive in schools it was unwieldy and overloaded, and left teachers scratching their heads in frustration, wondering how they were going to teach it all. The first version, beautifully produced in shiny ring binders, quickly found its way into my school museum as a new, simpler version was hurriedly designed and, of course, changes and amendments have taken place ever since. Nevertheless, I was a supporter of a national curriculum, because it got rid of things like 'the dinosaur effect.' Young children love learning about dinosaurs, but in the Plowden days a child could end up learning about dinosaurs for several years on the trot… simply because teachers knew the topic would go down well with their classes and they liked teaching it. The strongest argument against a national curriculum was that teachers would become bored stiff teaching the same thing each year, but this to me didn't hold a great deal of water because any capable teacher could ring the changes and find innovative roads into a topic, and it is unusual for primary school teachers to teach the same age group year after year.

Kenneth Baker made two other important changes, one which was useful and one which wasn't. The first was the introduction of in-service training days at the start of each half term. These were intended to be days in which guest speakers could be invited in to talk to the staff (usually headteachers felt money could be spent in better ways unless the speaker was exceptional), or the staff could work their way through the latest initiatives that land so often in schools. Many schools used it as a day in which teachers could prepare their classrooms for the new term, and this is usually what I did, although since my teachers always came in for at least a day or two… and often for a whole week at the end of a summer holiday, this wasn't really needed.

Baker's other initiative was an annual meeting between school governors and parents, so that any issues that parents were concerned about or matters they wanted more information about, such as the national curriculum, could be discussed. Once again, it was an evening where the headteacher had to stay at school until late, because it was often only the headteacher who could answer the questions. Again, this was all reasonably successful in the shires, but much less so in the inner cities where often only a handful of parents and a few governors turned up, so nothing really worthwhile came of these meetings.

Often, a new education minister would try to repair the damage done, usually expensively, by the previous administration. When

Tony Blair became prime minister he declared that his three priorities would be 'education, education and education' and there's no doubt that he poured a huge amount of funding into schools. David Blunkett, probably his best known education minister, was responsible for The Literacy Hour, created because there was great concern that far too many primary school children, especially in the inner cities, were leaving school at eleven with poor literacy skills, much of it caused by the lax attitude to reading and writing in the past, even though this freedom had been insisted upon by the inspectorate. I remember an inspector holding a meeting with teachers and parents at a school I taught at, sarcastically pulling to pieces a phonics practice booklet, saying what a lot of nonsense it was. But now, under Blair's reign, phonics was back in again, and primary schools were required to teach an hour of literacy (and later 45 minutes of numeracy) each morning. It wasn't actually mandatory, but if you didn't do it you were in trouble when Ofsted came knocking at your door, unless you could show you were teaching a literacy programme that was equal to it. The Literacy Hour cost a fortune, and the hour had to be divided into whole class reading or writing, a session on work with words such as phonics and spelling, some directed group activities and then a plenary session at the end. Every school was provided with a huge kit of teaching materials and masses of information for teachers to become familiar with (most could only study it at home because there wasn't time in school) and they were even told what they had to say when delivering the lessons. Many teachers were horrified... it gave them no leeway to design their own exciting creative writing lessons, and by the time it... and the numeracy strategy... were no longer used it hadn't made that much difference to children's achievement anyway.

An important member of Tony Blair's Education Delivery Unit even suggested that, with the rapid increase and versatility of computer based assessment, 'automated essay marking' would shortly be on the horizon. When I read this, I wondered if I had misinterpreted what he was saying. Was he really suggesting that a computer would soon be able to assess the quality of children's writing? Would the teacher feed the essay into a piece of software, where the text would be scanned and points awarded for the use of acceptable adjectives, adverbs, metaphors and similes? Would the computer offer a smiling face and say, 'That's great, Neville. You've scored a level 5 and I've just reduced your teacher's marking workload'?

Looking back, I understand exactly how I became a writer. At a very young age, my mother constantly read interesting stories to me. At primary school, my teachers instilled a love of creative writing. I wrote about pirates, daring jungle expeditions and thrilling crime sagas where I was the boy detective who thwarted the villain. When I reached headship, I resolved that my staff would share my enthusiasm for creative writing and communicate it to their students; I organised workshops to make sure this happened. But gradually, I found myself battling against the government's determination to grind everything into data, levels and measurable outcomes. It seemed that the young teachers I was recruiting had been trained to give out worksheets containing chunks of prose and then ask children to identify points of grammar, with little consideration for the writing itself.

One newly qualified teacher read George Layton's *The Fib* with her pupils, a wonderful short story that really resonates with primary classes. I asked how the children had reacted. 'Oh, we're just looking at extracts,' the teacher said. In this brave new world, strange things were occurring, especially with Year 6 attainment tests. I marvelled at a child's description of the joy he experienced when he ate a plate of his mother's spag bol… a delightful piece of writing that scored a mere level 3. Another piece, a dull and repetitive zoo visit, scored a level 5. The latter contained perfect spelling and punctuation and the former didn't, so the examiners were clearly playing it safe. The next year, my Year 6 teachers compiled lists of complex words, punctuation and grammar for the children to slip into their tests and they were rewarded by the highest scores for years. If children's imagination will count for nothing because the outcome is determined by a computer, then I fear for the future of creative writing. Years ago, when a whale was stranded in the river Thames, my Year 6 teacher jumped on a bus with her children to record the experience. The writing produced was among the best student work I'd read for a long time. But now, she would probably be advised to give out a couple of photocopied paragraphs from Moby Dick instead.

However hard primary schools try to improve young children's literacy these days, there's little doubt that they have a real task on their hands, because many of them spend so much time watching and often joining in with social media conversations on phones and tablets. And there's always television of course. Consider this snippet of a TV host recently congratulating a contestant on a talent show:

Host: 'That was fantastic! You were, like, brilliant. Like, just brilliant! What a fantastic voice!'

Contestant: 'It was, like, so fantastic. I've had, like, such a fantastic time.'

Host: 'That's so fantastic to hear.'

Or this announcement from a BBC continuity announcer last night...

'At seven firty there's part one of the noo drama series you won't want ter miss. There's somethink dodgy in the farmhouse and all is not what it seems. It contains scenes viewers might find upsettin' and some very strong langwidge.'

Or this conversation I overheard between two teenagers on a bus recently:

'Where did you went?'

'Where did I went when?'

'That time. When you wasn't in school, innit.'

'I weren't well, Bro.'

'I see your mum in the shop. Innit you've had a chicken's pox though?'

Or this from an 'expert' on a recent antiques programme...

'I fink it's probly worf about twenty pound. A bargain. Specially as you only paid five pound for it.'

Since when has the 'g' disappeared from the end of words like something and nothing, and a 'k' substituted? Chat to any young person today and their speech will be peppered with the word 'like', so where has that come from? Last week my wife and I sat in a restaurant listening to a couple of teachers at the next table adding 'like' to their conversation every few seconds, to the extent that it became so annoying we wanted to slap their table and say 'For heaven's sake, <u>why</u>?'

And do you remember when the words 'fantastic' and 'awesome' were used in their proper context, and not as nouns to indicate that something was rather good? Similarly, the word 'sick' used to mean being ill. Now it replaces excellent. And greet somebody with the words 'Hello, nice to see you. How are you?' they won't say 'I'm very well, thank you.' They'll usually say 'I'm good.' As opposed to naughty, perhaps? And instead of talking about 'strong language', why don't TV announcers just say 'There's a lot of swearing in this programme?'

What is happening to our language? Forty years ago, an older teacher on the staff of a school I was working at walked into a shoe repairer and complained about a sign in the window that said, 'Shoes mended while U wait'. How could we teach children to use English well, he asked, if they were being subjected to signs like that? But how utterly trivial that seems now. We can accept text messages peppered with shorthand such as 'IMHO ('in my humble opinion') and 'FWIW ('for what it's worth') because there is a reason for the brevity, but the poverty of language and standard of spelling and grammar in everyday life is truly worrying, proved by the merest glance at social media conversations, reviews on Amazon or the Internet Movie Database, or comments on YouTube. Even printed books have far more grammar and spelling mistakes than they ever used to. I can't recall a single book I've read in the past year that didn't have several spelling mistakes or other errors. And I read a lot.

A free newspaper I picked up at the train station recently was riddled with errors. Train services were still largely 'unacceptible'. On another occasion, it said that London teachers had too many discipline problems 'dispite' smaller classes, and patients were still having far too many difficulties trying to book an appointment with a doctor at their local 'practise'. I love reading a newspaper, and people who write in them usually have a fondness for the correct use of language, but I began to wonder if I was witnessing the birth of a worrying new journalistic standard. These days, no one seems to have heard of colons or semi-colons, either; commas have taken their place and sentences are merely run into each other. One advertisement in the paper said: 'Mortgage brokers receive fees, these are paid by the lender.'

Even the BBC got into the act. I could imagine the conference that preceded an embarrassing series of programmes on children's literacy...

'Morning, Tristram.'

'Morning, Skye, Pennie, Gareth. Now, we've got a spare slot in our programming, and I'm wondering if we can do something on primary education. What about children's inability to read or spell properly these days? That's always a contentious issue.'

'We need to be careful, Tristram. Remember that disastrous programme recently, where we sent a reporter undercover to show how poor teachers aren't being sacked? The one the editor of the *Times Educational Supplement* tore to pieces?'

'Well, I accept it was scantily researched, shoddily edited, badly narrated and most of the evidence didn't stack up. But apart from that it was pretty good. Filled a slot in the schedules. No, this time let's go for something more entertaining. We'd need a minor celebrity to front it, of course...'

'I've got it, Tristram. Why don't we get hold of that nice Gareth chappie who does the choir thing with lots of different groups of people?'

'I don't think the public would thank us for yet another programme where he gets people who hate singing to form a choir, Skye. I suppose we could make it even more gimmicky. We could get him to teach a herd of cows to sing.'

'No, I meant getting him to solve the reading thingy. Here's the scenario. There's bound to be a bit of research somewhere that says boys don't read as quickly as girls. Then we find a school out in the Styx where the head is worried about her reading results, so she calls in an expert… that's Gareth of course…'

'Hold it there, Skye. Gareth's not an expert on reading. He teaches people who can't sing. To… um.. sing.'

'No, but he's a celebrity, Tris, and he's cheaper than Simon Cowell. Gareth bounds in and has just eight weeks to raise the reading standards of the boys. We can rack up the tension over three programmes. Will he or won't he get the boys to read? And he's bound to have all sorts of whacky ideas….'

'Skye's right, Tris. He'll probably take the boys into the woods and get them building bivouacs and skinning rabbits, or he'll prance around pretending to be a highwayman and get them all excited.'

'Take them in the woods? Good God, has he been CRB checked? And we'd have to get all the children wearing hard hats…'

'Oh, we can sort all that. We'd start with the boys saying how they hate reading and how boring they think school is and how crap their teachers are and take things from there. Slip in a few parents saying they can't tear their kids from their play stations. And we could do some fun things with the sound … a bit of Ron Goodwin as Gareth rides in to improve the children's speaking and listening skills. Perhaps that rollicking piece from *'The Trap...'*"

'Steer clear of that, Gareth. The older viewers who've seen the film will think of Olly Reed being nasty to Rita Tushingham. What about a blast of *'633 Squadron'* or *'The Great Escape?'* Cliched, yes, but always works. You're very quiet, Pennie. Share your thoughts...'

'Well Tris, my son is really happy at school. And it seems to me there are thousands of teachers out there making learning exciting for children, despite all the ridiculous constraints they're under. Couldn't we just have a short season of programmes showing outstanding teachers and the amazing things they achieve...'

'Sorry Pennie, but that idea's a non-starter. Where's the celebrity factor? Where's the tension, or as we in the trade call it, the jeopardy? And what would we do with our Ron Goodwin records? No, we could get a lot of mileage out of this. We could film a follow-up series with Alan Tichmarsh teaching Nursery children to speak Swahili. He'd have eight weeks to do it...'

And then there was Jamie Oliver's *Dream School* series. Apart from the fact that it was an insult to the teaching profession, its sheer naiveté was astonishing. Now, I've certainly nothing against Jamie Oliver. I cook his recipes regularly and they are extremely tasty. I also greatly admired his determination in trying to improve school meals... but those things were within his zone of expertise, and I strongly feel he should have remained within it. *Dream School* was well outside it.

At the start of each programme, we watched Jamie announcing that the education system had failed him, but he was lucky because he discovered cookery. He then told us he'd gathered together twenty disaffected youngsters who were also failed by the system. It would have been interesting to hear the views of the teachers who'd tried to get them to learn, but this programme wasn't about serious debate. It was corny edu-tainment. Then we watched a short sequence of an old building being tarted up to become his 'dream school'.

Jamie felt the youngsters had been turned off education because every lesson wasn't whizz-bang excitement, so he'd gathered a host of celebrities to enthuse them. Simon Callow for drama, Alastair Campbell for politics, Ellen McArthur for sailing, David Starkey for history, Arnie Schwarzenegger for Language (move aside, asshole), Lady Gaga for deportment and dress sense. Okay, I made the last two up, but you get the general idea. There was also a 'real' headteacher on hand, just in case things got a bit sticky.

The format for the series was boringly predictable. You knew that things would go horribly wrong at first, then there would be much angst and soul searching, the celebs would admit there's actually more to teaching than they first thought and at least some of the youngsters would regret they'd missed out somewhere along the educational route.

And go wrong things certainly did. Simon Callow's patience ran out and he roared at his charges, Robert Winston sliced up an animal with a circular saw and caused some girls to throw up, and poor David Starkey got hammered for saying one of the boys was so fat he could hardly move, which caused him to be severely admonished by the real head. One just doesn't say that sort of thing these days, although, of course, it's okay if it's the teacher who is on the receiving end of a load of teenage abuse. Ellen McArthur's group had a wonderful time with her on the boat, but then they would, wouldn't they? And I rather suspect she got her education sorted out first. By programme three I'd had enough, and I gave up watching.

Years ago, in the days of black and white television, BBC2 made a series of programmes about primary school teachers who were truly inspiring. Each week, we watched an outstanding teacher throughout the course of just one day, and I remember a class of very young children visiting a pond to do what was then called nature study. The excitement on the children's faces as they gathered a remarkable collection of flora and wriggling fauna in jam jars was a delight to behold, as was the teacher's knowledge, love of the children and her sheer enthusiasm for learning. The viewers were left in no doubt about how inspirational a good teacher can be. These days, of course, a lengthy risk assessment would be required in case anybody fell in the water, but I can't say I noticed Robert Winston filling in one before he got slicing.

So, in the end, who's to blame for falling literacy standards? Well, we'd better start with the teachers. Many younger teachers were educated in the days when everything in literacy was subordinate to the 'creative flow'. Grammar, spelling and syntax weren't important; the main thing was to get your ideas on paper. Teachers were told not to correct errors on their pupils' work because it might put them off writing forever. Looking back, it seems amazing that so-called 'educational experts' can have been so daft, but they certainly did some damage.

But parents must take some of the blame, too, and there are many reasons. Often, they are hard-working people who simply haven't got enough time to spend with their children. Others, who do have the time, don't talk to them, let alone read a book with them or have a conversation, even though such basic activities are crucial in developing language skills. A child who has been given a rich literacy start at home stands out, from nursery age onwards. Yesterday, walking down our high street, I watched a mother twiddling on her mobile phone, while her youngster sat in the pushchair, facing away from her. How much nicer it would have been to see the mother chatting to her child as she walked.

Nevertheless, I believe that David Blunkett's aims all those years ago were made with the best of intentions, and I was extremely annoyed when he was shoved and pilloried by ill-tempered delegates at the annual conference of one of the teaching unions. As a blind man, this must have been excruciating for him, and it was totally unacceptable. It was quite clear that he wanted to improve the quality of children's learning, and undoubtedly his aim was to raise the standard of literacy.

Just occasionally though, some serious heckling of secretaries of state was thoroughly deserved. It was reported that John Patten was often physically sick before facing a vast number of delegates at an annual union conference, and there was no doubt that teachers had very little time for him. One of the great educators that I had the utmost admiration for, but never had the opportunity to meet, was Sir Tim Brighouse, and not simply because his philosophy of primary education was identical to mine. During my headship, I attended a 'broader perspectives' course with other headteachers, and we spent a couple of days visiting several schools in Birmingham, where Tim was the chief education officer. Every school we went into had only fine words to say about him. His interest, passion, and enthusiasm for education was legendary. John Patten, incredibly, called him a 'nutter', saying that he 'feared for Birmingham with this madman wandering the streets frightening the children.' Rightly, Sir Tim sued, won substantially, and donated the money to charity. And John Patten disappeared without trace.

In the last decade or so under the Conservatives, the secretary of state for education has become something of a sour joke for teachers, and they have come and gone with astonishing rapidity. Gavin Williamson, dogged by scandal and controversy, who kept a pet tarantula called Cronus in his office and allegedly told a senior civil servant to go and slit his throat. Then, during the Covid crisis, he was forced to perform a U-turn on the decision to award students grades based on a computer algorithm, forty eight hours after the results were issued. There's no doubt these were extremely difficult times with the pandemic raging, but Williamson was criticised for ignoring warnings and defending his position. As chaos erupted on results day, damaging student's university prospects as well as their faith in the education system, the teaching unions lost confidence in the secretary of state as they prepared for another year of school disruption and headaches.

Nadhim Zahawi held the post for ten months and I'm yet to find a teacher who remembers anything he did. James Cleverly lasted for just two months and Kit Malthouse, lasted for days. No wonder teachers feel that many secretaries of state, unless they have the clout of a Kenneth Baker, or the genuine enthusiasm of an Estelle Morris, herself originally a secondary school teacher, make precious little difference at all.

At one point, a Labour government even suggested that it might be a good idea if teachers had a 'license to teach', with a check every five years to make sure they hadn't gone to seed. The idea was that teachers would become more respected and have the same sort of status as doctors and lawyers, but of all the strategies, about-turns and half-baked initiatives heaped on the teaching profession I found this idea to be one of the most idiotic and I wasn't surprised that the education minister who introduced the idea wore such a glazed expression when announcing it. At a stroke, I suspected he'd managed to alienate almost the entire teaching profession, and he didn't seem to have the slightest idea about the microscopic examination class teachers were already under. At least the idea crawled back under the stone it came from.

There was, after all, a time when teachers were actually trusted. A time when teachers were respected as people who were inventive, interesting and dedicated; people who could think for themselves and inspire youngsters with a thirst for learning. But in the nineties and noughties, unless they showed a determination to fight back, schools were bludgeoned into submission by endless monitoring under the highly dubious excuse of 'driving up standards'. There were Ofsted inspectors who often hadn't taught for years and sometimes not at all. There were School Improvement Partners, who weren't partners at all, but minor inspectors checking up on what you were doing six times a year. Local authorities were sending in 'teaching and learning' monitoring teams to make sure you weren't sitting in the corner silently weeping with your head in a bucket. Teachers were performance managed every year to make sure they hit their targets, and if you were a class teacher your headteacher... if he or she had nothing more sensible to do... was likely to visit your classroom regularly with a clipboard and comment on your ability to deliver a decent lesson.

And in order to progress and earn a half decent salary, a teacher was suddenly subjected to another pile of rigmarole called 'crossing the threshold'. It could equally have been called 'we don't want to give the teachers any more money, so if they want some, we're really going to make them work for it.' After six years, a teacher would have reached the top of a pretty unexciting salary scale, but to earn any more, a great deal of evidence had to be collected to prove they were worth it. Headteachers, never trusted by the powers that be, weren't allowed to assess this evidence, even though they knew their teachers far better than anyone else. An army of consultant assessors was recruited to march into schools to pass or fail the poor souls whose knees trembled with worry over whether their forms and 'evidence' would pass muster with a stranger. During its first year, seven of my staff were eligible for the threshold. Two found the forms so patronising they threw them in the bin. One found the whole idea objectionable and said sod the relatively small salary increase. Another two waited to see what would happen as this new system got under way. The remaining two found it objectionable as well, but both were single with high mortgages, and teaching salaries don't lie easily with London property prices.

Was the new initiative expensive to set up? Well, of course. The explanatory video for schools had to be prepared and distributed, and there was the usual ton of paperwork. A website had to be created, and all the special forms for the local education authorities across the country. And then there was the recruiting and training of the assessors. It wasn't actually too taxing to become one. So long as you had a couple of GCEs and a certificate saying you'd been in the scouts and could tie a reef knot, you were away. A few hours training made you fully competent in deciding whether qualified teachers, who had trained for years and then spent at least six more in a classroom perfecting their skills, could do their job properly. And you wouldn't have to use your own initiative; the DfES had put questions on tick sheets and even helped you with what you were supposed to say. The cost of setting this up? Well, what was £25 million among friends? Your average consultancy could easily spend half of that preparing a paper on why chalk isn't the best medium for writing on a white board.

I remember the half-term week my wife spent with a group of colleagues, sitting in our lounge frantically justifying themselves for 'Threshold Man' on bits of paper. I ministered coffee and sandwiches to keep them buoyant, and listened to the earnest and worried conversations as they questioned each other and wondered if what they'd written would get them through. And I remember thinking how utterly demeaning it all was. Any competent inspector need only spend two minutes in their classrooms to appreciate their commitment and ability.

Interestingly, it suddenly became harder to recruit Ofsted inspectors than threshold assessors. Shorter hours, an easier workload and good pay caused the inspection army to don their marching boots and shift camps. Even the guide for headteachers was patronising. 'When the assessment has been completed,' it said, 'promptly notify the assessed teachers of their application outcome.' I suspected that most headteachers had actually worked that bit out for themselves! And what happened ultimately? Well, the army of gravy train consultants had to move elsewhere. The schools and the government couldn't afford it, and headteachers were told they had to do the appraising. Just another little addition to all the other jobs they were required to do.

Any competent primary school headteacher should know, in considerable depth, what is happening in their classrooms and how to move learning forward. Which teachers need a little extra support, who is doing really well, who needs a bit of assistance with behaviour management or lesson planning. Ofsted inspectors and local authority inspectors were never particularly happy about the way I 'monitored' my teaching staff. Apparently, to do it correctly, I had to sit in a corner of a classroom taking notes, and I had a real problem with that. I don't mean I couldn't do it, I just didn't see the point of it. During one of our Ofsted inspections, the lead inspector (who hadn't taught for the last century) asked how much time I spent monitoring teaching. I said I monitored constantly. I chatted to children in the playground at lunchtime every day. I discussed work whenever I popped into classrooms on errands. I talked to teachers at breaktimes and after school. I spoke with parents, and I taught regularly. So I had a commanding overview of progress. I said spending a great deal of time with children was the finest indicator of how the teachers were doing. Apparently, though, this wasn't proper monitoring. To do it correctly, it was essential to take notes from the classroom corner and then give the teachers verbal and written feedback, which would be filed in a binder for important people to look at. Needless to say, Ofsted failed my monitoring abilities.

Nevertheless, for a very short time afterwards, I did try, just to see what would happen. It seemed the prescribed way forward was to plan my monitoring sessions so that everybody went under the microscope regularly. I was required to tell a teacher formally that I'd be monitoring her that day, study her lesson plans (which should be very detailed), sit in the corner with clipboard and pen, and ensure she carried out her plans exactly as written. If she didn't, I could criticise the lesson pace, even though Charlie had asked her an interesting question that happened to lead off at a tangent; if she did, I could criticise her for giving Charlie a short answer. After school, I would be required to sit with the teacher, tell her what she's done well, to lull her into a sense of false security. Then I should home in on what needs to improve. She'd be very grateful, and rush home to rewrite her lesson plans for the rest of the term.

Okay, I'm cynical. But when I explained to the staff that Ofsted had suggested my monitoring should be more formal, my teachers groaned. 'That's what we've moved here to get away from,' they said. 'We had all that at our last schools and it didn't help at all.' One said he'd even had the head and deputy monitoring him simultaneously, which terrified him and caused him to make a complete mess of his lesson.

So I visited a nearby school I admired. 'I've had that stuff about monitoring too,' said the headteacher. 'I spend one session a term in each class and write a 'visit sheet' afterwards. I say mostly nice things, because I've appointed good staff and I know them well. I photocopy each sheet three times and file them in this.' She lifted a binder from a shelf. 'Ofsted didn't even look at it. The inspectors were impressed because it's a fat file and jam full of paper... and that's what it's all about.'

I monitored for a term before I went back to more important things, such as teaching music and producing the school play. Wearing my monitoring cap, I'd joined in some superb lessons. Nobody resented me being in their classrooms, and the children were always pleased to welcome me. But I learned nothing new, and discovered no hidden defects in my teachers. After all, even Ofsted had said that of the ninety lessons they'd seen in our previous inspection, only three were unsatisfactory, and that was probably because they'd scared the young teachers stiff.

Shortly after that, I heard about another wheeze that really concerned me. I was chatting to a teacher whose son was currently attending secondary school. That day, he'd been taught by a newly qualified teacher, and the *class* had been required to evaluate his geography lesson. This was done verbally, the children pointing out the good and bad parts of the lesson, and then via individual 'evaluation forms'. At the bottom was a space for giving the lesson a mark out of ten. This seemed very odd to me, just a trifle sinister, and naturally the children had widely differing views. One child thought the lesson 'brilliant'. Another said there wasn't enough 'entertainment and stuff'. One thought it was 'really boring', but qualified that by saying he hated geography anyway.

Useful feedback? I wouldn't have thought so. I've always loved MG sports cars and I drove them for years. Jeremy Clarkson hates them and avoids sitting next to MG enthusiasts at a dinner because he fears they might start talking about their failing track rod ends. But who's to say his view is more valid than mine? Hi-fi is another of my lifelong passions, and I recently read a rave review of a new amplifier in an audio magazine. A different magazine, reading between the lines, thought it was awful. Both reviews were written by respected audio journalists, so who was right? A prospective purchaser would surely have been bewildered. So what should he do? Go and listen and make up his own mind, I'd have thought.

And that's what I think the young teacher should have done. After all, he's had training and undertaken several teaching practices. Surely he should know whether the lesson he's prepared is likely to be any good. And if he wasn't sure, why not seek the advice of another teacher whose lessons and teaching style he admired?

But I suspect I know the answers to these questions. These days, we're supposed to think of the child as 'the stakeholder', and what a truly awful description this is. No longer is a child a small person with a unique, relatively unformed and fascinating view of the world around him. Now he's supposed to be an adult in miniature, with the corresponding reasoning power, knowledge, and experience of an adult. Yes, I accept that we want to get as far away as possible from the days when children were seen and not heard, but let's retain a little common sense here. Children look to adults… particularly parents and teachers, to offer a secure, loving environment tempered by wisdom and experience. A parent who uses the child as an equal, friend or confidante almost invariably ends up with a highly insecure youngster.

For a time my education authority issued an annual questionnaire for children. The idea was to collate all the gathered information and then issue a folder of graphs purporting to show, for example, whether bullying was a major problem across its schools. It seemed a very shaky premise to me. However simple and straightforward the compiler tried to make the questions, many children would still struggle to interpret them. Even 'Are you bullied in school?' could easily be misunderstood; a minor falling out with friends can cause a child to say they are being bullied. And 'Are you happy in school?' seemed particularly daft. A child's world is often of the moment, and it can be full of joy one day and angst the next. A caring, well run school will always be listening to children sensitively. And it seemed to me that if an education authority needed to thrust regular questionnaires at its schoolchildren its officers needed to visit the schools more often. They'd have quickly found out what was working. And what wasn't.

Dedicated teachers will always listen to children and colleagues and want to improve their practice. They'll attend training courses to find ways to improve their skills and, because they are fascinated by the processes of education, they'll soak it up like a sponge. And truly inspirational teachers, the sort I was always anxious to employ, will stay that way throughout their careers, despite the fashionable claptrap piled on their shoulders every few years. Being monitored by somebody who's abandoned the classroom for the clipboard is the very last thing they need.

Of course, teachers should always be good enough to ensure children make steady progress from year to year, and assessment of their progress is important, just as the inspection of schools is important. It's all a question of how you're going to do it, and when I became a headteacher there was hardly any guidance on what 'working class' children could, or should, be expected to achieve. One of the teachers I inherited, who fortunately left very quickly after I arrived, thought her children were doing pretty well if they could write their names correctly. I quickly realised the importance of work assessment though, so I evolved a system for evaluating children's work that was quick, easy, and over time seemed to work rather well. Throughout my first year, I used school assemblies to show examples of excellent work, to give the children… and teachers… reminders of the standard I wanted. I spent much time in classrooms… not monitoring aggressively, simply encouraging and coaxing, and often teaching classes myself to show what I felt could be produced. At the end of that year, I collected books, topic work and folders in a range of curriculum areas from the three most able children in every class, and I put them in display boxes in my room for teachers and children to look through. It was a fascinating exercise. The work from one very able Year 4 teacher outshone that of the top class, and it was obvious that progression from year to year was erratic to say the least.

But over the next six years, as standards steadily climbed, the work collections proved extremely helpful. Teachers learned what they were aiming for at the end of each primary year, and the books provided a quality benchmark. At staff meetings, we discussed the work, argued about it, came to decisions about how we should mark and assess it. Because the system was *simple*, it left everybody with bags of time to do what they were employed to do… teach the children.

These days, of course, that system would probably seem arbitrary. Computers enable masses of data to be gathered on every child, and most senior managers insist their teachers spend many hours doing just that, even if the teachers are perfectly well aware of what Charlie needs to do next to improve his sentence structure. Data Co-ordinators spend days collating, tracking, investigating unexpected trends, and then printing it all out in line graph and colourful block format. A School Improvement Partner or a local authority Link Inspector looks at it all and asks why Cynthia has slipped to a 2b and what you intend to do about it. She doesn't show any interest in actually meeting Cynthia, of course, or want to listen to the human reasons behind Cynthia's modest slippage. Cynthia is a speck on the graph, amongst all the other specks. I remember watching two parallel class teachers, masters at their trade, levelling writing and taking forty minutes per child… simply because an LEA moderator was due to visit, and they were nervous.

We've gone so far into this bottomless barrel that many teachers spend half their waking hours recording data and studying graphs before resorting to worksheets because they don't have time to prepare a proper, exciting lesson. Senior managers no longer teach, they moderate. Even in my own school, where we avoided this sort of thing like the plague, we spent three staff meetings on assessment because we'd bought in a new data handling program insisted on by the local authority, and quickly became bogged down in mindless and irrelevant detail until we made a really determined effort to see the wood for the trees. Which gives me a sneaking suspicion that my work collection system wasn't so outdated after all.

But how do you choose a primary school for your child, one where you are sure they will be happy, make good progress from year to year and not be relentlessly pushed through hoops to please the inspectorate? There was a time when parents, moving into a new area, evaluated primary schools by talking to neighbours and then drawing up a very short list. Then they'd visit one or two of them, ask for a tour, talk to teachers in their classrooms, meet the headteacher, ask some pupils about their school, and get a general 'feel' for whether or not they wanted their child to go there, presuming, of course, that a place might become available. I always insisted the prospective child should be brought along too, since it was the child who was going to come to the school, not the parent. But now, parents have been conditioned to evaluate schools by looking at Ofsted reports and league tables, and so often neither of these give an accurate description of a school at all.

During my headship, my local education authority was in a socially diverse area, with exceptional deprivation in some parts and tiny pockets of extreme privilege in others. It also had a large number of primary schools. My school was usually high in the league tables because the children were extremely well taught, and in one particular year, we were almost at the top of the tables. Why did we achieve this? Because the Year 6 cohort was an exceptionally able one for an inner city primary, but they had been a notable group throughout the school. The following year, prior to an Ofsted inspection, we had slipped back half a dozen places, and a member of my governing body showed great concern. I explained that the current cohort wasn't as able as the previous year's. 'Well, if we are going back down the league tables,' he said, 'standards must be dropping. We should always be moving steadily upwards.'

For a supposedly intelligent man, it was hard to believe he could make such an ill-informed comment… but then, he hardly ever visited the school, knew little about the children we taught, and was merely using our governing body as a political stepping stone to local government. In fact, the cohort had been taught just as well as any other, but reality dictates that you can't spin every piece of flax into gold. You just have to do the best you can… and the league tables have no real recognition of that, despite various attempts at value-adding.

League tables also encourage schools to become cramming institutions. Good results are utterly essential in warding off the aggressive glare of Ofsted, the LEA, the School Improvement Partner. In many cases, schools abandoned an interesting curriculum at the top of the school in order to relentlessly ensure the maximum numbers of children achieved the required Level 4, force feeding them old SATs papers to the point where some parents pleaded for them to be allowed to do a bit of art, or model making. Cramming like this has no justification.

When it was time for the Ofsted inspection, the lead inspector had looked at our data, seen that our results were lower than usual, and made up her mind that we were falling apart. I suspect she'd virtually written her report before she walked into the building, and she showed little interest in our explanation that, due to an exodus of families to newer estates outside London, over half the current Year 6 children hadn't been with us in Years 3 and 4. We'd lost many able children, and taken in many with social problems and low ability. Twelve were on the additional needs register. Incontrovertible proof of these things was demanded, before agreement was grudgingly given.

The league tables won't disappear, but are there any good reasons for retaining them? I don't think so. They put schools in challenging areas, whose teachers are often highly skilled and exceptionally hard working, in an unacceptably invidious position. They pit school against school. And, as I discussed above, they give potential parents no real idea of what a school is like.

Of course, there's always the parent who's been conditioned to believe something that simply isn't true. I remember two youngish parents bringing their son to my school, to have a tour and see whether they felt it was the right place for their child. I always asked two Year 6 children to escort prospective parents around the classrooms and then I would make myself available afterwards to elaborate on anything the two Year 6 children hadn't been able to answer. After forty five minutes, the parents had been enormously impressed with what they'd seen, and Simon, their son, was obviously very excited about the possibility of joining us. We were asked to put his name down on our waiting list immediately, and then, almost as an aside, the mother said 'Oh, I should tell you that we've got Simon's name down for St James's as well. After all, church schools are always so much better than state schools, aren't they.'

Needless to say, Simon wasn't invited to join us.

8

I CAN JUST LOOK IT UP ONLINE

The Pace Of Technology

When I began teaching, technology in the classroom was in its infancy. There was no internet, there were no iPhones, tablets, or computers or, of course, any kind of social media. There wasn't even a pocket calculator. You made phone calls either from a heavy black handset at home, or you queued at your nearest public red telephone box and waited your turn, coins in hand, while hoping the handset would actually be working. Television had two black and white channels. If you saw a computer, it would be at the cinema, in a futuristic film like *2001 A Space Odyssey*.

If your school was at the cutting edge of technology, it would have a couple of cassette recorders for classroom use, an overhead projector on which acetate slides could be placed so that the image could be thrown onto a screen, (saving a great deal of money on hymn books if you were a church school!) a reel to reel tape recorder which sometimes chewed up the tape, a slide projector, (which was great for history and geography if your school could afford enough slides), a 35mm camera for recording school events, and if funds could run to it and somebody could work them, a standard 8mm cine camera and projector.

If you worked for the Inner London education Authority, as I did, your school would also have a 16 millimetre film projector. This was an expensive piece of kit and highly prized, because the ILEA had a massive library of 16 millimetre films on every conceivable subject housed in County Hall on the River Thames. When I became a deputy head, and was put in charge of the projector because I enjoyed working with anything technical, I'd ask each teacher which topics they'd be studying with their classes that half term, browse the ILEA library catalogue and order a suitable range of films. The school would then troop into the main hall on Fridays, to enjoy two hours of cinematic but educational entertainment, and it was a weekly treat to be looked forward to.

Even if the school was burgled, nobody bothered to steal the projector, because simply heaving it out of the door would have given anybody a double hernia. Cassette recorders and 35mm cameras sometimes disappeared, but most items were relatively safe. Until the arrival of the videotape recorder. Here was a coveted piece of kit that revolutionised everything cinematic. You'd slip a sealed cassette of tape into the machine, and then you could record a television programme, even while watching a different channel if you so fancied, and if there was a programme on that might prove to be a good visual teaching aid, that was an added bonus. If you were a film buff, you could now buy complete feature films on videotape instead of the cobbled together poor focus 8mm extracts of cinema films that had been available in the past. The pictures were much sharper, and there was a wider choice virtually every week in the shops. Video libraries sprang up in every high street, where for a small payment and an annual subscription you could hire whatever you wanted. Small wonder these machines were so popular at home, in schools, and in every institution. You could even buy a video camera to record school or family events, but they were heavy, inefficient and not really much use for schools. The small reels of recording tape, once you'd recorded on them, had to be slotted into a bigger shell for acceptance by the video player, and it was all rather cumbersome.

But the video player itself wasn't, and as a lover of films I desperately wanted one for home. They were expensive... good ones cost upwards of £700... a lot of money at the time, but fortunately a friend worked for Hitachi, and he was able to get me one at a discount. I proudly set it up underneath our television, and spent many hours recording favourite films, programmes, and bits for school, labelling them all neatly to be enjoyed again whenever I wanted. At the same time, schools were being given VCRs by their education authorities, the ILEA being one of the first to recognise the significance of these amazing machines for visual learning in the classroom.

But Burglar Bill had realised their value, too. One morning I came down to the lounge and found our VCR wasn't under the television any more. My wife was in the shower and I called up to her, asking why she'd moved it. She answered, unsurprisingly, 'Why on earth would I have moved it?' And then I noticed the forced window and scratched paint left by BB and his likely lads as they'd made off with our expensive new toy during the night.

At the same time, video recorders were disappearing from schools daily because they were fetching great prices down at the Frog and Nightgown, even when they'd been carefully locked away in a cupboard. Children had obviously related excitedly about the school's new audio-visual possession to their families, and in socially deprived areas such as the ones I taught in, big brothers were quick to lend an opportunistic ear.

And then, even more desirable, home computers had arrived, in the form of the Commodore, the Sinclair Spectrum, the Atari, the Vic20, and the Dragon. These were fascinating machines, because you could type your own 'programme' into the computer using a coding language such as BBC 'BASIC', save it on a standard compact cassette, and then load it back into the computer whenever you wanted, to play through a television. There was soon a proliferation of games available for purchase on cassette that could be loaded into the computer, and played over and over again. And there was a rapidly growing range of home computer magazines available too, listing a wide variety of programmes you could type in. There were serious downsides though… you usually sat up half the night typing in a lengthy program, and then it wouldn't work because a tiny bit of code had been missed out. When it was all working… at last… you saved it on cassette and prayed that the tape didn't mess up or have oxide 'drop outs' when you tried to re-load it, because the much faster and far more reliable disk storage system wasn't then widely available.

As a headteacher, my first experience of a home computer came when Alan, our chair of governors and a keen technophobe offered to come to a staff meeting and demonstrate this amazing machine, for which he'd spent a week developing a learning programme for children. He brought along a small but chunky black and white TV, his Sinclair Spectrum, a cassette recorder, spare tapes in case one didn't load, and all the necessary wires, leads and plugs. We all sat waiting with bated breath as he started the demonstration. Suddenly, a simple addition sum appeared on the screen. A teacher was asked to type in the answer, and a smiley face appeared with a message saying 'Well Done!' 'What happens if you type in the wrong answer?' the teacher asked. 'Try it and see,' said a beaming Alan. This time, the computer said 'Ooops, wrong answer!' To Alan's disappointment, the staff weren't that impressed. They didn't really need a machine to teach their children how to add up, however clever it might be.

The pace of technology being what it is, however, it wasn't long before the Acorn BBC Micro came along, with a much bigger memory. (a mighty 32k, no less!) For the time, it was a superb machine, with a full size keyboard, a range of programmable function keys, excellent sound quality and the ability to pair up easily with ancillaries, such as a fast disc drive, a dot matrix printer and a special colour monitor which gave far sharper pictures than a television. You could also plug in sophisticated 'chips' containing programmes for word processing, drawing, designing, or desktop publishing. The modern computing era had arrived with a bang, alongside a superb range of games, useful home software and, for the education market, a wide range of educational programmes designed by teachers and other people experienced in education. A favourite, for example, showed an animated picture of a cuddly little orange creature called Podd from another planet, and children were invited to find out what Podd could do by typing in a verb. If Podd recognised the word, he'd perform the activity amusingly, and there were well over a hundred actions he could perform... and many surprising things too. He could fly, change colour, explode, inflate, levitate and balance on one digit. All of which greatly amused young children and rapidly increased their vocabulary as they tried to discover everything this amusing little creature could do. Virtually every education authority in the country wanted, at the very least, one of these machines in their schools and demand far outstripped supply for a long time.

For reasons known only to themselves, however, the powers that be at the Inner London Education Authority made an arrangement with a different company to supply computers to their schools. With the enticing name of the RM480Z, this computer was big, black, made of heavy metal and as attractive as a Sherman tank. It was also expensive, so schools could only have one, and it came with a chunky cassette recorder for software loading, a monitor, a trolley for trundling the kit from one classroom to another, and a small set of educational software. Unfortunately, these software programmes had been designed by people in the Authority's computing department, who had no real idea of what teachers needed or wanted, and most of them were extremely tedious, quickly tired of, and demonstrated curriculum principles which could be achieved just as easily using normal classroom materials. Since virtually all ILEA primary schools had at least three floors, (one close to mine had thirteen!) moving the machine from one floor to another was a Herculean task needing two people, and many teachers simply didn't bother, particularly as children would only have a few minutes computing time each week. Meanwhile, the highly portable and attractive BBC Micro used everywhere else was becoming in greater demand daily.

Although I had asked for a BBC Micro instead of the 480Z, I was told this wasn't possible, and when I asked why, on the mandatory 480Z training course, I was told that the BBC Micro was made of plastic and children could break it. Well, had they attacked it with a sledgehammer I suppose there would have been some truth in this, but given the paucity of good software for the 480Z and the impossibility of lumbering it around, I determined that my school should go for the BBC Micro. We ran regular raffles, second hand toy fairs, cake making sales, sponsored events and within a year had enough money to put one BBC Micro in every classroom, and the children loved using them. Although the Authority didn't stop us doing this, I certainly wasn't supported, and I was told that if anything went wrong it was down to us to sort it out. Fortunately, the machines were extremely reliable, apart from an internal chip that handled software loading from cassette, and when they began to fail it cost £25 to have the computer serviced... a lot of money at the time. Until I discovered that I could buy the chip for nineteen pence from a specialist firm advertising in one of the computing magazines, and fit it myself.

Then, another big move forward for our school. My deputy headteacher's brother, who taught in a London technical college, was re-equipping the computer department with the newly emerging PCs running early Microsoft Windows software, and he had thirty BBC Micros to give away. We jumped at the chance, fetched the computers in a van, and we could now have something very few primary schools had... a specialist ICT room where a class of twenty five children could be taken for lessons in computing, each child having their own computer to work with. Since I had a BBC Micro at home and had a lot of experience with it, I ran a course for the staff and for eighteen months things went exceptionally well.

But technology was advancing ever more rapidly, and during our first Ofsted inspection we were told that the time had come for our BBC Micros to be retired. This seemed a little ridiculous to me, since the BBC Micro could word-process, desktop publish, design databases, enable children to code easily, design with an electronic pen and do everything that a primary aged child could possibly need to experience. But no, sorry, if we wanted to pass our Ofsted inspections in future we'd have to junk our Micros and buy in some modern PCs. Since the ILEA had been disbanded by the Thatcher government, and its computing department closed down, each borough now had its own education authority and we were given some money to buy a handful of Windows PCs… which because our budget was tight had to be the cheapest we could find. Unsurprisingly these tended to break down with monotonous regularity. And now, children would no longer be able to have a computer to themselves when the class had a lesson in the ICT room.

Once again, things changed rapidly, computers began to have much higher specifications, and Tony Blair's government wanted to make sure primary teachers were computer literate and knew how to integrate ICT across a range of curriculum subjects, while recognising how important computer learning and technology was becoming for schools. Most primary school teachers were still very wary and unsure about computers in the classroom, so I had no argument with that, but the way the government went about it was, again, an expensive mess.

A rigorous computer training course had been quickly designed for all teachers, even though most schools were chasing their tails desperately trying to find enough money to keep up with the constantly accelerating pace of technology, meaning quite a few of their computers were probably already becoming obsolete. Nevertheless, there was an enticing crock of government gold available for any firms who fancied running a little course for teachers, so they stepped forward in their hundreds. Many hadn't a clue, apart from knowing a quick buck when they saw one, but a handful survived, and I invited one of them to show me his wares.

Perhaps I should have been warned when the salesman's laptop demo broke down twice, but the firm was highly recommended by our local authority, we signed on the dotted line, and on the first training day, while the children were still on holiday, we duly assembled in our ICT room for the first session. My ICT co-ordinator had provided croissants and fresh coffee, to bribe those who were still a bit wary about the pace of everything electronic.

The first surprise had been that all the training would be done via the internet. No fresh-faced, bright eyed young chappie guiding us through the jargon… just a handful of CDs and faceless mentors somewhere across the ether, gently forgiving every daft mistake and showing us the way forward. Since I'd been into computers since the very early days of home computing and written a popular educational programme for the BBC Micro published by the Mirror group, the second surprise was finding the first two hours of this course so boring even the croissants and coffee couldn't compensate. The e-mail system, then in e-mail infancy, was incomprehensible, the electronic form-filling (that's all the course really consisted of) was deadly dull and the literature an unbeatable cure for insomnia. Nevertheless, my wonderful staff, with the spirit that won us the war, slogged at it, all determined to achieve their certificate for completing the course. I gave up at session two, simply turning up to smile at everybody else and brew the coffee. Strong and sweet, as it needed to be.

And then, in session three, things suddenly turned interesting. We'd noticed that although everyone supposedly had an individual mentor somewhere across the internet, the feedback was remarkably similar. Identical, in fact. 'Well done Zoe, you are realising your learning and teaching objectives.' 'Well done Philip, you are realising your objectives for teaching and learning.' By session four, we thought we'd test the water. So, in answer to 'How did the children respond?' Terry wrote: 'By asking themselves basic questions like, 'Am I a sardine?"' And back came the response: 'Well done Terry, you are realising your objectives for teaching and learning.' Was there a human across the ether, we wondered, or were we being mentored by R2D2 and a sophisticated software program of stock responses, an early and primitive computer 'bot'? Intrigued, Terry became bolder. 'What are your aims for the lesson?' the electronic form asked. 'For the children to have skills with the mouse, and for the mouse to have children skills,' he wrote. 'Well done Terry,' came the mentor's response over the ether, 'You are progressing well with your objectives for teaching and learning.'

By session six, and e-mails outlining how he'd found ICT lessons to be more successful when undertaken at the deep end of a swimming bath, somebody twigged and chastised him gently. Amazingly, he was still awarded his certificate though. And I got one too, although all I'd done really was make the coffee. At the end of the six mandatory full day sessions, I can't say my staff felt enlightened, or especially computer literate, but the firm providing the course had no doubt bankrolled a fair bit of cash. How much better it would have been for one member of staff, fully immersed in the possibilities offered by computers in the classroom, to attend a short course and then train the staff themselves. It would certainly have been much cheaper, and far more money would have been available for the provision of badly needed hardware.

With increasingly clever technology moving into the foreground, attending a course or lecture at the local authority's learning centre suddenly changed dramatically. I saw my first PowerPoint presentation when our education authority invited its headteachers to discuss its latest initiative. Instead of the ubiquitous overhead projector and transparencies, a large electronic whiteboard hung impressively on the wall, connected to a laptop and a device that looked like a slide projector. For a moment I wondered if we were about to enjoy the chief inspector and his wife on Brighton beach in glorious widescreen, but no, this was a discussion about raising achievement for boys. And it was a lot more entertaining than the average LEA meeting.

Each time the introductory speaker made what he thought was an important point, he'd push a button and the sentence he'd just said would animate its letters across the whiteboard and then underline itself. Was this new whizzo presentation of wise words intended for ageing headteachers who tend to nod off as soon as somebody other than themselves starts talking? No, the new flashy technology was there to impress. Later in the day, I investigated the cost. For the same price, I could have bought over eighty guitars for my school.

Of course, Sod's Law clearly states that the reliability of a piece of technology is in inverse proportion to the size and importance of the audience watching you use it, and the law was certainly in operation that day. The three main speakers were using PowerPoint presentations, although their talks didn't seem that much better for it. They just looked prettier. At the end of the afternoon, the laptop crashed, and the embarrassed female presenter stared at it in bewilderment. Male technophile headteachers quickly leapt to her rescue, and for ten minutes bodies were bent over the apparatus while plugs were pushed and pulled, cables substituted and buttons pressed. Confronted from my front row seat by a line of bums, I peered up at the screen, which, almost gleefully I felt, kept displaying those annoying little Windows messages saying it couldn't make any sense of the input. In the end, the poor lady was forced to improvise her talk.

But the technophiles won the day, of course. The headteacher who managed to fix the laptop proudly gave a PowerPoint presentation that amounted to a set of visual fireworks. Animated characters jumped and jiggled on the screen, words and sentences exploded in dazzling colour. It was so eye-popping I still couldn't remember what his talk was actually about afterwards, and it must have taken weeks to prepare, although I couldn't help wondering whether his time might have been more profitably spent listening to children read.

Teachers soon realised the interactive whiteboard was by far the greatest leap forward in classroom computer technology. It was an electronic marvel, soon to be fully embraced by primary and infant teachers, even those who had been suspicious about the benefits of computers in their classrooms previously. And it was also straightforward and easy to use.

Since the dawn of time, classrooms always had a blackboard at the front of the classroom. It was there during my primary school days, it was green and stretched right across the classroom in my secondary days, (and the ubiquitous wooden board rubber was thrown at you if you weren't working hard enough), there was one in every lecture room at college, throughout my teaching career I used one, and they were written on with sticks of white and coloured chalk, chalkdust filling the air when the board was wiped. Compared with the new whiteboard, however, the blackboard was truly a relic from the ark. The interactive electronic whiteboard allowed teachers to display crisp moving and still images in full colour from a computer onto an electric screen, using a projector fixed to the ceiling in a small cage. Presentations and videos could be shown to the whole class at the same time. The interactive whiteboard didn't need chalk or marker pens, and as well as projecting images on them, they could be written on using a special stylus. The boards could also detect more than one person writing on them at a time, which was ideal for a teacher posing problems and a pupil trying to solve them at the same time. Software also enabled 'touch screen' facilities, like modern tablets. It was a really useful and exciting invention as it presented information to children in a most exciting way, easy to assimilate, and the ability to include images and videos on the screen provided children with a visual aid that would further encourage and stimulate their learning. A great benefit for the teacher was that first class interactive presentations could be prepared well in advance of the lesson.

Once again, schools were anxious to include these modern miracles in their classrooms, but as with all the technologies that had gone before, they were expensive. The boards needed to be installed and set up by a specialist firm, and few schools could afford to install more than a few at a time. And, of course, Burglar Bill had rapidly moved on from videotape recorders, now worth very little, to these new and flashy items. It wasn't the whiteboard he was interested in, it was the projector... small, light, easily smuggled out of a building and infinitively desirable, because interest in home cinema was rocketing and all you needed was one of these projectors, a DVD player and a surround sound system in your lounge and you had something approaching the quality and scale of the local multiplex. They began to disappear from schools with monotonous regularity around the same time that local authorities decided their schools could do without the expense of a resident premises officer, so schools then had to invest in heavy steel ceiling cages, with massive padlocks and chains, to house their projectors. The other downside was that, although the lamps for the projectors lasted a long time, they were hideously expensive to replace and usually several would go at the same time, especially if teachers left their classrooms at hometime without remembering to turn them off.

And what is it about technology that causes it to have such a mind of its own? My iPhone often does things I haven't asked it to, the electronic key to my car suddenly refused to open the car door after I'd fitted a new battery, the pages on my wife's tablet sometimes flip backwards and forwards annoyingly when she's reading a book on it, my computer printer suddenly displayed a message saying 'Urgent! Call the service agent immediately!' and then carried on working normally and the electronic alarm in the secondary school at the bottom of our garden will go off in the middle of the night for no reason whatsoever and there's no on-site premises officer to turn the thing off. And even when the technology seems to be working well, there's the human element.

During one summer holiday, I'd arranged for three more interactive whiteboards to be installed. Holidays were always a good time for this sort of thing because something always goes wrong. This time, one of the projectors once installed, didn't work. No particular reason. It just stopped working. In fact, I'd begun to feel I was developing a slightly negative view towards technology because it was eating hungrily into the school budget, so near the end of term I'd attended an ICT course for school leaders. The idea was to do some blue skies thinking about your school: where you were now, where you were going, and where would educational ICT be in twenty years' time. That sort of thing. As I pointed out to the course leader, the stuff was still too unreliable. Very clever, yes, but children give the hardware a lot of heavy use and it can break down, or the software can crash. Plus the fact that everything goes out of date with alarming speed, and if you can't afford a technician to come in regularly to keep things running smoothly, you're walking on eggshells. Not so, said our instructor. He took his mobile from his pocket and said that five years ago it would have been four times the size and prone to all kinds of faults. This one, he said, hadn't gone wrong once... even when he'd accidentally dropped it down the toilet.

I wasn't sure how much contact he'd had with reality in schools, but to prove my point four things happened the very next day. The server in our ICT room packed up. Speakers on a whiteboard refused to work. Our Admin Officer couldn't upload some census data, and the local authority said that a data disc we'd sent had somehow acquired a virus. Could we possibly send the data on paper instead? Of course, the government doesn't seem to have had much success, either. It has been known to spend billions on computer systems in the public arena that are often unreliable at best.

Because the pace of technology waits for nobody, a brilliantly clever piece of software will be released, then a new, improved, uncrashable version comes along, quickly followed by a third when that turns out not to be infallible. Take the suite of programs our school office used, for example. Yes, it worked well most of the time, but we had to pay for regular updates, as well as telephone support. And the contract certainly didn't include a visit from a technician. That would have been several hundred extra.

But back to my ICT course... on day two, we were shown a government video of some primary schools supposedly at the cutting edge of ICT. In one sequence, we watched a literacy lesson, with each child sitting at a computer screen holding a 'voting stick'... a sort of remote control with coloured buttons to push, indicating the child's choice of connectives for sentences. It looked incredibly boring, but the teacher was on a high, saying that each push of a button sent results straight to a pupil-specific data bank, which even did away with marking. I sat there thinking that if that was the direction in which things were moving, I was only too glad that my own children weren't at primary school any more.

As whiteboards became increasingly essential to the modern classroom, I read three articles about ICT in primary education. The first talked about the importance of the electronic whiteboard in the nursery class. We know, of course, that many parents think it's fine for very young children to twiddle on tablets and mobile phones, but I couldn't think of anything more dismal than having tiny children in a school nursery spending a chunk of their day gawping at a screen instead of painting, constructing, socialising, dressing up, role-playing, mark-making… and most important of all, listening to stories read excitingly by an imaginative and creative teacher. A newly qualified teacher recently told me her college advised the use of an electronic board for story telling because 'it could show the children lots of scenes from the book and animate them.' What happened to imagination, then?

Another article talked about Luddite primary school teachers, unwilling to keep abreast of new technology and rapidly falling behind the skills of the average techy seven year old. Schools, the writer said, should be incorporating the children's personal bits of electronic wizardry… which they spend much leisure time getting to know intimately… into their classroom learning. Bring in your touch screen phones! Bring in your personal players that store a million tunes, your tablets that hold the entire works of Shakespeare on a chip the size of an aspirin! After all, at the touch of a finger the entire content of the web is available on a phone, as well as the location of the nearest kebab shop for a bit of lunch, with voice-guidance leading you to it while avoiding traffic jams and motorways.

It must be obvious by now that I'm certainly not against the technological revolution. But to say 'Teachers, if your school can't afford the latest equipment, get your headteacher to allow phones and tablets into school so that the children can access information in their lessons,' seems to me a little foolhardy and probably dangerous. Imagine the lesson and look at the downside. Children wouldn't be using their touch phones when instructed. These pieces of wizardry are compulsive, and the children would fiddle with them under the table. They wouldn't necessarily be accessing what you wanted them to, either. A teacher recently told me one of his Year 5's was using a phone to show his mates a website where a gentleman was doing some very naughty things with a turkey.

Then, of course, there's always the security problem. I remember, years ago, a parent making an incredible fuss because her child's Beyblade, a popular toy you set spinning on the floor, disappeared from the teacher's desk after she'd confiscated it. The teacher took it, so the school should pay for it, the parent demanded. When I refused she phoned the local education authority, who phoned the chair of governors, who phoned me, and it actually became an agenda item for the governing body meeting three days later. Just imagine the fuss if a current mobile phone disappeared. It's bad enough if somebody nicks a sherbet lemon.

And then there's the bullying aspect. I am often appalled by some of the things children get up to with mobile phones. Cyber bullying can be horrific, and I can remember a serious incident at our school which took a great deal of time and effort to resolve. Yet children still tried to smuggle their mobiles into school if they could. There is so much glibness from the 'experts' about personalised learning and technology. They need to spend a bit more time talking to teachers who are dealing, day in and day out, with the issues it brings.

Parents were often astonished when they rang the school and their call would usually be answered within seconds, either by me or our Admin Officer. There was no message saying 'Thank you for ringing our school, now please choose from the following twelve options...' But phone virtually any company or public service these days (tried ringing your doctor?) and you'll be subjected to layers and sub-layers of choices. By the time you push the final button, hoping you've made the right choices at each level and expecting to talk to a human being, you'll be told that all the operators are currently busy, but you must continue to hold because 'Your call is incredibly important to us.' Even if you've phoned your insurance company one minute past opening time. You'll sit listening to an electronic Boccherini minuet, and after ten minutes you'll probably have had enough and given up, unless you fancy chatting to an on-line 'bot', and even then it probably won't be able to answer your question and you'll have to hang on until you can talk to an adviser.

I remember when I tried to discover why a piece of equipment hadn't been delivered and spent twenty five minutes getting through to customer services. The lady said she'd check with the warehouse people... and then found she couldn't get through to them. It seems amazing, in the age of supposedly easy global communication, that we have so much trouble getting in touch with anybody. I began to dread phoning local secondary schools, or colleges that supplied us with student teachers, or the social agencies we needed to deal with. If I got through the layers, the phone often just rang and rang. Or the person I wanted wasn't working that day. Or nobody bothered to phone back even when I'd left a message.

It did make me feel a bit of sympathy for local education officers trying to contact their schools. Yes, they could send a collective e-mail, but sometimes they needed to phone directly, and it must be incredibly frustrating to be up against automated machinery constantly, and then having to leave a message at the end. We began to experience the same problems when we tried to get in touch with parents whose children were sick, or left uncollected after school. Although we asked one main number and a back-up contact, we invariably had to leave messages on answer phones. Or the line went dead because the parent had moved to a new network provider and nobody had bothered to let us know.

Shortly before I retired, I was sorting through boxes of old school documents and I came across some faded letters sent to me by the local education office in my first weeks as a school leader. There was no email in those days, of course: everything was done on a typewriter. One letter in particular grabbed my attention. 'Dear headteacher, now that the borough has moved its education office to larger premises, we'd like to make it a special place for parents and visitors. The entrance and waiting area is rather plain, and since we know our schools produce some outstanding work, we'd like to celebrate that by setting up exhibitions of children's work. If your school has been working on a project, and you'd like lots of people in the borough to see it, please get in touch.'

I jumped at the chance. I'd recently instigated a whole-school topic on famous artists. We had filled one of our halls with work and we had plenty left over, so we were able to create a lively mini-exhibition of artwork, models and creative writing for the education office. It was quite a hit. I received letters and phone calls from visitors complimenting us on the quality of the children's work, and even more importantly, increasing numbers of parents began to visit our school, seeking a place for their children. And then, many years later, I received an email saying 'Dear headteacher, the Department for Education has made available a 'beta' release of the Autumn school census, and they recommend that all schools load a file output from their administration system, which will allow a check that all the required data is being output from the school's system into the Autumn census return. This will indicate whether validation errors or queries are being generated, against your data when loaded into 'Collect', and any errors will need to be resolved before the collection goes live. Please note, the test blade is available for only a short period.' Could there be, I thought, a starker contrast between what was deemed important when I began as a headteacher and what was considered essential by the receipt of this email?

Almost weekly, I was receiving emails from companies desperate to sell me their latest electronic tool, which would tell me, at the touch of a button, just how my school was doing in the driving-up-standards stakes. One said that the dashboard provided by the school inspectorate was a wondrous thing, but that their program went into even greater depth, with meaningful benchmarks, adaptive management systems, weighted FSM, SEN and EAL, and data crunching for 'a broader context'. My governors, I was told, would be especially grateful for the tool. Frankly, I thought they'd be terrified, and, like me, wouldn't have the slightest idea what a test blade was. Perhaps, I thought, years down the line we'll realise what we've done and the word 'child' will appear again in letters to school leaders, provided we have an education secretary who actually knows what one is.

So, at a governing body meeting just before I retired, I was very amused to find we were being asked to adopt the local authority's new Code of Conduct policy, which included a statement that telephones should be answered within five rings and that further information could be found in its TAP, or 'Telephone Answering Policy'. After a little investigation, I discovered that most LEAs had a TAP, long statements of the obvious that must have been incredibly dull to write. I found one sporting two highlighted, important headlines. Calls should be answered 'promptly and politely', and messages should be replied to 'quickly and effectively'. That was a revelation. Who'd have thought that! There was lots more information too. Pass on the details of the caller and the enquiry to the appropriate person. Put a smile on your face when answering the telephone, because it makes your voice sound friendlier. Establish the identity of the caller. Gosh. So many things we had no idea about. I made a mental note to tell my admin staff not to keep saying 'Oi, what do you want...'

And just occasionally, I was tempted to install an answer phone. Especially when Mrs White rang up to tell me why Cynthia wasn't at school and then launched into long descriptions of the trouble she's having with her 'various' veins and why the canary had to be put down. 'Thank you for ringing and welcome to our school. Push button one if you want to tell us your medical history, button two if you want to discuss avian medicinal practices…'

There is, of course, no holding back technology, either in schools or anywhere else, and much of it is enormously exciting. But as I write, there are increasing concerns about the pace being far too fast and the enormous concerns it could bring. And this was hammered home when I watched a television programme showing a line of human robots who could mimic human behaviour and movement with incredible and somehow quite unnerving precision. It certainly made we wonder what my grandchildren might be experiencing twenty years down the line…

9

TESTING, TESTING!

Children And The Standard Attainment Tests

At the age of eleven, I failed my eleven plus. The eleven plus tests were important enough for my final year of primary school to include a fair amount of regular weekly practice on mock papers and our headteacher even gave us compulsory homework, to make sure we were as ready as possible.

I didn't fail through any fault of my own. I'd had a severe bout of chicken pox and I was still feeling pretty fragile and unwell when I took the tests. I failed the Arithmetic by just one mark. Nevertheless, in those days, virtually all education authorities used the eleven plus tests of Arithmetic, Intelligence and English, and they were the great arbiter of life chances. I lived in the London suburb of Ealing, and my parents knew just how important it was to pass. Fail, and you were doomed to the local secondary modern school, with its reputation of intimidating initiation rituals for new boys and its failure to turn out anything more worthwhile than fodder for a dead-end job at the Walls ice cream factory. Pass, and you attended Ealing Grammar, and a bright outlook would be mine if I worked hard enough. Unfortunately, even though I'd failed by just the one mark, failure it was, and it was going to be the secondary mod for me. I still remember the despair on my mother's face when she opened the letter.

And then... a sort of reprieve. My primary school headteacher called my parents in, and told them that he was astonished that I should have failed, and that there were places in the grammar stream of a newly built 'comprehensive' school, and he would strongly recommend me for a place if my parents so wished. Comprehensive schools were a very new idea at the time and naturally they were delighted, but there was a downside. The school was nine miles away, so it would mean getting up very early and travelling by trolleybus… an unreliable kind of electric tram which ran on overhead wires. However, it seemed far preferable to me than having my head thrust down the toilet on day one at the secondary modern, and so the place was duly taken up. Early Comprehensive schools were a mixture of the able and less able. For the less able, there was the possibility of working hard and transferring quickly into the grammar stream, with all the opportunities that offered.

It seems dreadful now that a test taken at eleven could more or less decide your future, even though some areas and authorities still use it, but of course life consists of many different tests, whether it's a regular test each year to gauge a child's performance in every curriculum subject, an entrance exam to get into university, an interview for a job, or a test to see if your car is in good enough condition for using on a public road. For a long time in my early teaching career, spent in socially challenging areas of London, children were not tested at eleven at all. Their ability was graded by the class teacher and headteacher, and applications could be made to any secondary school that parents preferred, although preferences had to be sensible and there was no certainty that a child would be accepted. Hence, after a talk with the school, they chose a shortlist of options. The system seemed to me, as a regular Year 6 teacher at the time, that the system worked pretty well, even though it involved a fair amount of paper work, discussion and long hours.

Then, in 1991, the Standard Attainment Tests (SATs) arrived, designed to measure children's educational achievement in Year 2 and Year 6. The aim was to hold all primary schools to account for the attainment of their pupils and the progress they'd made. After all, a national curriculum for primaries had been introduced a couple of years beforehand, one of the ideas being that if all schools were studying the same curriculum, and a family moved from one part of the country to another, the child could pick up the curriculum at the new school from where they'd left off at the old one.

The Year 2 tests, or their preferred title 'assessments', take place at age seven and they test children's ability in maths and reading (plus an optional test in English grammar, punctuation and spelling). These assessments are intended to be quite informal, so they aren't timed and they take place in a normal classroom setting, so that children are hopefully not frightened or worried about them, and that parents won't pressure their children to pass. From September 2023, Key Stage 1 SATs became non-statutory, so schools could choose whether they wanted to administer them or not.

The assessments for children aged eleven are more formal tests, in English grammar, punctuation, spelling and reading, and maths. The papers are forty five minutes long and they are usually taken in exam conditions. Key Stage 1 SATs are marked by teachers within the school, while Key Stage 2 SATs are sent away to be marked externally. Key Stage 1 parents won't necessarily be told their child's results, because the whole thing is designed to be downplayed as much as possible, but they can always ask, and they'll be told, usually on a school open evening, whether their child is working to the expected standard.

Key Stage 2 parents get their child's scaled score in July and are told whether or not they have reached the expected level. The results of Key Stage 2 SATS are also published annually in the Department for Education's primary school league tables, where an online facility enables users to compare schools against other schools, as well as against the national average. Naturally, the government says SATs are not about passing or failing. They're simply about showing the level a child is working at.

So that's the theory, anyway. But when examined more closely, the whole thing is quite a can of worms and every year there is a considerable amount of dialogue about the tests. Many believe they place children under undue pressure at too young an age. A study in 2017 found that anxiety and panic attacks had increased in more than three-quarters of primary schools over the previous two years and that SATs also affected the morale and general well-being of teachers.

When SATs began in 1991, I made careful preparation and decided that I would invigilate them myself, together with my two year 6 teachers. I purchased fifty second-hand individual folding desks to set out in the top hall, and bought new sets of pencils, rubbers, rulers, set squares, and calculators for the children to use. I certainly didn't want to worry the children, but I did want them to feel a sense of occasion, especially as the tests were going to be administered over the period of a whole week. I had no idea of what I was about to experience.

Since we knew these tests were on their way, and since we suspected schools were going to be judged on their SATs results, my two dedicated Year 6 teachers had worked exceptionally hard all year, lessening the time spent on the construction of technological miracles from cornflakes boxes so that they could give a fair amount of time to the all-important core subjects. On the big day, I realised that I was almost as nervous as my teachers, so I arrived at school even earlier than usual.

At nine o'clock the sky was filled with sunshine, and so were all the faces of Year 6. A beautiful May Monday, and not a single absence. Really, I thought, we should have been in the park, studying nature and this beautiful season, but every one of them is here: the able, the less able, the unable, the unstable. I realised that, spurred on by the powers that be, parents had been persuaded that these new SATs tests were *very important,* like Ofsted inspections and league tables. My Year 6 trooped excitedly into the hall and sat at the individual foldaway tables. Then they examined their new pencils and unchewed rubbers with relish, as we explained the mechanics of SATs week, and the tests began in earnest. The silence and concentration was wonderful, and the day passed quietly.

They were all here on Tuesday, too. Even the unable. Especially the unable. Damn it, I thought, we're about to be judged on the results of these things, and this could muck up our position in the coming league table position. The parents had obviously continued to view the week as extremely important. Gary's hair had been cut for the occasion, and Jade had been provided with a box of scented tissues to mop her troubled brow. It was mental maths day, and as I listened to the careful articulation of the voice on the CD I wondered why, just a few years ago, the powers that be were telling us that doing whole-class mental tests wasn't 'good practice'. The voice asks the children to circle the approximate weight of an apple. What apple are we talking about here, I wondered? A Granny Smith? A cooking apple? A crab apple? The children hurriedly scribbled answers into the boxes. Just as Haji's facial contortions suggest he's been moving towards an answer, the voice moved on, throwing him completely.

We ground through Wednesday, and on Thursday it was maths test B. My wife and I had eaten the usual quick breakfast before dashing off to our respective schools. 'How much does an apple weigh?' I'd asked her. 'Haven't a clue,' she'd replied. At school I gathered together the implements needed for the maths test: calculators, rulers, protractors, tracing paper. I noticed that Year 6 were astonished at the daily production of new accessories and studied their immaculately sharpened pencil points with interest and not a little disbelief.

In Question Two of the test, the children were shown six shapes, all differing slightly, and they're asked to find which one is identical to a seventh shape. The examiners have assumed tracing paper would be helpful and said they can use it. Silly examiners. Nine of the children, who managed to turn their tracing paper upside down and inside out during the process, became totally confused and got it all wrong. Gary had wrapped his comb in his tracing paper and looked as though he might attempt to play it.

But children are adaptable creatures and by Friday they were almost blasé about the tests. I knew when they'd finished now, because they turned to their neighbours to see how things were going and accidentally knocked their pencils off the desks. As they bent to retrieve them, they knocked their rulers, rubbers and protractors off as well. If I told them to try very hard not to drop pencils, three more would immediately clatter to the floor. On Friday afternoon the science test began, and I watched as Mark buried himself in the food chain question. What will happen to the otters if an item earlier in the food chain disappears? 'Otters might go very dark,' he writes with supreme confidence. I am constantly awed by the intricacies of young minds.

At four o'clock on Friday I joined my Year 6 teachers to study the incredibly detailed packing instructions and post them off for marking. When I arrived home that evening, my wife handed me an apple. 'About a hundred grams,' she said. 'Oh well,' I thought, 'quite a few of them got that one wrong.' But then, apples didn't seem to feature regularly in their daily lives…

Come to that, nor did tree houses, a prominent feature in the English test two years later. Throughout my career, I taught in areas where most of the children would hardly recognise a tree, let alone the fact that you could build a house in one. What kind of house would the children envisage mentally, I wondered? Virtually all of them lived in high rise flats. As I read through the booklet, and the questions, it occurred to me that the compilers hadn't really thought things through.

The piece the children had to read, and then answer questions on, was about a little boy called Norman, who'd had a serious argument with his parents and taken himself off to live in a tree house, built in an oak at the end of his sizeable garden. The booklet consisted of letters written to Norman by family and friends. There are indications that he wrote back, so I presumed he'd stormed up the tree, complete with a pad of Basildon Bond and a Sharpie or two.

The first letters are from his Mum and Dad. Dad wishes him all the best for his exciting new life (no doubt before filling his pipe, retiring to his favourite armchair and doing the *Sunday Times* crossword) and understands that his decision to leave the family is a serious one. Mum is grateful to him for explaining all the things she and dad got wrong, and says his advice is very helpful, so thank you Norman. Good bit of middle class psychology here. Pander to your child's every whim, pretend he's a miniature adult instead of a little boy... and, get this... even allow him to lug a television up the tree. Good thing health and safety officers weren't in the neighbourhood, although they could explain that Norm wasn't in much danger of electrocution, since electricity isn't normally found up trees.

Then comes a sour little note from his sister. She's nicked his bedroom! 'Ha Ha,' she says, 'Mum and Dad said I could have it.' This is followed by a formal letter from his class teacher, undoubtedly taking time out in the evening from targeting and tracking, to advise him on life skills he'll need in his new leafy retreat. It seems his parents popped in to see her, explaining that Norman wouldn't be coming to school anymore because he was now living in a tree. (Mind you, perhaps that wasn't so strange. A parent once came to see me asking if I could have a word with Andrew because he kept climbing into wheelie-bins and closing the lid, only opening it to frighten passers-by by shouting 'boo!')

Turn the page and we meet Grandma.. aurally and visually because there's a photo with her letter. And a miserable old harridan she looks, too. She witters on about how lonely she is, how her grandchildren don't visit often enough and how Norman's father hasn't written to her for ages. Frankly, if she was coming for lunch, I thought, I'd be up there with Norm. She was certainly unlike any grandparent I've ever known. I'd always thought grandparents were elderly cuddly people who bought their grandchildren loads of stuff they didn't need, and always said 'of course you can have another ice cream, whatever your mum says.'

Still, Norman has one good friend. Alfred writes and says how totally cool living up a tree is, because he won't have to wash or brush his teeth. Presumably he doesn't realise he'll have to keep his distance after a couple of weeks, because Norm will smell like Pepe Le Pew. And then he says 'Can I have your bike?' A charming friend, then.

It all ends well. Mr Precocious eventually climbs down from his tree because… wait for it… he's won a competition about solving the world's problems and he's off to meet the President of the US of A. Before he does that, I hoped that he'd get sent to bed with a severe wigging and no supper. Similarly, the compiler of this piece of nonsense, which bore no relevance whatsoever to anything my Year 6 children had experienced, and morally, was quite reprehensible.

And then, some years later, the government decided that tests for children in Year 6 should be tougher. There was even a suggestion that failing children might have to spend part of their summer holiday in a local secondary school as teachers tried to get them up to speed. I suspected this might be an attempt by an increasingly unpopular government to prove that the SATs were worthwhile.

When I was able to look at the new tests once again I began to question the minds compiling them. Take English, for example. We were told that pupils would be asked to identify subordinate clauses, recognise adverbials and use the subjunctive. Then the children would be asked whether a given sentence contained a simile, onomatopoeia or alliteration. Were the compilers trying to put children off literature for life, I wondered? At the age of eleven, I wouldn't have known onomatopoeia if it had jumped up and bitten me, but I was already strongly fired by literature, because I was fortunate in having a mother who had read widely, cared deeply about books and whose greatest wish was to instil a similar love in her children. Unlike today, there wasn't a massive amount of literature aimed at young people, so we had explored many classics together: *The Coral Island, Swallows and Amazons, Treasure Island, Peter Pan.* She would often stop and savour a paragraph, asking me to listen to the way the sentences had been assembled, or to the rhythm of a sequence of words.

And at primary school, there were teachers who loved reading aloud to the class. I particularly remember Miss Webb's skill at dividing a story into segments, enabling her to stop at a cliff-hanger. How well I remember fearing for the little girl, in *Old Peter's Russian Tales*, being chased across the hills by Baba Yaga, the evil iron-toothed witch. And, oh, the anxiety I felt for Pinocchio as he hammered on the door of the fairy's house to escape the murderous fox and cat. Would the fairy come down in time? I had to wait on tenterhooks for a whole day to find out.

As a headteacher, I felt the rot had really started to set in when I watched student teachers handing out extracts of a well-known story with a set of questions underneath, asking the children to identify verbs, adverbs, subordinate clauses and metaphors. Wouldn't it be better, I often asked, if they simply read the story in its entirety, enthused over the use of language and pointed out how certain words and phrases made the sentences come alive? Usually the student teacher would say that, yes, they would much prefer to do that, but their lecturers had suggested that this way would help the children with their tests. There was no doubt that it would have done, but was that really what the aim should have been?

Young children are wonderfully alive to the world around them, and if they are sufficiently excited about the language they are exposed to, they will be inspired to create their own stories, poems and plays. And they will want to share their joy with others. I wasn't optimistic though. The politicians had spoken, the world was a stage and we teachers merely obedient players. There's a metaphor in there somewhere. Not that it matters, of course.

Over the years, as computers rapidly became increasingly sophisticated and data-gathering a massive feature at the Department for Education, schools became increasingly worried about the SATs, particularly the Year 6 ones. Parents were using them to compare one school with another, the local authority used them to determine whether their inspectors needed to pay you a swift visit, and Ofsted homed in on them like hounds on a fox.

One year, after tossing a bit of data around, we calculated that only 55 per cent of our children would attain SATs Level 4, the required level Year 6 children should be achieving. Really, this shouldn't have caused us any concern at all. All the teachers they'd been taught by were superb, and some of the children would perform very well indeed. But there was a significant number in the cohort who had additional educational needs, and a fair proportion who simply weren't very able academically. In many ways, it was remarkable they had achieved as much as they had. The parents were well aware of how much we'd done for these children and they knew how much they enjoyed school. We should have been celebrating instead of feeling our stomachs churn with anxiety.

If our calculations were correct, we knew the results wouldn't be acceptable. Little lights on the DfE's electronic map of attainment in schools across the country would flash red and sound an alarm. The suits would notice that our results were usually in the high seventies or eighties, and the year before had been in the nineties…(even getting results in the seventies was considered admirable for a school in a socially deprived inner city area)… and now they were about to drop dramatically. How would the dip in results be interpreted in those high offices? The school must be failing, they'd think. Not enough rigour is being applied. Senior management wasn't monitoring the quality of teaching and learning properly. The children weren't attentive enough, and assessment by the teaching staff must be poor. Undoubtedly, inappropriate targets were being set. Marshall the cavalry, send for the guard… and look, the school hasn't been inspected for three years. Get Ofsted down there immediately!

And that, of course, is what caused my staff to get so worked up. What could we do about it, they cried, it's utterly unfair. And it was, but whatever we said, we knew perfectly well that Ofsted wouldn't accept the real reasons for the drop and we'd plummet to a 'satisfactory' rating… or worse. Although nothing could be further from the truth, people have been so conditioned by current and past governments to think Ofsted reports are an accurate reflection of a school, everybody in the neighbourhood would think our wonderful school was rapidly sliding down the pan.

So, what to do? Well, we did what other schools do in this position. The teachers looked carefully at the children who weren't that far from the Level 4 threshold, put them in a special group, and force fed additional mathematics in the hope they'd just about be able to crawl through the necessary hoops. It was 'protecting our backs' so that the school wasn't labelled 'satisfactory'. Because, as teachers were only too aware, satisfactory was almost a pseudonym for 'unsatisfactory'.

With a smidgen of luck, we knew that two thirds of this cohort would just achieve a Level 4. Then, having forgotten in the summer holidays the stuff they were crammed with, we also knew the children would move on to their secondary schools, and their new teachers would say 'We've just given these children a preliminary test, and they are nowhere near a secure Level 4… what on earth was the primary school thinking of?' And they'd become worried too, because they would be up against the same problem. And so the ridiculous cycle would continue. Sometimes I sat in my office wondering how this juggernaut of stupidity had been created, because it certainly couldn't be called effective education.

And there was another worry, too. Brian was one of my friends at secondary school and he used to cheat in exams, because his parents placed him under enormous pressure to do well. He was able, but not especially so, and he dreaded facing his parents if he performed badly. So he took a calculated risk and prepared crib cards with all the information he needed. The invigilators in those days became rapidly bored from walking up and down and often settled into a chair to read the paper, or, in one instance that astonished me, play cricket in the corridor outside the classroom. Brian would then sneak his crib cards from his pocket. I was appalled but fascinated, especially as he usually achieved his aim of finishing among the top five.

As a weekly columnist on the *Times Educational Supplement*, the SATs, data collection and Ofsted were always the three things readers wrote most often to me about and I was reminded of Brian by an email from a primary teacher who was at her wit's end. 'I really love my job, but things are becoming intolerable,' she said. 'My headteacher demands that every child makes measurable progress every term, but a third of my class have special educational needs, some of them quite severe. If I don't achieve the levels he wants, I'm hauled into his room and given a dressing-down. At the end of last term I started massaging results. I felt awful, but I'm sure other teachers do it and it seemed the only way to retain my sanity.'

My advice was simple. Either get together with colleagues and challenge these ridiculous demands or move to a new school. The trouble was, more and more senior managers seemed to think that harassing teachers was the only way to get the results that would satisfy their governing bodies, their local authorities and Ofsted. And, of course, headteachers are under enormous pressure themselves. I suspect that rather more 'massaging' of data goes on than schools care to admit.

I knew of one school in my borough that consistently achieved almost perfect results, earning a congratulatory visit from the education secretary of state. Since it had a similar intake to mine, with a high number of children who struggled with academic subjects, it was difficult to see how this was possible. In fact, it wasn't. When the headteacher moved on, it was discovered that some subtle manipulation of children's answers on the test papers had taken place.

Despite random visits from local authority inspectors to check that all is above board, primary schools know how easy it is for invigilating teachers, who naturally have a vested interest in pupils achieving high results, to surreptitiously point a finger at a careless spelling, a poorly answered question, a wrongly calculated sum. Indeed, the government has cottoned on to this, insisting that every child has to make progress each year that can be measured and recorded, with some schools using this data to calculate the performance pay of their teachers. All of which means that staff stress levels are higher than ever before. Because some children, like my friend Brian, simply cannot achieve the academic level demanded.

Occasionally, my mind drifts back to what was probably one of the two nastiest experiences in thirty years of headship. Our school was accused of possible maladministration of our SATs tests. Cheating, in other words.

On the maths test day, a local education authority officer visited my school on an unannounced monitoring visit. Most schools experienced these, so we weren't at all concerned… we'd had no problems with these visits before, and our SATs team had administered tests for years. But I immediately felt uncomfortably wary, because I'd crossed paths with this lady on a number of occasions. Indeed, I was aware that she'd reduced one excellent local headteacher to tears recently, then, presumably feeling a little guilt, offered her a tissue and said 'I do hope we can still be friends?' After spending twenty minutes with us, the lady announced that what she was witnessing wasn't totally in line with the SATs rules and regulations. She would need to report back to the LEA tests consultant, and we might be investigated by the National Assessment Agency. Despite my asking repeatedly what, exactly, she felt we were doing wrong, she refused to say. Though my headship years had coated me in Teflon, I felt I'd been hit in the head with a brick. God knows how my teachers felt at that moment. Stunned hardly coveyed the emotion. Soon, the hurt we felt turned to extreme anger, especially as everybody had worked so hard with that year's group. It felt like something of a vendetta. We knew we'd kept strictly to the test procedures and done nothing wrong. But within days, we were told we were indeed going to be investigated, that there was a 'procedure' for this, and that it wouldn't be appropriate for us to respond until the investigation had been completed.

Frankly, I wasn't having any of that. I wrote a lengthy letter to the National Assessment Agency, with copies to the local education authority, countering the vague accusation in detail. Two days later, we learned that the NAA had asked two of the LEA officers to investigate. Just prior to the investigation, I met one of them at the annual deputy head's conference, because my school orchestra had been asked to play at the event. I'd not met him before, and we both felt uncomfortable, knowing our next meeting would be in far less pleasant circumstances.

Next morning, my teachers phoned their unions and I phoned mine. I was astonished to hear that there were hundreds of these allegations every year. Not just from monitoring visits, but from disgruntled parents, pupils bearing a grudge, and anonymous whistle-blowers. Which must, I assumed, give rise to a massive bureaucracy… and so it proved on reading the documents I'd been sent about investigative procedures. Panels to assess this, committees to verify that, rules and regulations that ran into the tiniest detail. I assumed this was partly to protect people, but I also thought the amount of money it consumed must have been staggering.

Every member of my SATs team, including myself, was interviewed for up to thirty minutes. Detailed notes were taken, compared, read back to us, typed up, and sent to the NAA. It wasn't pleasant, but at least it was handled with sensitivity. Impassioned statements were given by some of my teachers. They were still appalled that this could happen to us… one of our authorities highest achieving schools. And the eventual outcome? No evidence at all of any maladministration could be found. Indeed, it appeared that we could have offered more reading help than we'd actually given.

In the last week of term, our test papers came back. The children had done incredibly well. But our experiences had left a bitter taste and we merely felt depressed. I could understand why checking needed to be done, but the hurt caused by false accusations is immeasurable. Following my vigorous complaint to the NAA, my only hope was that future monitoring visits would be undertaken by properly trained staff, and that the officer visiting me had been given an extremely sharp rap on the knuckles.

As the years went by, instead of learning from early mistakes and procedures, it seemed the Qualifications and Curriculum Agency, responsible for tests and examinations, simply became a victim of Parkinson's Law. When SATs tests were being delivered to schools, it seemed to me that the QCA constantly felt they needed to spell everything out to me in excruciating detail on the assumption, presumably, that I was a twit. Yes, of course we didn't want boxes of test papers just dumped in the ground floor corridor by the postman, where all and sundry could take a pair of scissors to the boxes and voraciously run their eyes over the tests. But I could hardly believe the long list of instructions that began to come with the tests, telling headteachers what methods should be used to make sure the packets weren't opened before they were supposed to be.

Firstly, somebody had to sign for the parcels. Not any old Tom, Dick or Harry, mind. It needed to be the headteacher, or a senior member of staff. And not just any senior manager: the person had to be especially appointed to that task. (Miss Robinson, you are appointed as SATs receiver this year. I trust you have the ability to sign your name legibly? Oh thank you headmaster, this a role I've coveted for many years…)

The boxes then had to be opened and the packets checked… making sure it was done by committee just in case somebody nicks one… after which it was permissible to inform the headteacher that everything seemed to be in order. Should something be missing, it had to be reported to the tests distribution helpline without further ado. That's if you could get hold of anybody, of course.

The next stage was to store all the boxes of tests in a location that was kept locked. Definitely not, we were told, in a room where there is a lot of ICT equipment, because such rooms tend to be targeted by burglars. ('Ere, 'Arry, we've fallen on our feet, lad. Leave the iPads and that Topstar five million gigawatt multi-drive computer where it is. There's a box of SATs papers over 'ere. That'll fetch a fortune down the market next Saturday....')

Then the actual lock had to be considered. The padlock and chain you put round your bicycle wouldn't do at all. It needed to be a high quality lock, of five levers. I summoned my Premises Officer immediately, who discovered that our secure location only had a lock with three levers, so I dispatched him in haste to Homebase to buy an updated one, before Year 6 had a chance to get their jemmies ready.

A list of the bleedin' obvious then followed: don't let people wander into the storeroom, keep the key in a safe place, keep a check on who goes into the room, compile a register to sign keys in and out. I was even required to conduct a couple of daily spot checks, just to make sure everything was still okay. I was even informed that the QCA had fully briefed the national crime prevention officers' network about the security of test materials. That's a relief, then, I thought. I was worn out after reading all this. And that year's tests hadn't even started....

In the early days, sending the tests to the external markers was relatively easy. Pop the test papers into large bags, attach a sticky label with the marker's address, and then take the bags to the post office. But then suddenly, that became more complicated too. The three subjects were never marked by the same person, and it seemed that many schools had mixed the papers in the bags, causing huge problems with getting the right papers to the right markers. So now all the packages were to go to a central depot, where the outer bags would be discarded, and the inner bags checked before mailing them on to the people who would mark them. I had no problem with that, provided it worked.

Unfortunately, we quickly discovered that it didn't. Checking through our mailing kit earlier in SATs week, we discovered that we had the outer bags for mailing to the depot, but no inner bags to put the markers' labels on. Without the inner bags we had nothing to seal the tests in, and therefore nothing to put in the outer bag. A fat booklet of rules and instructions came with the kit as usual, and since it included a phone number, one of my Year 6 teachers rang it immediately.

It took a while to get through, as she was sixth in line, but eventually a lady answered the phone. 'No problem,' she said, 'We'll get some off to you immediately. When nothing had arrived three days later, my teacher rang again, just to make certain the bags were on their way. This time, she was fifteenth in line and after forty minutes she spoke to an operator who asked her to hang on, because she'd check. Within seconds, my teacher was cut off. She rang again. Tenth in line this time. A disgruntled voice eventually told her it wasn't possible to check whether the bags had been posted, because the place was in chaos, but here was the depot number, so give that a try. The number was unobtainable.

Meanwhile, my other Year 6 teacher was attempting to log on to the National Assessment Agency, to complete the now mandatory register of children who'd taken the tests. The new 'streamlined process' meant we had to do it on line, rather than using pencil and paper. As usual with this kind of site, an ID number and a PIN number were required, just in case a band of ruffians was out to flog our SATs results to the highest bidder in Khazakstan. Our PIN, so carefully stored, didn't work.

Never mind, there was a helpdesk, so I rang the number. Could they give me another PIN? I just need to tick the register. No, it seemed they couldn't… security, you understand. But they could post or e-mail another one to me, although unfortunately it would take at least 72 hours. Four nights later, our new PIN arrived at my in-box and, hurrah, it worked. Until the next morning, when the site refused to let me in again. After a fortnight past the SATS, and after three more PINS, I seemed to have something that worked. But I still hadn't received my mailing bags and the words piss-up and brewery kept springing readily to mind.

It wasn't just us though. Interestingly, but unsurprisingly, the Department of Education, the QCA, the contractors, and teachers in general viewed that year's problems with the SATs very differently. The first three seemed to see it as 'an unfortunate situation', 'a disappointment' and 'a regrettable delay with processing and marking', while everybody at the coalface called it 'a complete and utter shambles'. Personally, I was with the coalface. My non-receipt of bags to put the tests in, PIN numbers that didn't work, a helpline that was anything but, e-mails that were ignored. The relief I felt when my tests actually returned before the end of term was immeasurable.

But even relief turned to shock when I received an e-mail telling me I hadn't put my teacher assessments on line. I tried... oh, how I tried... but the stress would have caused even Bill Gates to take up knitting. Apparently I had to create something called a common transfer file, and if I wasn't sure how, the NAA site would tell me. It didn't, so back to the helpdesk. 'Um.. I'm really not certain,' said the lady at the end of the phone. 'Hang on, I'll ask'. I hung on. And I hung on some more. And then the line went dead. After the sacks saga, I wasn't prepared to waste more time, so I e-mailed and said I'd send a copy via fax or carrier pigeon if they were desperate for it. Frankly, I couldn't see what use teacher assessments would have been to them anyway. Presumably just an excuse to employ some more civil servants.

As the whole sorry story unfolded during the last weeks of that year's summer term, I'm sure teachers all over the land must have gasped with astonishment. Why was that particular contractor selected? Well, would you believe, they gave the cheapest tender. Who checked them out? Ah, the same consultancy that charged the government four million to produce a report on what makes a good teacher. But there you go, I thought, at least the government didn't have to use the same contractor next year, did it? Well it did, actually. The company had been given a five year contract...

Over the years I have thought that the ongoing problems and difficulties, and the seeming inability to resolve them efficiently, could have been the beginning of the end for primary school SATs. We're only too aware that nowadays our children are tested constantly. Most teachers will tell you the tests are unsuitable, the results unreliable, and that they tell you nothing their teachers or parents didn't know already. They don't affect which secondary schools the children go to, nor do the secondaries use them as indicators of the children's ability, because they test the children themselves when they arrive. The reason for them seems purely as a government tool to showing the public whether 'standards' are rising.

In reality, they don't even do that. Any headteacher who's been in post for a few years knows how to handle the SATs, and how to jump through their hoops. Take my own school. We got very good results in KS2 year after year, but my experienced Years 5 and 6 teachers knew how to prepare the children to maximum effect. And I never worried too much if Key Stage 1 results were a bit down, because as the children moved through the school the 'value added' then looked terrific. Much as I disliked the SATs, good results at least meant we got no interference from the LEA, Ofsted or the Department for Education, whose sole criterion for success at the time was, sadly, high test scores.. and we were then relatively free to give primary children the educational experience I was insistent they ought to have… filled with art, drama, music, creativity and, yes, a great deal of fun.

There was also a problem of another kind. I had a mother and her five children arrive at my school one morning, together with an interpreter because none of them spoke any English. They had recently arrived in the country, and wanted school places. I had nothing to offer them as the year groups were full and I had to send them on their way. Three of the children were Year 6 and they would have had to take SATs, and no doubt been bewildered by it all. Which would mean it would have pulled our results down. And the government doesn't like that, so schools naturally try to avoid taking on children who would have difficulty with SATs even if they want to. Talk about being between a rock and a hard place....

Occasionally, I think back to my first year of headship. No SATs, testing, or anything like it, but I still needed to make sure that children were progressing each year. Firstly we decided that every child should be able to read by the time they left Key Stage 1, known as the infant department in those days, and we organised part of our mornings with group work to facilitate that. Then, looking at a number of printed maths text books, we worked out what each child should be aiming for by the end of that year. Finally, we took examples of handwriting, story writing, factual writing and grammar so that again, each teacher knew what standard their children should be aiming for. It took many staff meetings, but once established we used the system very successfully in the pre-SATs era. Of course, in those days far more trust was placed in headteachers, and most of them would have been highly successful practitioners in the classroom and very knowledgeable about primary school children's attainment in general.

Perhaps the government could have designed something similar. It wouldn't, unlike the SATs, have cost over fifty million a year.

10

MRS SMITH IS IN THE OFFICE AGAIN!

What Parents Expect From Schools

When you are lucky enough to have a child, you realise there is suddenly a tiny human being who is more important than you. Someone you would, literally, give up your life for. Someone you will nurture, guide and look after through their early years with a fierce determination. Someone you will try to cope with as best you can when they reach their difficult years. And then someone you hope you'll have a strong and loving relationship with as you, and they, grow older. When they, in turn, have a family you hope they'll give you grandchildren to spoil. The circle of life, and it was ever thus.

As a newly minted class teacher all those years ago, I was in charge of thirty young people, each one with an individual character, each one fascinated by the world around them, and each shaped by their home and early life experiences. Their parents expected me to look after them, care for them, teach them effectively, and show equal interest in every one. My very first Open Evening, when parents could come to the school, look at all the work the children had produced throughout the year, talk to me candidly about their progress, and take home the written report I had produced for them, was an evening I looked forward to with enormous pleasure. A class of fascinating little characters, whose company and enthusiasm for learning fired me continuously, and the cause of great pride when their parents were delighted with what their offspring had achieved. I can still picture most of them, and I can certainly remember most of their names.

Twenty years on, as a headteacher, I had four hundred children to look after… and a large group of teachers who expected strong, decisive leadership and a sympathetic ear when they had problems. Although I still did a fair amount of teaching, because that's what I loved doing, parents were often surprised at how much I knew about their children, and the amount of time I was able to give to nurturing their individual talents and enthusiasms. As a class teacher, I had quickly learned how vital it was to make parents feel I knew their child well, and it was important to me that they went home and told their parents they'd had an interesting, enjoyable day of learning and activity. As a headteacher, I wanted the children… and the teachers… to feel they belonged to a school they could be intensely proud of. I felt I'd achieved this when one of my teachers said, as I chatted to her when she stood on playground duty watching the children, 'You know Mike, this job may be hard and demanding, but it's a joy to come to work in the mornings.'

It seems incredible that thirty years ago, if you needed a doctor you could phone up and one would actually come to your house, often the same day. If you were unwell, or had a health problem but didn't need a home visit, you could walk to the surgery, sit in the waiting room, and usually be seen within half an hour. These days, trying to book an appointment with a doctor is a nightmare of bureaucracy, and you'll probably have to try booking one on line. If you're lucky, and your problem isn't too serious, you'll be seen within two or three weeks for ten minutes. A dentist on the NHS? Well, keep your fingers crossed in trying to find one. Similarly, years ago, there was a building called a police station in most localities, and usually at least one beat officer who knew your area well and spent a great deal of time around the locality. Nowadays, the police stations are no longer there, and access to a police officer is fraught with difficulty. Most people, if they've been burgled, simply contact the police because their insurance company insists they have a crime number. You'll be very lucky if a police officer actually comes to visit. And banks? Well, they've mostly disappeared, and posting a letter costs an arm and a leg, while you wonder if your letter is actually going to arrive at its destination. Schools aren't that bad, but if you ring up you'll often encounter a set of instructions… push 1 if you want to tell us your child is ill… push 2 if you wish to speak to the school office… and if you want an appointment with the headteacher, well, it's likely you'll have to wait a good couple of days.

When I was a teenager, there was a stage when my parents were worried that my education didn't seem to be as progressing as well as they'd hoped, so they telephoned the school to make an appointment with the head. The secretary booked them in for the following day, and, pleased that they'd received such promising service, my father dressed in his best suit, my mother took great care with her make-up, and they set off with the intention of sorting things out. Unfortunately, it went downhill from there. They quickly realised the head hadn't a clue who I was. He'd merely asked my class teacher for my timetable of lessons, and then he'd pencilled some out, given other subjects greater prominence, and told my parents he'd be letting the relevant teachers know all about the changes. He forgot all about it as soon as my parents had left the building, and when I questioned my teachers about the alterations to my learning timetable, they were as bewildered as I was.

In great contrast, my youngest daughter had an exceptionally dedicated teacher for two years at primary school. Not only was she a delightful person who taught inspiring lessons and was willing to chat with parents at any time, her end of year reports, often two or three pages long, made us feel that she knew our daughter intimately… and we knew other parents felt exactly the same.

The usual way for schools to keep in touch with parents is by holding open evenings in the classrooms, usually twice a year, when the teacher can show the child's work to the parent, chat about progress and discuss any ways in which the parent can help the child at home. Usually, since it is difficult for primary school teachers to hear every child read as often as they'd like, they ask for half an hour's reading to be done with the child in the evening. Then, at the end of the year, the parent receives a written report which describes in detail the child's progress and the levels reached in the core curriculum subjects.

It's interesting to consider how much school reports for parents have changed over the years. As a teenager, I regularly expected my teachers to come up with pithy and often witty put-downs, which tended to be par for the course and which the teachers thought would be very amusing. I suspected they were often in contest to see who could cause the most laughter in the staffroom. 'It would be most helpful if he could enclose his garrulous tongue between the jaws of discretion in my lessons.' 'I suspect, if his brain were examined by a medical professional, it would be found to be made of Teflon. As far as I can discern, only a modicum of learning sticks to it.' 'Seems to consider that life is a bowl of cherries. If he isn't careful, he will soon be grinding his teeth on the stones.' 'His progress in my subject is, sadly, akin to that of a tortoise ascending a rocky incline.' Nowadays, fortunately, nobody could get away with that sort of sarcastic and unhelpful remark.

But the quality of school reports often say just as much about the teacher as they do the child. When I began headship, I inherited two teachers whose use of grammar and spelling left a great deal to be desired. No computers in those days, so end of year reports were all hand written. I always read every report, and often, if I'd had experience of the child in lessons or activities I taught, I would be able to add a sentence or two. It was always such a pleasure when I could praise the child. 'It has been so enjoyable to work with David in our summer musical. I know you thought his performance was an absolute delight. And so did I.'

I was horrified, therefore, to discover that one of these teachers had written 'verble' instead of verbal at least once on every one of her reports. Yes, a bottle of Tippex helped, but it made the report look very untidy. The other teacher, in writing about three of her boys, said that they had big heads. She meant she felt they were conceited, (frankly, her teaching wasn't up to much, anyway) but heaven knows what their parents would have made of that. Taken the children to the doctor?

Around then, the Inner London Education Authority, whose banner my school came under at the time, had sent a missive around its schools saying that inspectors were concerned about the poor level of 'litracy' in its primary schools. Worse, by the time an urgent message had been sent out to withdraw the circular, somebody had leaked it to the press, who had a field day. I wouldn't have wanted to be the poor soul who'd typed that letter up…

Visiting some neighbours recently, we were talking about school reports, because their daughter had just received hers. What did my wife and I think of the report, our friends asked… a natural question since we were both heavily involved in the business of educating the young. As far as you could tell, the report was very flattering, but it was littered with irritating jargon and chunks of numerical data… with no explanation of what they meant. The tone was also oddly cold, and… crucially and a big give-away… much of it could have been describing any child. There was little that summed up the unique characteristics of the child we all knew so well. The reason was obvious; the report had been written using a piece of computer software.

Just as companies were quick to produce model school policies that you just had to add your school's name to and then consider the job done, so it was with school reports. You chose what you thought was an appropriate comment from a bank of open-ended phrases that didn't really tell a parent very much at all. 'Could do better', (well, couldn't they all?) 'Is making progress in this subject' (now regularly writes three words for a story instead of one), 'Has a sound grasp of concepts' (but can't apply any of them?), 'Has moved one step up the P Scales and is working towards Level 1 (You what?)

I'm aware that secondary teachers, who often have to write a short subject-specific piece for the two hundred students they teach, often swear by computerised assistance. But primary teachers have thirty reports to write at most, and by doing a handful a night in the last term they should be able to produce interesting, worthwhile documents. My teachers were even luckier. It was my policy that no class had more than twenty three children. Even so, I never asked them to produce any kind of documentation that wasn't important and relevant, but I did ask them to take their time over report writing. What a parent wants to know is actually very simple. Is my child working well? Is she happy and motivated at school? How does she compare with her peers, how does she relate to them, what are her strengths and weaknesses... and how can we help?

Writing reports on challenging children can be quite an art. Dealing with them daily is much harder. Indeed, it's often the reason teachers leave the profession, because day after day being submitted to youngsters who want to be disruptive is utterly exhausting, particularly if no backing or help from the school's senior management is received. 'Difficult' parents, however, can be even worse, and I tended to find that the three main issues for contention were sex, religion, and a belief that their child could do no wrong.

My first wake-up call came when, as a young teacher in my first year, I offered to help organise a Saturday morning football match against a neighbouring school because the teacher who normally did it was ill. A fair number of dads from both schools had turned up to watch the match, and after it had been under way for about fifteen minutes, one parent began to question a decision the referee had made when a boy on the opposing team had fouled his son by barging him. The barger's dad seemed to think his son's action was fine, and laughed as the bargee picked himself up from the mud. This caused both parents to start a heated argument... which led to a short bout of fisticuffs before other parents intervened and stopped it. I could hardly believe what I was seeing. What an awful model of behaviour for the youngsters from the two teams to be watching, although later on I realised that witnessing it had stood me in good stead for the future.

During my headship, most of our parents were friendly, supportive, and interested in their children's education, and they fully appreciated how hard we were all working for their children. Nevertheless, I always had to be prepared for the determined trouble maker, since aggression could explode at a moment's notice. Many families were living in high rise blocks, often in crowded accommodation where repairs were slow to be undertaken. Lifts would regularly break down, large dustbins would overflow, boilers and essential services would often cease to function in the winter and vandalism was rife. It was hardly surprising that tempers could be short and often the school tended to be a soft target for parental angst. I soon discovered this during the steep learning curve of headship's first year. On the opening night of our Summer musical we were less than fifteen minutes into the action when I noticed a commotion on the other side of the hall. A mother had accused a woman in the next row of sleeping with her husband. She'd obviously come with the intention of accosting her and was well oiled with lager. In seconds, a scuffle had broken out, and while the children valiantly carried on acting, my tall, newly qualified male teacher, who happened to be nearest to them, bundled the pair into the corridor and down the stairs, receiving a knee in the groin for his trouble. On stage, my little actors hardly skipped a beat, but in that shocked instant I wondered whether I might have to breathalyse the audience before the next performance.

A belief that her child could do no wrong was amply demonstrated by Jasmine's mother, who followed the class into the corridor and pushed Andrea's mum forcibly, saying that Andrea had stolen Jasmine's coloured pencils and she wanted them back, right now. Andrea's mum, no stranger to a bit of confrontation, snorted angrily in denial, saying that her daughter would never do anything like that. Things quickly became heated, and fortunately the teacher had moved her class safely inside the classroom by that time, distracting them by reading a story very loudly. In the corridor, the two parents began shoving each other, and minutes later they were tussling against the wall, at which point our cook strode out of the kitchen and threatened to pour cold water over the pair of them.

School lunches, or 'school dinners' as they've always been known, were another contentious and regular issue with parents. Packed lunches do our children more harm than good, some say. We should get rid of them and return to healthy school meals cooked on the premises. Well, I certainly applaud that, with the accent on 'healthy'. At the start of my headship, my school had a superb cook. There wasn't a great deal of choice, but the children knew that what was on offer would be tasty and, if unfamiliar, probably worth a try. Packed lunches were unheard of and I was anxious that they should remain that way.

And then, some years later, a forceful parent governor wanted them introduced. It was her right, she said, to give her child a packed lunch, and she didn't need a lecture on which food items would be nutritious, thank you very much. Sadly, some of the other governors felt obliged to back her. The rot set in. Yes, she provided her child with a balanced packed lunch but many other parents didn't. Chocolate, crisps, long cheesy stringy things full of fat and precious little cheese, weirdly coloured fizzy liquids and a distinct lack of healthy sandwiches or fruit were the order of the day.

All I could do was compromise. I had to allow packed lunches, but I regularly sent out newsletters extolling the virtues of our school meals. We held evening taster sessions and invited the parents to drop in and sample the food. Meanwhile, as in most other primary schools, child obesity began to rear its ugly head. And then, one Friday evening, I listened to an intense radio debate on school meals. At the time, a secondary school was in trouble because the children weren't being allowed to eat what they liked. Parents weren't happy. 'Our kids should have whatever they want,' said one. 'They don't like the stuff the school gives them and I don't see why they should eat it,' said another. So what did they do about it? They stood outside the school in the mornings, took lunch orders from the children and then, at mid-day, one mum went to the fast food shop, filled a pram with heavily processed food and passed it through the fence.

I listened in horror. The disregard for the damage being done to their children was beyond belief. Even more frightening, but of course understandable, was the attitude of the chip shop owner. 'I'm with the parents,' he said, the sound of lunchtime frying in the background indicating the excellent and unexpected business he was doing. 'The kids should be able to eat what they want.'

Why do so many parents abuse their children in this way? Ask them what a packed lunch should contain and you'll find few who can't tell you. These days, of course, many families are really struggling with ever rising rent, energy and food bills and cannot afford to give their children good food in the evenings, but many parents of children at my school didn't want to cook anyway. It was so much easier to send out for a cheap kebab. One child was given one every day of the week. Another child, in the nursery and bordering on obesity, ate only pot noodles. He just won't eat anything else, his mother told me. Who, I wondered, was the parent in that relationship?

But count the number of cookery programmes on television or the number of celebrity recipe books the public buys and you could be forgiven for thinking that cooking is a national pastime. Many children are becoming unhealthier by the day, and only the fact that primary aged children are generally active creatures who like running around and playing energetic games keeps an epidemic of obesity away. All because parents demand that their children have the 'right' to eat whatever they like.

Readers may remember *Educating Essex*, a television programme featuring a secondary school that had bravely agreed to a 'warts and all' filming, using content from a multitude of planted CCTV cameras and additional no holds barred documentary footage. By the end of the programme I was hooked. It was a rare and honest look at the problems secondary schools face.

The first programme centred around the highly capable deputy headteacher, Mr Drew. Looking back, most of us would agree that the teachers who taught us best were fascinated by their subject, eager to enthuse, amusing… and just a little eccentric. Mr Drew covered all those bases. He followed children around the school… how shall I put it… purposefully, homing in on poor behaviour and inappropriate clothing. 'Dead animals shouldn't be worn in the corridors, Julie,' he mentioned lightly to a girl wearing what looked like the skin from a cheetah.

We watched, fascinated, as Mr Drew taught a history lesson, talking animatedly about public health conditions in times past. 'You have no idea,' he said to his class, 'how much I love teaching you'. Actually, I think they had; their attentive enthusiasm and affection was aptly demonstrated. Several times we cut to teachers chatting and enjoying each other's company. There was much laughter, and at one point, Mr Drew hid behind a door to surprise the headteacher. 'Government ministers watching,' Mr Drew observed, 'will probably think we're all fucking mad.'

But he doesn't do a great deal of teaching because most of his time is taken up with sorting out challenging children and parents, something he seems exceptionally good at. 'At the heart of every difficult child is a nice person, and we have to find it,' he says. 'Excluding children permanently is useless, and just puts them nearer bad influences and prison. Our main problem is that today's children simply don't recognise the word 'No' and their parents either can't handle it or they talk about their offspring's 'rights''. (Oh, how true, I thought.) We watched him politely but firmly wearing children down, until they ended up smiling at him and agreeing to try connecting with the class teacher one more time. Mr Drew recognised the tightrope situation, because not all teachers are as good as he is.

And then came the most extraordinary sequence. A particularly disruptive child who had been given repeated chances to alter her behaviour accused Mr Drew of shoving her in the corridor, always an exceptionally difficult situation and becoming increasingly common. The head of year conversed with the parent and then put the phone down after being subjected to verbal abuse. 'My child would never'.... etc.'

The headteacher became involved, explaining to the child that he took all such allegations seriously, that his main concern was that children should be safe in his school, and that what she was saying could be checked by examining CCTV footage, which he then did. The child had been lying and the parent was phoned again, the head explaining apologetically... far too apologetically in my view... that the child would be sent home for the next few days but could return after Christmas. The sequence forcibly demonstrated what a teacher is up against these days. Years ago, the parent would immediately have sided with the teacher and punished their daughter. I could imagine teachers all over the country watching the programmes and nodding their heads as they recognised the situations that were being revealed.

When I was a child, you attended the primary school nearest to you, whether it had a good reputation or not. But successive governments have persuaded parents they have a choice, and that it is their 'right' to have their child attend the primary or secondary school they want. This, of course, is a nonsense, logistically if nothing else. The best and most popular schools will always be over-subscribed and the poorest ones will always have plenty of places. Nevertheless, most parents these days are pretty astute at knowing what they want from education for their children, and they'll soon find which schools in their locality are worth attending. A parent new to an area will simply chat to her neighbours, assemble a shortlist, usually a very short one, and off they'll go to the one they've chosen. Which will be full. The headteacher will then have to explain the admission criteria, and the more he or she tries to explain it, the less the parent understands. Kafka is a doddle in comparison.

'But I only live two streets away,' Mrs Jones says.

'That's true,' I reply, 'but everybody we've admitted into that year group lives nearer.'

'Well, how is it that Mrs Smith has got her children in here then?' Mrs Jones persists. 'She lives further away than me.'

'Because Mrs Smith's children are in a different year group, and there were spaces.' Mrs Jones begins to get a little irritated. 'Well, what about Mrs Brown, then? Her kids come from East Dulwich and that's miles away.'

I sigh, having been over this ground so often. 'But Mrs Brown originally lived just over the road,' I explain. 'She's been rehoused in East Dulwich but her children are still entitled to come here.'

'Then how did Mrs Green get her Jimmy in here? She lives in the same flats as me.'

'True. But Jimmy lives one floor lower than you.'

'So what?'

'It makes Jimmy ten yards nearer. And we have to measure it all out on a large-scale map. As the crow flies.'

'What crow?'

The conversation normally continued in this vein for twenty minutes and I always ended up explaining the classic Catch-22 situation about the first admission rule, which is that other members of the family can come in if one of them is already attending. The trouble is, of course, you've got to get one on roll in the first place, which brings everything back to distance again. It's all very confusing for parents, but they do have one potent weapon: the admission appeal.

Provided they can make an extremely convincing case for getting a child into the school they've chosen, or prove maladministration, it's possible they'll win, and the school is then obliged to take the child over and above the legally specified intake number. If there are lots of appeals, and half a dozen are successful, the school can have a real problem. As I quickly discovered, more and more parents opted for this route, some of them becoming increasingly wily in the methods they used to gain entry. Appeals were heard by three independent panel members, with the parent and school putting their respective cases. The appeals committees weren't daft, of course, but as my school became increasingly popular I found I was spending more and more time at appeal sessions and several times I had to battle with parents who simply lied about their addresses and family situations, and had even gone to extremes such as forging a doctor's letter. I knew that most parents appealed these days when their child didn't get into their school of first choice, but I was amazed to read that in a recent year there had been 83,000 appeals. This is a staggering number and, if nothing else, reinforces the fact that for many parents choice in the state school sector simply isn't a reality.

I was always sympathetic to the parents I had to turn away. As the years went by, I felt that we were offering a truly first-class primary school experience and it was natural that people wanted their children to be part of it. It was therefore a frightening experience when my daughter, a bright and hard-working child, was turned down for the secondary school we wanted. She was offered an alternative, a truly dreadful school, and when the rejection letter arrived we spent a dismal weekend wondering what to do, knowing that a high number of appeals failed. Fortunately after rigorous investigation we proved that the school had been at fault. Our daughter had been unwell just before the series of entrance tests and we had phoned to change the date. When the original day dawned, however, she was determined to go and had passed easily, but somebody had assumed our phone call was a request to remove her from the list of applicants. I shudder to think of how her education could have been wrecked if she'd attended the sink school. But what a game of chance it all is. Even local authorities can be highly skilled at mucking up an application or three. A friend had put five schools on her form. She didn't mind which her son David attended, but the one thing she definitely didn't want was a church school. David was turned down for all five but he was offered an alternative. It was a church school.

Children's relationships with each other were often at the forefront of my dealings with parents, but particularly when there seemed a hint of sexuality. Majid and Cerice were a prime example. They were both in the same maths group, and Cerice, kind soul, had lent Majid her calculator. Impressed, Majid lent her his colouring pencils. Things moved rapidly, and soon Majid was passing notes expressing his affection and spending much of his lunch hour chasing Cerice around the playground because, at that age, that's what you did and Cerise thoroughly enjoyed the attention. Then, finding himself financially embarrassed on the day of our St Valentine's cake sale, he persuaded me to lend him 25p so that he could buy her a little cake with a heart on top. Being in love is one of life's great pleasures, the daffodils were out, spring was in the air, and as usual, it had all started innocently enough.

Other Year 6 boys, impressed by Majid's infatuation, also began directing their attention to the girls. Unfortunately, their approach was less refined. Huddling in packs by the boiler house wall like teenage boys at their first dance, they suddenly swarmed towards the girls, their hands raised as they pretended to smack them across the bottom. The girls squealed and ran away until, breathless and giggling, they regrouped by the water fountain and then made faces at the boys, whereupon the whole cycle started again. The calm before the storm.

Next morning Mrs Brown asked to see me. She was very concerned about the inappropriate sexual behaviour her daughter was experiencing, and that wasn't what she sent her to school for. Several boys, and Beyjou in particular, had been cavorting around the girls in a disgracefully sexual manner and her daughter had been extremely distressed by it. She hadn't even been able to eat her TV dinner.

I was taken aback, since according to the lunchtime playground supervisors Andrea had been prominent in the goading of the boys. Nevertheless, I listened politely, pointing out that most days I always spent the last fifteen minutes of the lunch hour in the playground chatting to the children, and that I would keep an eye on things for the rest of the week. I also remembered that Andrea was extremely skilled at winding her mother up. It wasn't the first time Mrs Brown had stormed into school.

'I've told Andrea to let me know if Beyjou comes anywhere near her today,' she concluded. 'And if he does, I'll fucking kill 'im.'

Later that morning, a delegation of three mothers appeared, demanding that I do something or they would go to the police. 'Do something about what?' I asked. 'Sex games,' said Mrs Stern. 'My husband is disgusted.' The others nodded. Presumably their husbands were wallowing in disgust, too. When they'd gone, I warned the lunchtime helpers to keep a very close watch, and I told them that I would come down to the playground too.

Early Thursday morning, at whistle time, I glanced out of my window. Mrs Stern was berating a crowd of older boys, wagging her finger at them. Then, she stalked across the playground and shouted at Beyjou's father, who was standing quietly with his son waiting for the whistle. Other parents became animated, and the teacher on duty motioned Mrs Stern towards my room. I sighed inwardly as she hurtled along the corridor.

'I wasn't making any trouble,' she protested. 'I was just telling the boys to keep away from our girls. I told them if they want a bum to slap they can come and slap mine, and see where that gets them...' By 9.30 I had the whole of Year 6 in the hall, pointing out that new, inoffensive games had to be found, or my hair would drop out from the stress of it all. At 10 o'clock, Mrs Brown was back in my room.

'I know what it is,' she said triumphantly. 'It's because they've started swimming on Tuesday mornings. They see each other's lumps and bumps. You'll have to take swimming off the curriculum...'

Frankly, I thought, it's not the children who were a concern. It's their parents we needed to worry about.

Sex of course is one of life's supreme pleasures, but there has been much concern for some time now about the frightening effect extreme images, so easily obtained, are having on young people. The internet and social media are mostly to blame, of course. Just a key press and a young person can view the most bizarre sexual practices and with AI moving along in frightening leaps and bounds it is easily possible for images to be manipulated alarmingly, even to the extent of putting well known faces onto pornography. The worry is that youngsters are coming to regard this kind of activity as the norm. By the age of thirteen, a recent survey said, a youngster could have watched more than two hundred strangers having sex in a disturbing variety of ways. Innocence has been well and truly lost, it seems, and it really has to be dealt with in frank discussions at school level, because it often won't happen at home.

Nevertheless, I don't think we were ever that innocent. The sexual urge is no different from hunger, and never has been. As a primary school child, I can remember Anne Wilkinson offering to show her wares behind the piano to any boy who was interested, and most of us were. During craft one afternoon, I recall Charlie Turner decorating his genitals with raffia instead of using it on the basket he was weaving, and then motioning the girls nearby to admire his handiwork. At my mixed secondary school, things took a more serious turn as puberty gained a stranglehold and French verbs took second place to daydreaming about girls. Occasionally there was enormous excitement when somebody managed to get hold of a naughty photo, and for those who were dating, there was much discussion about 'how far we had got' with our partners.

But although our parents would have been horrified to know what we were doing, it was all relatively innocent and harmless in those days. Even at teachers' training college, there were strict rules about how much time you spent in a young lady's study bedroom, especially in the evening, and this was supposedly the permissive sixties. I remember one unfortunate couple being caught, and they were banished from college the next morning, their future careers in tatters. And whereas sexual issues in my childhood were rarely something that teachers had to deal with, this is not so nowadays and situations crop up which can be very tricky to handle, particularly for a headteacher.

I recall the fury of a strict, church-going mother when she discovered that her daughter had given Andrew several kisses in the Play Hut at lunchtime, and she demanded that I exclude the boy for several days to teach him a lesson, because 'you never know what these things will lead to.' In fact, the daughter had instigated the activity, but they simply liked each other's company, and I saw nothing harmful in it. A week later I had to deal with a boy lying on top of a girl in the cloakroom. Again, the girl had instigated things, but investigation proved she had been watching some very unsavoury stuff with Mum's boyfriend. Knowing what to do will always involve tightrope decisions. You want children to grow up strong and true, but you also want them to understand that physical attraction should be a source of joy and pleasure, not something demeaning and ugly.

And then of course, there's race.

One playtime, Tunde, a new and immature boy admitted to the Reception class, asked Oliver to play with him. Oliver said that he only liked bright colours and, as Tunde was a dark colour, he couldn't play with him. Tunde reported this to his mother after school, and she asked the teacher what was going to be done, because this was racism. The teacher, a talented and patient youngster in her second year of teaching, agreed that the comment was very worrying, and she said she'd talk to Oliver's parents about it.

However, she added, Oliver is only just five, and he'd been enthusing about colours because the class had been doing a topic on rainbows and colours in the natural world. That could possibly explain it. Nevertheless, Oliver's parents agreed to sit him down that evening and talk the incident through, and they discovered that what the teacher had said did seem to be right. The next day Tunde, as usual, wouldn't line up when the whistle went. Since he'd been cautioned innumerable times, his teacher thought a word from me might help, so he was brought upstairs. His behaviour was better during the afternoon playtime.

But then, after school, Tunde's mother found me in the school hall and demanded a meeting. Tunde was in tow, and he careered around the hall whooping loudly as I tried to speak. Tunde's mother was clearly fired up and accused me of condoning racism from my staff. What's more, why had her son been sent up to me the day after the teacher had been racist? It was discrimination, and victimisation as well, she said, and somebody was going to swing for it. The conversation suddenly became very intense and I spoke carefully.

'So what are you going to do about that teacher being racist?'

'She wasn't being racist. She was just offering a possible reason why Oliver might have said what he did.'

'I don't accept that. And why were you victimising him for not lining up in the playground?'

'I wasn't. He can't run around when the rest of his class are lining up. He was simply being naughty.'

'No, he wasn't. He's hyperactive. You're discriminating against him for being hyperactive. The clinic said so. It's in his special needs report.'

'Really? I don't think it is. I didn't notice that when I read it.'

'You haven't read it properly then. Don't you read the reports of children in your own school?'

I hurried to my room, and pulled out his file. She hunted desperately through it. No hyperactivity. But she was quite determined. 'The clinic sent another report. You must have lost it. I'm going to make a formal complaint.'

I sighed inwardly, and handed her a form. She didn't complain, of course. Tunde's teacher was an excellent practitioner, despite being a ludicrously indulged child Tunde was making real progress, and his mother knew it. But as I consoled an extremely upset teacher, I knew who should really be making the complaint.

And then, religion, and that can be the worst of all.

Easter and Christmas were the times when religion came to the fore. Christmas at school was always wonderful. The concerts, the music, the parties.... even the disco, with the animated leaping about and 'Who Let The Dogs Out?' played loudly enough to rattle the windows. Nevertheless, as we began the Christmas preparations, I always wondered what parents would find to complain about that year.

'I'd like Cheryl withdrawn from Christmas activities,' says Mrs Stebbin. 'We don't celebrate it, you see.' I steer Mrs Stebbin into my room.

'We teach the children tolerance of everybody's beliefs,' I say, 'and there are certain things in the national curriculum we are obliged to teach. Christianity simply being one of them.'

She nods. 'Yes, well, I'm a tolerant person, but I still want Cheryl put in another classroom when her teacher's talking about Christmas.'

I explain that this isn't at all practical. All the classes are working on Christmas activities, so perhaps Cheryl should be kept at home? Inwardly, I know the local authority wouldn't support my advice, but then the local authority doesn't have to shuffle children around to prevent their minds from being tainted from the mere mention of the word 'Christmas'.

By the time we get to parent number three, I'm a trifle irritated. 'I don't want Femi in the concert,' says Mrs Amit two days before the show. 'It's against our religion.' Femi has been rehearsing enthusiastically, the concert isn't in any way religious and I simply can't believe that she hasn't mentioned it at home. I explain that Femi will be bitterly disappointed, and after heavy bargaining Mrs Amit says, 'Well, perhaps she could just hold the curtain or something... so long as she doesn't look towards the manger in the nativity play, if you're doing one.'

Mrs Banner doesn't want her child in the concert either, even though I say there isn't any religion in it. 'But hang on,' I say. 'Jeremiah's just bought a ticket for the Christmas disco.' 'Yes,' she says. 'He can go to the disco and the parties, but he can't join in the concert. It's against our religion.' Obviously Jeremiah, adept at twisting his mother around his little finger, has been assessing our Christmas agenda and selecting the items he fancies most.

Post Covid, there has been a great deal on the news about the number of children who haven't returned to school, and on a news bulletin recently three parents were stating that they had no intention of sending their children back. It was their 'right' to keep their children at home. Naturally the first thought that occurred to me was 'what will happen about their education? Not just the academic stuff, but school is essential for developing the child's social experiences. How else are they going to learn to get along with others?' And will anybody from an education department bother to follow this up?

When I was in junior school a grey-haired gentleman called Mr Thistlewaite visited once a term, opened the register and called out a handful of names. If he didn't hear a 'Yes, Sir' and he couldn't find a reason, he went knocking on the absentee's house that morning. I only tried truanting once. On the way to school, and a dreaded arithmetic test, I told my mother I felt sick. She looked at me sympathetically, walked me back home and told me to get into bed. When I said I didn't feel sick enough to go to bed, I was immediately taken back to school. These days, I'm astonished at how easily children avoid school.

'It's your birthday? Have the day off, son, and ask your friends too. We'll go to Thorpe Park.'

'Sorry Gavin wasn't in yesterday, but his hair needed cutting and we didn't want to waste any of the weekend."

And then there are all the other events. OK, it's sad the rabbit died, but two days to get over the burial? Or the flight to Disneyland that George's parents booked during term time. 'I'm afraid he'll be off for two weeks, Could his teacher give him some homework to do?'

Although English primary schools are closed for thirteen weeks a year, an increasing number of parents take their children out of school in term time. Why? To go abroad on holiday, because flights are much cheaper then. Understandably, there's considerable concern about this, because two or three weeks is a sizeable chunk of missed education, especially in the later primary years. It's certainly an inconvenience for the teacher, who will have embarked on a topic and will then be required to help the child catch up. I'm not without sympathy for the parents, though, especially those who struggle to make ends meet. The temptation to have a very brief, affordable holiday must be very strong, however much parents value their children's education. And does it harm their schooling? Probably not, if it happens only occasionally, and the more able children will usually catch up quickly. At my school, children came from a wide range of ethnic backgrounds and families often needed to return to their home countries when elderly relatives were dying. This meant the child being absent for anything up to six weeks, and that is far too much time to miss. Although I was obliged only to hold the place for two weeks, it seemed churlish not to accept the child on their return, especially as we had already put a lot of hard work into their education.

Early on in my headship, I found the best way to interact with parents was… quickly. If a parent came up to see me with a problem, or had a complaint, I always tried to see them immediately, and any difficulties would usually be resolved in a friendly but determined manner. If a parent phoned, it wasn't difficult to speak to me. There were no button choices, just a direct line to our secretary, who would call me if she felt I needed to speak to the parent on the phone. And it was always a great pleasure when a new parent popped her head round the door and told us how much her child was enjoying school. On one occasion, after a parent who was obviously very unhappy came barging into the office and went out of my room again fifteen minutes later, my secretary said 'Honestly, I really don't know how you do it. The difficult ones go into your room with faces like thunder, and they always seem to come out smiling.'

When I retired, after thirty year's headship, I knew I would miss the job enormously, so I balanced that against the pleasure of not having to rise early on winter mornings. Being able to spend whole days sitting in the warm, reading, writing and listening to music certainly had its attractions. Nevertheless, retirement brought constant reminders and memories of school. On my first morning, as I tidied the front garden, cars drove up the road towards the primary school at the top of the hill, fixed, determined expressions on mothers' faces as they prepared to battle for parking places. Then I watched a mother wheeling a baby in a pushchair, her daughter skipping happily by her side and telling her excitedly all about the book she was reading at school. Mum was listening intently, thoroughly enjoying the early morning conversation with her child.

Now that, I thought, is the right way to travel to school... and parenting at its best.

11

HORSES FOR COURSES.
AND TEACHERS

Professional Development

One picture is worth a thousand words, as the saying goes. If you've ever tried to assemble a piece of flat-packed furniture, you'll undoubtedly agree.

Just as being kept abreast of developments in any other profession or trade, headteachers and classroom teachers need to be kept up to date with everything that is happening in the world of education. Much of it isn't mandatory of course, but nobody in a school wants something sprung on them by an inspector or local official, only to be completely bewildered by what they're being asked to do. There are several ways to gain this knowledge; by attending a professional development course that can run for just one day or perhaps a day a week over a short period, by reading the material you're sent and watching a talk on-line, by reading a newspaper's education column, or by talking to informed colleagues. I always encouraged my teachers to go on a course if I was certain it would help their professional development, but I had to be sure it would be worthwhile.

The best professional development course I ever attended was given by an extraordinary lady, a maths specialist, named Edith Biggs. Her brief, over the course of three days, was to tell and show us how we could make maths really exciting in the primary classroom. I learned more in those three days than in all my maths lectures at teacher's training college. Ms Biggs demonstrated a vast range of techniques, mainly using simple but colourful apparatus, that would ensure children fully understood basic concepts in arithmetic, geometry, algebra and much else. I remember at one point, as lunchtime rapidly approached, she said 'I'd really like to finish this topic. Anybody mind if I strayed into your lunch hour just for another ten minutes or so? Ten minutes turned into twenty... and nobody minded in the slightest. I came away from the course armed with enough information to try out in the classroom for many weeks.

But there was a strong contrast with this and a residential weekend course I went on shortly afterwards as a young deputy headteacher. The idea was to provide us with a range of exciting ideas for creative story writing and language development, and tips to improve the reading ability of our primary aged children. In fact, apart from the enjoyment of chatting to the twenty other bewildered teachers, it was a complete waste of a weekend. It began on the Friday night, when we were all assembled in a hall, divided into groups, and given copies of a poem. Each group was given twenty minutes to dramatise the poem, and then perform it for everyone else. Then, on Saturday morning, our groups were sent into the local woods, armed with a cassette tape recorder, to record the sounds of nature. On our return each group had to make up a short play, complete with the sound effects we had recorded... and again perform it to everyone else. On Saturday afternoon, each group had to choose a children's book from a large box and demonstrate our ability to hold children's attention by... yes, you've guessed it, reading a page or so to everyone else. On Saturday evening, the authority's senior English inspector, who had organised all this, sat in the lounge with a pint of beer in front of him inviting anybody to come and solve the logic puzzles he had printed out on cards. On Sunday morning, some sort of academic professor arrived to give us a lecture on the history of the English language. It was an exercise in stultifying boredom. I suppose I should have been warned.

I had never known the inspector to get out of his lofty tower and visit any schools, and his main contribution to the education of London's children seemed to be organising an annual poetry competition. I came back to my school having learned nothing I wasn't already doing.

Professional development DVDs from the government were sent to schools at regular intervals, and we would watch them during staff meetings. Some were interesting, many weren't. And some were truly awful. I still recall the one we sat watching one winter Thursday. It had been raining all day, the children hadn't been out to play, and everybody felt that they'd hardly had a break, so tolerance was on a short string. The DVD was forty five minutes long and as logical as Alice in Wonderland. It was also excruciatingly, staggeringly, mind-numbingly boring. I simply couldn't believe professionals were meant to take it seriously. Are doctors required to watch a video telling them it's a good idea to ask a patient how he's feeling before attempting to try a diagnosis? Are dentists told that before they can start any work, it's sensible to get the patient to open his mouth?

Yes, I often complained about much of the documentation that emanated from our educational lords and masters and I suspect it's the same in all professions these days, but I was always passionately interested in education and I always tried to keep up with it all. When this package arrived I attempted, as always, to look on the glass half full side. *'Excellence and Enjoyment!'* shouted the headline from the glossy booklet. *'Continuing Professional Development'* declared the beautiful white lettering on the DVD, above a photo of three immaculately dressed women (who obviously hadn't been near the paint pots and papier-mache recently) poring over their laptops and no doubt still at school at 7pm busily setting new targets for driving up standards.

As I thumbed through the booklet, remembering that this costly package had been posted to every primary school in the country, I simply couldn't believe the nonsense I was reading. One of the principles underlying teaching young children, we were told, is 'the use of assessment to help learners improve their work'. Really? Gosh. And I wouldn't mind betting that two of the prime requisites for a brickie would be a trowel and a bit of cement to stick the bricks together with.

I read further. As a teacher, I'm told, I should 'set high expectations' and 'establish what learners already know'. Then (wait for it...) 'I could build on it.' Had our young teachers spent a lot of time training without being told these illuminating basics? More to the point, were teachers so daft they couldn't work out this sort of thing for themselves? And that was just the booklet. When we got to the DVD, things became even worse.

Now, I had a dedicated and enthusiastic team of teachers, always open to new ideas and techniques, but they were unwilling to suffer fools gladly. For the first five minutes they dutifully watched the video, while I watched their faces. Soon, they began to glance at each other; then the smiles began to appear. After ten minutes everyone was laughing uproariously, because even though the people on the screen were talking non-stop, none of us had the slightest idea what they were trying to tell us. Where, I wondered, did the Department for Education find people like this? Did you have to win some sort of silliness contest?

The worthy ladies on screen sat wittering away about structure and scaffolding and whole-staff reflection and scrutiny and systems of trialling (whatever they were), and none of them seemed to be hearing each other in any meaningful way. Samuel Beckett would have loved it. Harold Pinter could have inserted lots of meaningful pauses and staged it at the National. After fifteen minutes we turned it off in disgust and talked instead about ways to improve children's handwriting.

Nevertheless, it worries me that schools continually put up with this expensive and unnecessary claptrap. It lands in staffrooms with monotonous regularity and teachers either don't look at it, or they watch it, decide it doesn't have the slightest bearing on any kind of educational reality and then dump it in Pseud's Corner where it rightly belongs, or use it to prop up the tea urn. Perhaps they shouldn't do that. Perhaps schools should do what I did. Send the package back, with a strongly worded letter saying what we thought of it. And if even 10 per cent of the 26,000 primary schools who receive this rubbish on a regular basis did the same thing, perhaps a little sense could be battered into the suited dullards who think this is really what we need in our staffrooms.

Jargon has always been rife, of course, and not just in education. If you take your car in for a service, and on collecting it the mechanic says there's a problem with the nearside rear calliper dustshield retainer, you probably won't have a clue what he means, but you won't want to appear a fool and you'll say 'I thought so. Could you fix it, please.' Although the retainer is really only a small metal clip, he knows you'll pay whatever he asks, because he's confused you with the jargon of his trade. Dodgy plumbers excel at this. When there was a small leak from my daughter's flat that seeped into the flat below, the plumber she called diagnosed a problem with the overflow from the toilet. By the time he'd finished totting everything up with his pencil and pad, he'd estimated a cost of £295 for labour and parts, as he said it would take him at least an hour to drive somewhere and source the part, and then he'd have to take the cistern to pieces. Horrified, I went to the Wickes store ten minutes away and fitted the part myself. It cost £8, and took ten minutes to fit.

Recently, a colleague sent one of her youngest teachers on a classroom management course for a day. Afterwards, the teacher had difficulty recalling anything useful she'd learned, but she did return with an expensively produced handout. Consider this statement from it…

'In the assessment context, the use of verbal/non-verbal technique can inform our judgements and isolate strategies we can categorise as those of assessment, as opposed to variants such as teaching or feedback.'

Would that sort of thing keep Billy in his seat? Of course not. It's waffle. Rubbish. Even worse, the school paid £180 (excluding lunch!) for the teacher to attend, and this sort of stuff was pedalled all day to the dewy-eyed. Added to the £175 for the supply teacher who covered the teacher's class for the day, learning a little jargon became a costly experience for the school. Personally, I'd have covered the class myself and asked her to spend the time with a good classroom practitioner. She'd have learned more… and the £355 could have been spent on extra equipment for her classroom.

But primary education seems to spend a lot of time re-inventing itself and designing suitable phrases to describe questionable techniques, and yet we never seem to spend enough time running with the things that really work. If I'd wanted to, I could have spent a lot of money bringing consultants, advisers and 'experts' of every description into school to lecture my staff. But when I looked through the lists of what was available, I was often baffled by the lecture titles, let alone the thought of a day struggling with the tedium behind them. What do you make of *'Building Bridges in Perspective Balancing'* or *'Targeting The Listening System'*? Precious little? Me too.

Looking back though, perhaps things have always been like this. As an eager young teacher in the 60's, I was concerned at how little my new class had previously achieved in mathematics. I spent a lot of time teaching basic concepts.. and was really getting somewhere.. until I was visited by the local inspector, who told me, incredibly, that maths 'wasn't about number.' My Year 3's should have been spending all their maths time exploring 'real life' issues and nothing else. Making traffic graphs with sticky paper, or constructing castles from cornflake packets to explore area would be a good start, she said. I wasn't sure the parents of my children would have been entirely happy about their offspring standing on the street corner counting the cars that went past, but early in your career you don't question whether an inspector has a commanding grip on reality.

Buzz words and phrases have always been prolific in education, but never more so than now. If we're not 'striving for excellence', we're 'driving up standards' by setting 'smart targets' or offering 'opportunities for all'. Laudable aims, usually accompanied by glossy booklets and not much else. There is, of course, the version of bingo played by young executives required to attend tedious business management courses. They decide on a group of buzz words, write them out on a grid and as soon as the lecturer says one, they put a tick through it. The idea is to be first at crossing out a line of words, at which point you jump up and shout 'bullshit!' I believe there is a movement to adopt Bullshit Bingo in education too…

Teachers have had several different unions to represent their interests and concerns for many years, and it is up to the individual teacher to decide which one he or she wishes to give their membership fee to, and which will be the most dependable if they have a problem. Headteachers, rightly, have a separate union. But occasionally an agency will come into being, usually from the government, which purports to be a helpful and representative body for teachers, rather like the medical council that doctors have. Enter the General Teaching Council for England, the professional body for teachers and teaching which arrived in the year 2000.

Its aims were twofold. It was intended to contribute to improving standards of teaching and the quality of learning, and to maintain standards of professional conduct. Every teacher was required to cough up monthly subscriptions, and almost from the start it was pretty much a disaster, causing teachers to resent having to contribute part of their hard-earned salary and to increasingly question what they actually gained from belonging to it, especially when they realised that, at one point, the GTC was playing with around £33,000,000 a year of their money.

Several times a year I would receive all kinds of literature from the GTC, hardly any of it any use. Soon after it had been formed, I received a booklet stating that the Council had been very busy evolving a revised 'Code of Conduct' for teachers, after which they'd carried out an important thing called an Equality Impact Assessment of it. After a rigorous and searching investigation, it had concluded that the likely impact for teachers was 'positive'. That came as a relief, then. I reached for my tranquillisers and opened my booklet to learn what our Code of Conduct should be, and it seemed there were eight important parameters for my teachers to consider and absorb...

1. ***Help children to become confident and successful learners.*** So that's what the little people were supposed to be doing! Learning! And I wouldn't mind betting we were supposed to be teaching them. Who'd have thought it?
2. ***Strive to establish productive partnerships with parents.*** Damn. I'll have to take down that sign saying 'No Parents Past This Point' and actually let them into the building. A bit much really. Next thing, we'll be asked to discuss their children's work with them and they'll be wanting to help their offspring at home. Could be a worrying trend.
3. ***Work as part of a whole school team.*** And there was I, thinking the idea was to fast track up the promotion ladder and say 'I'm more important than you. I've got people under me and I can swan around monitoring everybody else.' And what's going to happen to Miss Gradgrind's staffroom chair? It's one of the only two really comfortable ones in the staffroom and she's laid claim to it for fifty years. The teachers enjoy getting to it first and irritating her. I suppose this means they'll have to talk to her now.
4. ***Put the wellbeing, development and progress of children first.*** This is a bit much, isn't it? I won't be able to send Year 6 children out to do my shopping. And I'll have to stop my rigorous targeting and tracking so that I've got time to talk to a child. How will I find the hours to spend with my School Improvement Partner, or prepare for Ofsted inspections if I'm supposed to consider the wellbeing of the children?

5. ***Co-operate with other professional colleagues.*** Oh come on! This is going to ruin the battle to retain our league tables position, showing we're better than all the other schools. At this rate, they'll want us to talk to other schools and give away our methods of forcing children through Level 4 hoops.
6. ***Demonstrate honesty and integrity and uphold public trust.*** Look, all I did was use a bit of the school budget to buy a second hand Porsche, and it's been down the garage three times already. Okay, and a new suit and a Rolex and some gold cufflinks. But schools are businesses these days, aren't they? I need to look the part.
7. ***Take responsibility for maintaining the quality of their teaching practice.*** Dear me, I suppose I'll have to let my teachers go on some courses. I don't encourage that kind of thing. Only leads to new ideas and demands on the budget. Can't see why they don't just repeat the same lessons year after year. After all, that's what teachers did when I was at school.
8. ***Demonstrate respect for diversity and promote equality.*** You mean we're not all exactly the same? Well blow me down, I had no idea.

My teachers reacted in the same way you are now. At least, said one, it is jolly good to know the General Teaching Council is spending our millions so wisely…

And then, in 2012, when asked what he intended to do about the General Teaching Council, MP Michael Gove gave an enigmatic smile and said 'I'm listening to the teachers. Watch this space'. We did, and suddenly it was gone.

Undoubtedly, when the GTC was first set up, there was considerable enthusiasm for it. A professional council to champion teachers and teaching. But ten years later any enthusiasm for it had long since dissipated. None of my staff had a clue what the GTC was doing. They knew it raked in millions, and a few knew it acted as judge and jury when teachers had been caught doing something naughty, but other than that? Nothing. Zilch. And only one had ever bothered to read the little magazine justifying its existence that occasionally popped through our doors.

But me? I loved the magazine. A huge source of amusement, because the GTC came up with eye-poppingly banal initiatives and professional development ideas that I'm astonished anyone ever took seriously. The Learning Conversation, for example; a jargon infested idea which, when unpicked, simply meant teachers talking to each other, which apparently encourages them to…um… learn from each other. A Learning Conversation, it said, may take place with a fellow teacher, an inspiring manager or even with a pupil. Fancy that! And a Learning Conversation could even take place in the staffroom at the end of the day. Extraordinary. Presumably though, Mrs Jones complaining loudly in the staffroom about the little sod who keeps yodelling during her lessons wouldn't qualify as a proper Learning Conversation.

By page five, we were into jargon, and we meet the 'check in, check out' approach. Apparently, this meant that staff meet and 'check-in' their daily pressures, known as baggage. Then they have a Learning Conversation, and sum up what they've learned at 'check-out' time. Finally, there is the 'double loop method', whereby those in conversation ask big questions like: 'Where are we going, and why?' It occurred to me that any half-decent school would already be doing this, though I suppose it would have been much more impressive to say: 'Yes, we're targeting staff cohesion with a double-looped check-out this week.'

When I was a young teacher, brim-full of enthusiasm, I knew I had a lot to learn. What did I do? I found the best practitioners on the staff and spent hours chatting with them. How did they organise their classrooms so effectively? How did they keep children so purposefully quiet and absorbed? How did they arrange their time so that all the children could have the individual attention they needed? Isn't that what all good teachers do? We talked, discussed, debated, argued. Hasn't it always been a feature of the job?

Often, there were questionnaires, mailed to all teachers and purporting to gather useful information for additional training and development. There were some real nuggets here. Not on the level of the DfE census that asked me to tick a box if I was too disabled to do my job. It occurred to me that if I'd been too disabled to do my job, I wouldn't have been doing it.

There was the sheer incompetence, too. One of my teachers received a letter demanding she pay her subscription or she'd be removed from the GTC register. Horrors! She replied and told them she'd retired seven years ago. And notified them at the time. Another teacher received a similar letter, and she wrote a polite letter back, saying she paid via the school payroll provider every year. The GTC wrote back and thanked her. And then sent another letter asking why she hadn't paid. If the money wasn't forthcoming immediately, it said, she'd be struck off and then, poor soul, she'd be stuffed because she wouldn't be able to get another job. Apart from the private sector, of course. You could always get a job in the private sector.

She telephoned again, irritated. Sorry, they said, our mistake. Relieved.. because she's a young teacher and doesn't need that kind of worry... she went back to her classroom and stopped thinking about it. A fortnight later, she received a letter saying she'd been removed from the register. Another phone call, another apology, and could she just be popped back on the register? No, she was told, it wasn't that simple. She'd have to re-apply...

So... what have the Romans ever done for us? Whoops, sorry, that's Monty Python. What I meant to say was: 'What did the General Teaching Council ever do for us?' But wasn't there a bit of Monty Python about the GTC anyway? Hardly a week went by without an item in the *Times Educational Supplement* about some poor soul who'd been hauled in front of it for getting inebriated on a plane and taking his trousers off, or going potty in the maths corner and eating the entire boxful of Dienes apparatus. It began to seem the main reason for the GTC's existence...

Teaching is such an endlessly fascinating profession it makes us continually seek better ways to educate our children, and there surely can't be a teacher in the land who'd disagree with that. Back to that booklet: the more I read, the more ridiculous it became. Fast on the heels of The Learning Conversation we had the 'Hot Lesson', the headline telling us that ideas like this are 'pushing the boundaries of teaching and learning.' Apparently, the hot lesson is one where the teacher tries something a little different, perhaps a lesson they haven't taught before. The 'hot' bit is the part where the teacher is 'pushed out of her comfort zone'. Again, this explanation was followed up with lots of jargon, including a reference to an Elgar hymn sheet! Basically, it was simply saying 'teachers... stretch yourself, and your pupils. It's good for them and it's good for you.' Frankly, isn't that what good teachers have been doing since the dawn of time?

But almost as soon as the GTC had disappeared, up popped 'Learning Matters'. Rather clever that. Learning is actually important, it was saying, but here are some matters you'll find useful. It was our local education authority's new pamphlet of news and information. Since it was intended to be a regular way for the authority to keep in touch with its schools, and a bit of a morale booster to boot, I applauded the idea. At first.

But when I settled down to give it a thorough read I became a little concerned. A piece on the back page was entitled 'Work smarter not harder,' (Dear God, how we constantly murder grammar these days!) and it purported to explain the benefits of joining something called the Teacher Learning Academy. Frankly, I'd never heard of it, so I was intrigued to learn more. The first paragraph says 'it underpins collaborative working and learning, building on strengths of the past to influence and achieve the aspirations of the future.' Okay, fair enough, but... well... what is it? And what does it do?

I read further. I learn that it gives schools a 'portable four stage framework'. Pretty exciting stuff so far, then, but I still don't really know what it is. The next sentence attempts to tell me. At the end of a long day, it made as much sense to me as a primer in serbo-croat. I quote it in full...

'It is a system which advocates for promoting action research by teachers based in their own professional practice which affords recognition of existing activities within their classrooms and schools.'

I read this six times but it didn't help much, so I read on. It seems that schools can register with the TLA, and once things are 'embedded' they get 'connection between pupil and teacher learning' and 'alignment between school improvement and teacher development'. There was even a quote from a headteacher. 'I want to work with other schools so that the total outcomes are more than the sum of the parts'. Wow.

At this point, I checked the date on the cover. Was it April 1st? No, this was all deadly serious and here was I, a headteacher with twenty five years at the coalface, unable to decipher what I was reading. Then I had a jolly good idea. I googled the TLA, and up came a colourful website with other snippets of information. It was all about having a personal programme for 'practice based learning', which would enhance 'teacher recognition'. (You're a teacher, aren't you? Thought so. I could tell by the cadaverous pallor brought on from reading indecipherable pamphlets...)

Then after another half hour, I was pretty sure I'd cracked it. I think of a useful idea... such as giving children a pencil to write with and a rubber to rub out what they've just written... then I join the TLA, become accredited, pay a fee, have a mentor, write some stuff, and then share it with the world, although I still wasn't sure how. But wait... there are lots of little tabs across the top of the screen and one of them is labelled 'Case Studies'. And there are seven of them. Now I can really find out what these schools have undertaken and how exciting it all is. Unfortunately, only one of the schools... a business and enterprise college... had written anything at all and even then it didn't tell me what they had done. Disappointed, I clicked on the tab that listed some of the topics TLA enrollers have opted to investigate. One says 'Use of the LASC wheel to develop independent creative learners.' The LASC wheel? No, I hadn't a clue, either. And then I spotted a tiny subtitle at the top of the home page 'Inspired by the General Teaching Council of England', it said. And that, of course, explained a great deal...

The National College of School Leadership was formed in 2000, to train future school leaders.. When it was recommended that our school became an accredited 'Leadership Development School', meaning that I'd be able to help train future headteachers, I was a little surprised, because I had always spent a fair amount of time criticising theories that simply didn't work out in practice. Nevertheless, our School Improvement Partner, who recommended us, recognised that our school worked well, and understood that there should always be room for an alternative view. (SIPs were like mini Ofsted inspectors, allocated to every school. They visited once a term. I have no idea why the government felt the need for them. Just to keep the pressure on school leaders, I suppose.)

That was certainly how our first trainee felt. He was delighted... and a little surprised... to find that you don't have to run around monitoring your teachers with a clipboard every five minutes. Neither do you have to scrutinise (what an ugly word this is) their planning every Monday morning, or insist they feed masses of irrelevant data into a computer to find out how their children are performing.

He discovered that if teachers are let off the leash, they'll have time to develop inventive, inspiring lessons, and they'll spend far more time simply enjoying their job. The children will benefit, achievement will be higher, and morale in the school will be lifted significantly. I stayed in contact until he got his first headship, not only because I liked him but also because I wanted to see whether he could survive the intense pressure that headteachers experience from above, which tries to make them lead their schools in whatever the currently prescribed manner happens to be.

After attempting to do the mandatory signing up with the College three times because they seemed to have lost the first two electronic applications, I eventually received a 22 page document about working in partnership with the NCSL. I put aside the Ofsted 98 page manual on writing your 'Self Evaluation Plan' and the 56 page guide to 'Completing Your Financial Management Systems Audit Form', and settled down to read it.

The first page told me I would be 'inspiring new leaders to improve children's lives.' Naturally, it hadn't occurred to me that headteachers might be influencing children's lives, so that was helpful. Next came a page with a big blank green square. 'Visual Identity Guidelines' was written beside it. Perhaps, I thought, I'll be required to send a nice photograph of myself. But no, 'visual identity' referred to the NCSL logo, and, lucky chap that I was, I was now allowed to use it on my headed notepaper. This was in line with the practice of putting a logo from a relevant body on your school notepaper when you achieve its particular goal. Healthy School status? Add the logo! An Inclusive School? There's a logo for it you can use. One morning I received a letter from a school with so many logos there was hardly any space to put the writing.

Five full pages told me how to use the NCSL logo. I was advised to employ the full colour version wherever possible, although I should observe the exclusion zone and minimum size rules. I could use the black and white version if I subscribed to the Ned Ludd school of printing and technology. It is important, I'm told, to give the NCSL logo 'room to breathe', and I must never use it in a size less than 40mm in width, or 252 pixels if I use it on line. On dark backgrounds it's best to use it in a light colour. Like.. um.. white. Then I'm shown what happens if you get it wrong, with a helpful diagram showing the logo a bit skew-wiff. If things are still not working out, I can phone their 'Marketing and Communications Team'. This was my first taste of the NCSL, but it did make me wonder whether its priorities for expenditure were actually in the best order...

Sometimes, when things seem to be getting out of hand, teachers decide to take action. It's highly unusual, because teachers are usually friendly, uncomplaining people, and they will put up with a great deal that many other professions wouldn't, which is why so much is put upon them, but testing, SATs and dodgy training have always been contentious issues.

In 2010, many schools decided to boycott the Key Stage 2 SATs. I'm not against testing, but I've never thought the formal sitting of SATs, rather like the eleven plus, was the best way to do it. The secondary schools don't take much notice of them because they don't indicate accurately what a child can do. They simply prove that primary teachers have become pretty adept at honing a narrow agenda for squeezing their children through that essential level 4... essential to the school even more than the child, to avoid Ofsted giving it a hard time.

But, as in most things the government does in education, rather than decrease the testing it decided to step it up, announcing its intention to publish school by school results after just one year of formal education. This was 'to give parents more information.' About what, exactly? The quality of education taking place in the school? If I were choosing a school for my child I'd visit a few, request a tour, see how accessible the headteacher was, check whether the class teachers seemed happy in their work and ask some in-depth questions. I'd learn nothing from a league table and precious little from an Ofsted report. In fact, in two of the most miserable schools I know, staff morale is so low new teachers usually have to be recruited every year,

Both had been labelled outstanding by Ofsted.

12

IS CHARLIE JUST BEING... NAUGHTY... AGAIN?

The Rise In Children With Additional Needs

'*All the world is queer save thee and me. And even thou's a little queer.*' This well-known quote was penned by a gentleman named Robert Stephen on severing business relations in 1828 with his partner. And I rather think there's a fair amount of truth in it.. we're all probably a little odd. Set in our ways with our opinions and our behaviours and our particular view of the world. Even when we're young. Even the things that interest us, irritate us, or make us laugh or cry.

When I look back at the children in my final year at primary school, I still have strong memories of most of them. There was Mickey Smith, who had a dreadful stammer. There was Emily Jones, a white faced little girl who sat quietly in her desk and hardly said a word. Her father, a coalman, regularly came home from the pub drunk and thumped his wife and there was never enough money to feed the family properly. There was Colin Blake, who had no hope of doing anything much, apart from failing at the awful local secondary modern school, and he could barely write his name, let alone a literate sentence. He used to write it as Conie Bikey, and he was known to everybody, including the class teachers, as Connie. There was Alan Stern, who was restless all the time and just couldn't sit still. His mother, apparently, was very unkind to him because he was an unwanted child. There was Julia Marchant, a girl so large she could barely sit on the narrow plank of the two seater desk and who apparently had an eating disorder and parents who constantly argued at home. Robert Stevenson enjoyed pinching people or prodding their thighs with the point of a pencil, especially when he'd just sharpened it, and there was poor Clive Goodwin, an effeminate child with a lisp, who for the whole of the school year was called Softie by the teacher. And most handicapped of all, Anthony Wake, who'd had polio and now had his leg in an iron cage, which meant that he couldn't run about like the other children. He'd be chased at playtime by the unkinder elements of the class, because they knew that however slow they were, Anthony was even slower.

I came from a good home with two very loving parents. They didn't have a great deal of money, but they rented a spacious Victorian home with four floors for some years and then the owner suddenly became bankrupt. Desperate for money, he offered the property to them at a very reasonable price and although it still required a hefty mortgage it was an offer they couldn't refuse.

My mother always trusted and assumed that I wasn't misbehaving, which for most of the time was correct, although this trust was seriously misplaced on a few occasions. In Year Six, for a very short period, I came under the influence of the Baker brothers who lived in the next road from me. They had something of a reputation for being troublesome, and I was persuaded to hang around with them after school, partly in fear and partly in awe of their derring-do. We'd knock on people's doors and then run off, stand in the foyer of jeweller's shops shouting out that we were going to rob the place that night, and then move on to the sweet shop, where one of the brothers would attempt to remove some sweets from the counter while the other kept the shopkeeper talking. Then we'd cram ourselves into the telephone box on The Green, dial some numbers and tell anybody who answered to get off the line because there was a train coming.

All this was very exciting and daring stuff until, one afternoon when we were inside the box, the door was suddenly barred by a heavily built man with a notebook and a very unamused face. He told us he was a police officer and he demanded our names and addresses. Terrified, I gave mine immediately, and although the Bakers attempted to give the wrong address, they changed their minds when the officer said he'd be checking up with our school and he'd insist we were given a thorough caning by the headteacher if we were lying. Since we were wearing school blazers he didn't need to be Sherlock Holmes to work out where we were receiving our education.

At eight o'clock that evening there was a loud knock on the front door, and two police officers, one female and the other the man who had caught us, asked to speak to my parents. I heard them talking in low tones for a while, and then they asked my mother to fetch me. As I stood trembling in front of them, they said that although they knew the Bakers because they'd been in trouble before, they hadn't expected to come to a home like mine, that I should consider how what I'd done had affected my parents, and that if I got into trouble again they'd see that I was taken to juvenile court. It all scared me stiff and I promised never to do anything like it again. They seemed satisfied, my mother showed them to the door, and I was left to face the fury of my parents.

I had never seen my father so angry. Pocket money was stopped, my journey home from school was timed, and I wasn't allowed to see my friends for many days. Although I tried to convince them that the Bakers had egged me on, my father was totally unsatisfied with that explanation, stating that there would be people egging me on throughout my entire life, and that I'd better aspire to a higher standard pretty quickly.

Now, consider this. If I'd exhibited that behaviour these days perhaps I could possibly have been dubbed a child who had 'special needs.' Someone who had problems at home, and setting fire to cardboard boxes round the back of Sainsburys, scaring old ladies or abusing people down the telephone was a way of getting rid of my angst. Perhaps I was a child with pyrotechnic tendencies. Perhaps an educational psychologist, or the school's Special Needs Co-ordinator would have interviewed me. In fact, there was nothing wrong with me at all. I was simply stepping over the line in the sand. Exploring the behaviour boundaries and being a bit of a rebel. Being naughty.

My mother and father never, ever, told me they loved me. Parents didn't in those days, but I was never in any doubt that they did. My father, a man of many hobbies and interests, encouraged me to have many hobbies too, and he shared his own with me. If I received a construction set for Christmas, or a build it yourself model aeroplane, he'd be there at the table working on it with me. He spent hours making me a go-cart with his small and primitive set of tools, building me a puppet show, and showing me how photography worked. He built me a useful blackboard and easel, something I played with for years and which probably pointed me in the direction of becoming a teacher. The only time he was ever concerned about a hobby I'd taken up was when I decided to do some French knitting with cotton reels and wool. I thought the technique was clever and great fun, but he thought any kind of knitting was a very inappropriate activity for a nine year old boy and although he didn't openly express his displeasure, it was quite obvious that he was unhappy about it, and he was very relieved when I moved on to something else.

Thinking back to those children in my class, these days most of them would have been given a label. Children we used to call 'special needs children,' or today, 'children with additional needs.' There was no additional help for any of them then, of course; no classroom support workers, no special provision, nobody in the school called a Special Educational Needs Co-ordinator (SENco), and certainly no real understanding of their needs or difficulties. They were just left to go it alone, so they were often bullied or mocked and they just had to cope with the ups and downs of life as best they could. And to their credit, most of them did.

It is certainly true that we are now beginning to have a much greater understanding of children who have additional needs, although we still don't have many concrete ideas about the causes of them. What, for example, causes autism? It's a very wide spectrum and many theories have been put forward, some saner than others. It's all the convenience food we eat these days because people can't be bothered to cook. It's all hereditary. It's the lack of exercise, with children spending far too much time on their phones, tablets, x-boxes and virtual reality headsets. It could be pre-natal exposure to air pollution, or certain pesticides. Or is it maternal obesity, diabetes, or immune system disorders? Or perhaps even extreme prematurity or very low birth weight, or any birth difficulty leading to periods of oxygen deprivation to the baby's brain, because these days, with so many advances in medical technique, a baby will almost certainly survive when they wouldn't have many years ago.

But there's also no doubt that children are very different now compared with even a decade ago. A very young child will stroke a television screen, expecting something to happen, because it does on mummy's tablet and phone. Many television shows or dramas, particularly children's television, have a sort of whizz bang hit you in the face quality about them, where the picture has to change every few seconds or the viewer will become distracted and lose concentration. Often, an adult viewer will be texting or scrolling on their phone at the same time as watching the TV. After twenty minutes of watching *Jurassic Park* with me for the first time, my grandson said 'When are the dinosaurs going to attack?' I explained that the first part of the film was character development. If you weren't made to care about the people on screen, you wouldn't fear for them when the attacks began in earnest, but so many films these days, especially the many that involve superheroes, are just pieces of computer generated action strung together.

Most headteachers nowadays are increasingly worried about the mental effect technology is having on the children in their schools.

Just this weekend I read about a headteacher who is trying to introduce a twelve hour school day in a bid to tackle pupils' addiction to smartphones. The children will be expected to arrive at 7am and stay until 7pm, and he intends to offer a wide variety of practical activities to wean them in the right direction. Like many of us, he is extremely concerned about children gaming through the night, sometimes with children in different countries and time zones, cyber bullying, blackmail and sexting, and children's growing inability to make eye contact, hold conversations or make strong friendships in real life. At the moment technology seems to be racing ahead so quickly that we are simply unable to keep abreast of it, even though it is enabling many miracles to be performed. Watch a surgeon on television carrying out a complicated operation and marvel at what can be achieved. Climb into any modern car and be astonished at what it can do and how pleasurable it is to drive, while safely guiding you towards the destination you've simply asked it to transport you to, because there's need to stop on a layby and look at a map any more. Attend the cinema or theatre, and watch pictures of the highest quality, without the need for highly skilled projectionists. **Modern high fidelity equipment can bring a concert into every room in the home with astonishing realism. But then, watch a programme showing how artificial intelligence has progressed in leaps and bounds, with robots simulating humans with ever increasing accuracy and, perhaps, be more than a little afraid.**

Truancy has also become a massive problem, not infrequently with the permission of parents, whose attitude tends to be 'What does it matter if they don't attend school all the time? It's a waste of some of the best years of their lives and going to school for two or three days a week is more than enough.' In a recent survey, three in ten parents said that it simply wasn't necessary for children to attend school every day. Well, perhaps this is true. Perhaps we are beginning to see a seismic shift in the way the young are educated. After all, virtually every bit of knowledge is available on the internet and eventually everything humans know will be accessible instantly. Or if you want to know how to put a new battery in your iPhone, or build a bookshelf, or replace your car battery, or put a new washer in your bathroom tap, you simply look at a step by step video guide on Youtube or your virtual reality headset. (And modern taps don't even have washers.)

The whole truancy problem has, of course, snowballed since the awfulness of the Covid pandemic, and schools are having to take unprecedented measures just to try and coax children back into school. Before Covid, one in ten children were labelled as persistently absent from school, but that number has recently doubled to a hugely worrying one in five. Many educationalists believe it is now the most concerning issue in schools across the nation, and are labelling it as a massive crisis. During the pandemic, remote learning was seen as unsatisfactory and very difficult for schools to manage successfully, but it was the only possible solution for trying to ensure continuity in children's learning. But there's little doubt that the long term impact has lingered worryingly.

As always, there is a scarcity of funding for tackling this crisis and much disagreement about what, in reality, can actually be done about it. Some schools are sending minibuses to collect children from home, or giving them pre-paid travel cards. Some schools help with the cost of uniforms for the children. They have always been expensive, and usually had to be bought from specialist shops, but a family consigned to visiting a food bank would hardly be able to consider the purchase of a school tie, let alone a jacket. And whereas at one time a child who deliberately stayed away from school would be visited at home by a truancy officer, now the police are getting involved. Which is truly a huge waste of police resources.

It has always been acknowledged that teaching is a job that has implications far wider than statutory responsibilities suggest. It was something I realised from my first week as a class teacher, but now some teachers are also becoming social workers in all but name. When I began headship in the eighties, some dreadful terms were in common use. Mixed race children were called 'half caste'. Children who had learning difficulties were labelled as 'educationally subnormal' or 'mentally defective'. Educational psychologists would visit schools regularly to discuss the most concerning cases and try to offer suggestions for learning that might make a difference to the child's academic progress. Nowadays, unfortunately, much of this has to be done on line. One or two educational psychologists who came to my school were genuinely interested in making a difference. A few were appalling. The first gentleman I dealt with, elderly and nearing retirement, told me that the previous headteacher always got out a bottle of sherry when he visited and they just had a chat about the needy children over several glassfuls of Croft's original. I was furious, and refused to have the man in my school any more.

But over the years, there was gradually a much greater determination to help children who needed additional support, whether it was physical or mental. Money was provided (though never enough, of course) and it became important for every primary school to have a SENco, who was experienced with children displaying learning problems or challenging behaviour. The idea was that the SENco would have a room of their own, where these children could take part in short but intensive lessons with just two or three others with similar needs and have plenty of time to talk, share problems, or experience activities which interested and motivated them. Ninety per cent of the SENco's time would be given over to a hands-on approach, and there would be very little form filling. Indeed, if there was form filling to be done, the SENco would usually do it at home, and good SENco's were worth their weight in gold, especially in an area of social deprivation. They would also be experienced enough to give assistance and advice to class teachers who needed it, and also liaise with the visiting educational psychologist if outside help or additional funding was needed.

But gradually, as usual, things began to take an annoying and frustrating turn. Allegedly, when Ronald and Nancy Reagan visited

London for the first time, Nancy turned to her aides and said 'Will they be showing us the orphans?' It was an astonishing question and I assumed she must have been shown some Dickensian pictures of slums in Victorian England, but I was reminded of her question in 2010 when I read the foreword to a booklet sent to schools by the Department for Education about maximising the progress of children with 'special needs.'

Excitingly titled 'The National Strategies and Progression Guidance', it was written by a brand new minister, the Parliamentary Under Secretary Of State For Schools and Learners. When I read it, I began to wonder if the lady had the slightest idea about children with additional needs. For too long, she said, we have not set high enough ambitions for these children, and that should be a prompt for putting in place the support required to help them learn and succeed.

A worthy sentiment, but for starters, I wondered who the 'we' was that she referred to. The government? Her? No, of course not. It was the poor bloody infantry again, those idle teachers who don't bother enough about poor old Charlie who can't do much and sits in the corner waiting to be 'stretched'. And 'support'? Actually, most kinds of support always require something called money. Even in those days, it was a miracle teachers managed to do what they did with special needs children on the very small budgets they'd got.

At the time, there was a growing emphasis on inclusion, and parents with SEN children gradually had a greater right to choose which school they wanted for their children, even if the child had extreme physical needs. Again, this was obviously laudable, but only provided the necessary resources were forthcoming, and far too often they weren't. I was told to admit a child who'd been in hospital almost constantly until he was three years old, and then spent a year at a local nursery, where he'd had several adults attending to his needs. It was a medical miracle that he'd survived. He needed to be fed via a machine linked to his stomach, and he had no control over his bowel movements. He needed full time support... which wasn't forthcoming, so I refused.

I received strong and threatening pressure from the local authority's inclusion officers, and I told them I'd be more than happy to take the boy, but only with the appropriate help and a refurbishment of my dowdy old shower room, because he'd need to be changed very often, usually several times during the course of a school day, and that wasn't a teacher's job as far as I was concerned... or, indeed, the job of a SENco. After a lengthy battle, I got what I wanted, and fortunately the child thrived. I knew from bitter experience that authorities can promise the earth, but help had a habit of disappearing mysteriously if you took a child before you'd actually got what you needed.

Following on from the report telling us to pull our socks up and work harder with additional needs children, there was a bizarre demand for these children to make at least two 'levels' of progress in a Key Stage, 'just like other children'? Well, tell that to Allan, I thought, whose mum had tried to commit suicide twice. Tell it to Jaynal, Year 5, whose brother had been seriously injured in a street fight. Tell it to Simon, looked after by a succession of 'uncles' because his mother was out half the night. Tell it to Annie, infant, who watched her father stab her mother, or Mercy, who was walloped with her father's belt. I thought it highly probable that The Parliamentary Under Secretary Of State For Schools and Learners had composed the introductory page but not actually read the booklet and I couldn't imagine any teacher bothering with it. From front to back, it was filled with the usual incomprehensible graphs and management speak.

With regard to helping children with additional needs, I was lucky. After a number of years of headship, I had gathered together a truly superb set of teachers who could cope with more or less anything and children who came to us with additional needs, some very concerning, did make remarkable progress in a settled and happy atmosphere. Leon, for example. Six years old and very small for his age, he and his angelic smile came into school accompanied by his mother, asking for a Year 2 place. A child had left recently, so we said we'd take Leon the following Monday. We never refused anyone, provided we felt we could cope, but we always rang the previous school for background on a new child before his personal file arrived. It meant we could find out what the child was good at, and whether they'd have difficulty settling in. On this occasion, the secretary at the other end of the phone paused, and then said 'Just hang on for a minute. I think I'd better I'll pass you to our SENCo....' When the SENCo came on the phone, she obviously couldn't believe her good fortune. 'He's coming to you? What a relief! His behaviour is appalling, he does no work, he hurts children, and he hides under tables and spits at staff. I wish you luck, because you're certainly going to need it.'

When Leon's file arrived, things looked even more depressing. Police often arrived to turn his home over, his older brothers and sisters collected ASBOs like trophies, and there had been continuous involvement with social services. We'd never excluded a child, but I worried about our chances with this one. Nevertheless, he was going into a class with the sort of teacher who tells you how delightful her children are, but doesn't realise it's because she's so good at her job.

Things went fairly well on day one. Leon was allocated a friend to help him during his first week, and apart from watching the other children cautiously, wandering around the classroom whenever he felt like it, and calling out during lessons occasionally, he seemed like most children we'd taken on from elsewhere. Leon seemed genuinely surprised at how well the class behaved. He obviously wasn't used to that.

The problems started on the fourth day. Leon arrived at school… late.. looking as if he'd just crawled out of bed. His mother had demanded he take the DVDs back to the rental shop before going to school. He'd had breakfast.. a small bar of chocolate as a reward for going to the shop. We gave him fruit and a hot drink, but he was clearly angry. Later on we discovered he'd had very little sleep… the police had found his baby sister wandering in the street. At breaktime, he wouldn't line up with his class, and he ran off and climbed onto the playtown.

A child was sent to fetch me. 'I'm not dragging you inside, Leon', I said, when I found him skulking in the corner of the structure. 'If you want to stay out here, that's entirely up to you, but it's cold and it's going to rain heavily. And your class is cooking cakes this morning.' I knew he was hungry so I crossed my fingers and went back inside. Ten minutes later, I found him under a table outside his classroom. 'Do you want to go back in?' I asked. He nodded and I slipped him back into the room. By the end of the week, he'd started to discover that our school was a place where you could do lots of interesting things instead of spending the time being told off. He was bright, alert, exceptionally talented at art, and desperately keen to learn how to read.. something that seemed to have been ignored at his previous school, and which our SENco gave a lot of time to in the sessions he spent with her. He quickly formed a strong relationship with his class teacher. He knew she liked him and he was anxious to please her, even arriving one morning at eight o' clock to see if she needed any help. In those first weeks, I often popped into his classroom, but he was fine. Apart from habitual lateness, which wasn't his fault, he continued to thrive, but I did find it extraordinary that two schools could perceive a small child so differently. When I returned to school after a few days on a course, Leon saw me, and ran up and hugged me. 'I missed you', he said quietly, and I was reminded, if I ever needed reminding, of just how awesome my responsibility as a headteacher was.

There was always the child who would be designated as somewhere on the autistic spectrum now, but who was a delight to have in school. Like eight-year-old Frankie, who had an all-consuming passion for buses. He'd joined us from another school and it was a fortnight before I met him properly. As I chatted to his teacher while she supervised playtime, he wandered up to us.

'Shall I do a bus, Miss?' he asked.

Seeing my baffled expression, his teacher smiled. 'Frankie's my very own bus service,' she said. 'Shut your eyes and listen.' Frankie launched into an impression of a bus in motion, with gear changes, stops and starts, and hissing air brakes. It was a pretty fair impression of the real thing.

'What bus was that?' he asked.

'I reckon it's a 53,' his teacher said.

'Of course not!' Frankie replied indignantly. 'It's a bendy bus. *This* is a 53...' He did a second impression, which sounded very different.

Each day, as I chatted to the children as they came in after playtime, Frankie would hurry past making motoring noises. I discovered that he'd drawn elaborate maps of the school, recreating the building as a large chunk of south-east London. Bus routes were illustrated with coloured lines and stops were marked at intervals. To catch the P13 to Streatham, also known as the dinner hall, you had to wait outside Class 9, where buses should appear at ten minute intervals if they were on schedule. Frankie could give any activity a transport slant. On an outing, while other boys compared the contents of their lunch boxes, Frankie unfolded a bus map, laid it out on an empty seat and carefully studied the route the coach was taking. I was relieved he wasn't sitting behind the driver, because I could imagine him pointing out that he wasn't taking the most expedient route. His South African class teacher was initially unfamiliar with London but after teaching Frankie for a year she felt she could travel anywhere by bus. Frankie simply loved them. He drew pictures of them whenever he had access to a pad of paper and some coloured pencils, he spent a lot of time in the London Transport Museum and he built models of buses with empty cereal packets that his grandparents gave him to bring to school. We were certain that he would eventually find a career working with them and I have often wondered if he did. Soon after Frankie had left us for secondary school, I met him one Saturday morning in a store miles from where he lived. He was shopping with his mother.

'Wow, you're a long way from home,' I said 'How did you get here?'

'Oh God, please don't ask him that!' his mother said. 'We'll be here all morning!'

But however hard we worked, there were always children who moved on to the far more difficult world of secondary education, where the work we had done, often for years, was rapidly undone. Andrew was 11, and his early years were dreadful. Abused physically and sexually by his natural parents and bullied mercilessly by an older brother, he was taken into care, and then adopted by a couple living near our school, which is how he came to us. He was understandably withdrawn and shy, and his emotional instability meant it took months for him to settle or relate to other children, let alone do any meaningful academic work. Nevertheless, with determined help from our SENCo, plus tireless support from his adoptive parents, he did manage to make progress. By the time he'd reached Year 6, he was a reasonably happy and contented child, and we felt he could move to secondary school with confidence. His adoptive parents had chosen his next school carefully, because he still had a 'statement' of special needs and would require much additional help. The school they'd selected certainly had its publicity angle sorted out. Andrew was promised the earth. The special needs department ran like an oiled machine, they said, and Andrew would receive his full entitlement from dedicated, specialist teachers.

The reality was different. As soon as he joined the school, Andrew was constantly bullied by three other Year 7 children. Money was demanded, and to celebrate his birthday, Andrew was beaten up. He received few of his special needs hours, and when his parents went to find out what was going on, the SENCo couldn't even make his laptop work, let alone offer any kind of explanation. The situation deteriorated rapidly. Andrew suffered nightmares and couldn't sleep unless a parent was in the same room with him. Meantime, it seemed the school had simply gave up, saying it wasn't possible to protect him from bullying without 'firm evidence' in writing, because the bullies' parents would object if accusations had been made without proof. Presumably Andrew should have carried a mobile phone around with him and taken a few snaps while he was being beaten up.

What particularly angered me was the age of the bullies. Barely twelve years old, and apparently renowned for their appalling behaviour at primary school. It's hardly unique, of course… we were reading about child victims every day, but my SENco was distraught when Andrew's parents fed back to her what was happening. Is it so impossible, she said, to mould children with decent life-values when they're very young? It was very easy to use every excuse under the sun for the bullies. They've got attention deficit disorder, they're 'reluctant learners', they've got rotten home lives, they need counselling, they're too young to be responsible for their actions… anything to excuse what they were doing. There is much pandering to poor behaviour, a great deal of money is spent on behavioural therapists and many schools tended to use fashionable techniques like Circle Time to give miscreants an opportunity to unload their angst. And, of course, schools had filing cabinets filled with written policies. Somehow, though, it didn't seem to be solving very much.

I never claimed to have more answers than anybody else, but I knew my school was getting something right. Great teaching and a high quality learning environment work wonders, but I suspected it was the massive effort we put into the early years that made such a difference. Like any sensible parent, we simply refused to tolerate any unsociable or aggressive behaviour from the moment children joined us. We allowed no excuses for it, and we made extremely clear boundaries for children when they were very small. It's hardly nuclear physics, and it worked. It really is the duty of schools to get children's values sorted out long before they reach secondary school. If they don't, what possible chance have children like Andrew got?

It was hardly unexpected when paperwork and form filling began to replace the practical roles of teachers involved with special needs children, and there now is a proliferation of labels for these children.

Dyslexia, Dyscalculia, Dysgraphia, Attention Deficit Hyperactive Disorder, Auditory Processing Disorder, Dyspraxia', Autism Spectrum Disorder, Anxiety Disorder, Bipolar Disorder… just to a name a few. And last week, when I was at the hospital for a health check-up, I was handed a 'patient experience' form to fill in which, as well as the usual things like name, age and colour of my underwear, I was invited to tick my sexual orientation. I had a choice of thirteen. I had no idea what four of them were. No wonder teenagers are so bewildered.

These days, the children come a poor second to the paperwork, but it has to be done, immaculately, if the school is to receive any additional money for pupils with the greatest need. Indeed, some special needs co-ordinators spend *all* their time form-filling, or nagging overworked teachers about handing in termly special needs reviews and 'individual education' plans.

Last weekend, I was speaking to a friend who is a primary headteacher in London's Hammersmith area. He loves the children, he was always a superb teacher, his school is popular and successful… but he is giving up headship, because trying to budget for children with additional needs is keeping him awake every night, and he fears if this continues, it will make him very unwell. Some of his classes contain one or two children whose behaviour is virtually out of control, and these children need an adult with them all the time. This he simply cannot afford. He says that affluent parents with money and a little legal knowledge can, firstly, afford to have their child assessed privately, and since they are paying for the report, the assessor, however experienced, is highly unlikely to say there's little wrong with the child apart from a lack of strong and determined parenting. Once they have their report, the parents will then approach the council and demand all day resourcing for their children, and the council, fearful of a legal challenge, will simply acquiesce. But the extra money often isn't forthcoming, particularly for the parents who don't want to make a fuss and wouldn't know how to challenge the system anyway, and the burden lands back on the school's resources. If no support is provided for the challenging or disruptive children, they can give a class teacher enormous problems, because the rest of the class will then be affected.

Even when a child has been allocated extra provision by a classroom assistant, the assistant is often afraid to challenge what the child is doing. Recently I spoke to a classroom assistant who said 'I have two children to look after and they can create havoc together. Last week when they ran out of the classroom and played on the grass they wouldn't come in. If I tried to hold their hands and walk them back in, I could have been in trouble with the parents for manhandling their offspring. I asked the school SENco what I should do and she just said 'Oh, those two, just leave them alone. They often do that. They'll come in for lunch.' What possible help could this piece of 'advice' be, either for the classroom assistant or the children? Shouldn't the parents have been summoned and told that the school simply wasn't accepting this sort of behaviour? Another teacher who does some regular supply work told me that in one school she worked at, several of the classes had more than fifty per cent of children with some sort of additional need. How can any school possibly hope to fund additional help for these children? And fifty per cent? Isn't it possible that there's not much wrong with these children, apart from the fact that their parents might have poor parenting skills? One of them, for example, is still in nappies at seven. Another eats only a particular flavour of crisps and other assorted unhealthy food. I can't imagine what that home is like, with the child ruling the roost. The poor teacher is left to try and cope with the result.

There will always be a few parents who try to play the system. One of the parents at my school decided that her son warranted a 'statement' of special needs, something that was essential at that time if extra provision was going to be allocated, and the 'statement' had to be drafted by an educational psychologist. The parent maintained that her son Jimmy wasn't making adequate progress, that the class teacher wasn't doing enough for him, that his health was suffering from worrying about his work, and that one to one support was absolutely essential for him. We didn't accept her case. The reason her son wasn't making progress was extremely simple… he was rarely at school, and when he did come he was worn out from being allowed to do whatever he liked at home by his consistently indulgent mother. The word 'bedtime' didn't feature anywhere in his vocabulary. The parent then managed to secure some financial help for a specialist to represent her, and the school was taken to a tribunal. We could hardly believe what we were hearing when her case was presented, and economy with the truth was well to the fore. Despite the fact that I could present irrefutable evidence to show his appalling attendance record, the panel of three accepted that he had a phobia about coming to school, and we were required to provide addition support for Jimmy. Which didn't achieve anything, because after a few weeks of reasonable attendance, he still didn't come to school, so fortunately we were able to cancel the support and save some money.

At the other end of the spectrum, there were parents who simply wouldn't accept that their child needed some extra support, even though it was being offered. I would hear my SENco on the telephone, patiently trying to explain why it was important for the parent to come to school to discuss the child's particular needs.

'Hello, is that Mr Ahmed? Oh hello. It's Amid's special needs teacher here.'

There's a pause.

'Yes, Amid's teacher is Miss Jones. But that's his class teacher. I'm the special needs teacher and I give him a little extra help. You were supposed to come to a meeting this morning.'

There's another pause.

'Well, it was going to be a meeting with the educational psychologist. And you. And me.'

She waits as Amid's father considers this piece of information.

'No, Amid isn't sick. The educational psychologist can help us to get some extra support for Amid. You promised you'd come.

Psychologists are very busy but I've managed to get one for half an hour. We can't get extra support for Amid unless you discuss it with us.'

There is a longer pause.

'I think you did know about the meeting. I've written three times and spoken to you twice on the telephone. Aren't you worried about Amid?'

Another pause.

'Yes, I'm sure he *is* very helpful in the shop. But he can't do lots of things that an eight-year-old should be able to do. No, I don't think hitting him with a big stick would help. Could you pop round for ten minutes, then?'

I hear her sigh deeply and put the phone down. I know that she has a steely determination and she won't give up, for the sake of the child, and I only remember one parent rendering her speechless. I sat in the meeting while she outlined, in detail, her concerns about Steven to his adoring father. 'You do realise,' she cautioned, 'that Steven doesn't even know which way up a book goes?'

His father smiled serenely. 'Well,' he said, 'show me a five-year-old who does…'

But perhaps the way things have changed is also summed up in this essay written by a Year 5 child at a friend's school. Shortly after the start of the school year, the class was asked to write about themselves, and what Simon wrote says, I think, a great deal…

'Hello. My name is Simon and I have just started in Year 5. I am not very clever but I have lots of things I'm intrested in. My favorite thing I am intrested in is cars. My uncle stan is mad about cars and he is always fixing them. He likes old cars best and his favorits are sports cars like the TR5 and the MGs. He shows me how to do things like tuning the carbretters. You have to listen to the air with rubber tubing to tune them up. He showed me what you have to do to change a wheel to.

When I grow up I want to have my own garridge and fix peeples cars. When I was small in Miss Browns Class I built this garridge out of all sorts of stuff. It took me a hole week but Kevin helped. We showed it in assembly and our headteecher Mr Andrews said it was briliant. We were so proud when he said that. Mr Andrews did grate assemblis becos he had loads of hobbies. He showed us how to mak things out of wood and how to play guitar and do lodes of amazing science experamants. He even showed us a book he had writen. He said life was about finding lodes of things you could do and its a hole lot better than sitting watching screens all the time. He said everybody is diffrent and it doesn't matter if you are not a genuis at sums or writing, you just have too find the things your good at.

I miss Mr Andrews. Our new headteecher Miss Fisher doesnt smile much or come too our classes too see what we are doing. That is sad becos our class does intresting stuff. My teecher is Mrs Wright and she gives us smashing lessons but she looks nervus when Miss Fisher comes in. Once she came in and said stand up the level fours and sum of us did not understand. She told Mrs Wright that all the children should no if they were level four becos that is what all children shood be. Miss fisher asked my teecher for lots of bits of paper and my teecher looked very worrid.

I asked Mrs Wright if I was won of those level fours and she said no but I was going to be in a specail group with our deputy head Mr Jones to make me won. Last week I started in Mr Jones specail group with some kids from Year 5 and Year 6 and we had to do this hard maths stuff. Some of us didnt understand it but Mr Jones said we had to do it. Mr Jones used to be nice but he look sad trying to get us to understand this stuff.

On Wendsday we did some writin. It was boring and we had to look at things called genres. I had to ask Mr Jones how to spell that. I used to like writin when we could do poems and stories and stuff. Miss Fisher has told Mrs Wright we have to do loads of tests in class and it seems that's about all we are doing. I used to really like school but its getting boring now. Sometimes I tell my mum I'm sick when I'm not reely.

Miss Fisher took asembly yesterday. She said we had to get good writin and maths marks becos it wood help the school and if we were really good at it we cood go to university. I don't want to do that. I want to have a garridge but now I'm wondring if I'm clever enough too do that.'

13

SORRY, I'M SNOWED UNDER

Teachers' Workload

Of all the things that are wrong in education today, it's the obsession with data gathering that annoys me the most.

Why do schools collect so much of it? Not, I think, because most of it is any use to them. Headteachers collect it because they need to protect their schools against inspectors, School Improvement Partners (known as SIPs) and local education officials who think that if you didn't predict Simon's slight slip back in mathematics during week two of the autumn term, you're an idiot and you shouldn't be in charge of a school.

I could never understand why SIPs were needed. They were intended, like school governors, to be a 'critical friend' of the school, who would visit regularly between Ofsted inspections, but did we really need governors, local authorities, Ofsted and SIPs breathing down our necks? A SIP visited a school about six times a year, for half a day, the idea being that he or she would help to identify priorities for improvement and help plan effective change. Ofsted could only inspect, not give detailed or useful advice, so SIPs were supposed to bridge that gap. Perhaps some headteachers couldn't see the wood for the trees and needed these interventions, but I simply found the visits an encumbrance. What really enraged me, however, was when I found a couple of local headteachers getting into the act because not enough SIPs could be recruited, and it then became the source of a second income when these people, I reasoned, should have been in their schools. One of them said to me 'You really ought to get into this, Mike, it's a real gravy train.'

I told my first SIP that I could happily gather together all the tracking data on our children, all the graphs and diagrams and percentages, all the numbers and tick-boxes and charts, and dump the lot in the recycling bin. And it wouldn't have made a scrap of difference to our school. The children would still thrive and achieve. In fact, they'd probably achieve even more, because their teachers would have more time for them. My SIP smiled, but didn't agree. Well, of course she didn't. She'd have been missing out on a lucrative piece of income. So, over tea and a jammy dodger or two, I expounded my non rocket science views yet again…

The teaching staff are the key factor to a school's success. We didn't have vacancies very often, but I took great care over appointments. I wanted lively, interesting people who thoroughly enjoyed being with children, who understood and appreciated their humour, who related well to each other and who could create stimulating classrooms. I wasn't interested in reading references or long application forms that spouted the government mantra that 'Every Child Mattered.' I'd known that every child mattered since the day I started teaching. After spending an hour taking prospective teachers round the school and chatting to them, I'd know whether I was likely to want them on my staff. The interviews for short-listed candidates were informal, interesting and humorous… and the right person would be bubbling over with enthusiasm for what he or she could bring to the school.

Secondly, we kept our classes small, although how we managed it I was never quite sure, because the local authority was always pressing me to take more children. All were under 25. Since I didn't ask my teachers to fill in reams of forms, plan in unnecessary depth, attend meetings every five minutes, or spend hours tracking everything, the children in their classes got a great deal of individual attention. This meant children progressed quickly, happily and well, and our

SATs results (however much I might disagree with the tests) were consistently high. The teachers then showed their appreciation of this freedom, by working exceptionally hard.

Thirdly, we spent money carefully. A school close to mine had a bursar and three administrative officers, one of whom had sole responsibility for collecting dinner money tins and registration. I just had Sandra, a gentle, thoroughly capable, unflappable gem, and Kelvin, an experienced and helpful accountant who popped in once a month to do budget reconciliations. My office was small, sparsely furnished.... and usually full of children showing me work they were proud of. The money we saved went straight back to the children. It was one of the reasons we had a thirty piece school orchestra, extremely rare for a primary school, especially one in a socially deprived area.

And finally, there was always a huge amount going on. Whether it was the opportunity to play in Jazz Group, or act in the summer musical, or write a poem for Poetry Week, or produce an animated film, or become a gymnast, or join the many activity clubs, there was always something to make every child want to get out of bed and come to school. Quality learning followed naturally.

I recently saw a sentence in an Ofsted report which said 'Teachers aren't making use of assessment data to match work to pupils' needs.' Frankly, I thought, this is just management-speak nonsense. If Mrs Smith needed to pore over a pile of data before she could work out why Charlie can't handle subtraction, then she shouldn't be teaching him. We all know most teachers work long hours without complaining, and yet their workload could be reduced instantly if they didn't have to waste time on endless paperwork.

A friend of mine works in a primary school where every lesson has to be planned, in detail, on a sheet of A4. All these have to be handed in to the deputy head, every week. The deputy doesn't teach any more, of course. She doesn't have time. She just looks through piles of planning sheets, writes comments on them, and passes them back. When the teachers have taught the lessons, they have to write a critical appraisal of them, and give them back to the deputy again. It's a wonder they've not collapsed from boredom. And yet a really enjoyable part of teaching, creating stimulating displays in the classroom, is now becoming a job that has to be delegated to classroom assistants. I even knew a school where several teachers had created superb artwork displays and then covered them up with cellophane, so that they could be kept in pristine condition ready for Ofsted's arrival.

Back in 2014, the government introduced the National Workload Agreement for teachers. This was quickly followed by a circular entitled 'Tackling The Workload', and what it contained was fascinating, but typical. Firstly, it told me that the Education Department had allocated money for implementing the scheme. Well fine, I thought, but I didn't get too excited about that, because I knew the money would be swallowed up in administrative committees and schemes. And so it turned out, as I read further. A 'Workforce Agreement Monitoring Group' had been formed, its brief being to turn out 'helpful advisory documents and supportive development material'. Then, I was told about the 'national remodelling team', whose members had all been recruited from the civil service to 'monitor compliance'.

Presumably anyone who wasn't meekly compliant would get taken round the back for a good slap on the wrist. The role of the local education authorities, we were told further down, was to appoint a 'lead facilitator' with 'enhanced resources'. It wasn't essential to appoint one, apparently, but I assumed you could kiss goodbye to any funding if you didn't. Then it was suggested that LEAs should consider buying in support from 'school remodelling advisers', swiftly creating yet another highly paid avenue for the armies of consultants and advisory 'experts' who specialise in helping to bleed schools dry. A week later, my LEA sent me a form to fill in, with lots of boxes in which I was supposed to describe how far I'd got with implementing the agreement, what remained to be done, and when I was likely to do it. Amusingly, though, the form quite obviously wouldn't have reduced my workload. It would have added considerably to it.

So, what did I do about the agreement? As I explained to my SIP, for a start, I didn't make my teachers play the 'pass the piles of paper' game, because all their efforts went to the right places: the classroom and the children's minds. We had no 'business manager.' My admin officer coped easily with her workload because she and I shared administration tasks. The money I saved on all this went back into the classrooms, giving teachers classes smaller than those of all our other local primaries. And that, I told her, really *was* a workload bonus.

I'm all for things that make a difference, but changing fashions are a constant turn-off for would-be teachers. It seems that schools are almost encouraged to be businesses, obsessed by data, charts, targets, value-added percentages, league tables. We must plan lessons down to the tiniest detail, and never deviate from our plans. All this is frequently forced on us by people who've never taught, or who've escaped from the classroom because they couldn't do it anyway.

As well as being visited by my SIP, I was also visited regularly by my LEA inspector, who'd been remodelled as a 'link adviser.' He was a pleasant man, but apart from checking up on my school occasionally to make sure I hadn't gone berserk and eaten the contents of the sand tray, he was also required to peddle some of the dafter documents produced by the local authority and central government, many of which I was always certain he didn't really agree with.

On one visit, he brought with him a document, then used by a number of LEAs, designed to help me decide how good my school was by using 'self-evaluation performance indicators'. The document had ninety pages and, as I thumbed through it, I wondered why it was deemed so necessary to patronise schools and teachers.

When I became a headteacher, much needed to be done in the school. We simply selected the most urgent things and attended to them. Nothing else was given any priority. Simple. As the situation changed, we moved on to the less important things, and then the minor ones. We didn't write it all down. There wasn't any need. We knew exactly where we were going because we discussed it endlessly.

After all, aren't heads, deputies and senior managers supposed to be appointed because they can see the wood for the trees? And doesn't the current practice of producing a mountain of paperwork take people away from actually getting things done?

A page in the document told us to 'identify the school aim you will use to indicate current expectations. For example, it could be to ensure that all pupils achieve and make steady progress in their learning.' I couldn't believe that somebody would be daft enough to write that, and expect teachers not to howl with laughter? You can imagine how I felt about the other eighty nine pages. Come here, Grandma, I need to teach you how to suck eggs.

Then along came a new initiative, a document called the PANDA, (Performance And Assessment Report) which had to be downloaded from the internet, all forty one pages of it, using our own ink, paper and printer. It was designed to show how your school was doing against all the other schools in the country. The report didn't actually get under way until page nine, but there you go; the Office For Standards in Education had never relished using one word when three hundred would do. I'm certain the people who compiled it must have insisted on being paid by the word.

Having sat down and studied the thing, which was rare for me, I didn't know whether to shrug in resignation at the mistakes, or phone up in anger. But as I couldn't stomach the thought of half a dozen button-pushing options and electronic Vivaldi while I was put on hold, I decided against it. Our SATs marking that year had been incorrect, we'd complained, had it corrected, and built the calculation into our own school data. But had the PANDA figures been adjusted? No, of course not. Cross-referencing between huge bureaucratic empires hadn't shown any signs of emerging, but, I thought, give it another millennium or two.

But it wasn't what was written on the paper that bothered me, because I didn't take much notice of it. I was concerned about the paper itself. Remember, my Panda had 41 pages. My governors, of course, all needed a copy to study, as it was an agenda item for the next two meetings and, wow, there were lots of exciting new targets to set. I had sixteen governors, so that was already 656 sheets of paper in total. Plus my copy, which made 697, and a copy for the clerk, which brought it to 738. Naturally, my staff wanted to see it, if only to tut and shake their heads at the inaccuracies, but to stop the photocopier exploding I gave copies to the curriculum leaders only, and they passed it on. This meant 328 more sheets of A4. Add this to the other 738 sheets, and we were up to 1,066 already.

Our school, of course, was a speck in the vast ocean of academia. At the time, there were 26,582 primary schools in the UK, and if they were all running off copies for their governors and senior management teams, we were looking at something like 23,336,412 sheets of paper. If they were making copies for the entire staff, it would have been a lot higher. And that was not counting photocopier wear, the toner cartridges, the printer ink, or the folders and binders. A huge and wasteful industry. And bear in mind, I'm talking about just one report. The PANDA was just a fraction of the tree decimation that reached our schools every year.

But the final straw was page eleven of my PANDA, giving a summary of our recent Ofsted findings. The 'management and efficiency' of the school required some improvement, it said. In our previous Ofsted, exactly the same management team was said to be 'strong, purposeful and efficient'. Perhaps, said one of my teachers, the best place for a PANDA was still up a tree in China. Assuming, of course, there were any trees left.

Three year's into the PANDA's life, my board of governors, understandably, still found many aspects of it bewildering. I was asked if we could arrange a special evening meeting so that I could explain it fully. That year, there was a newly designed PANDA, supposedly a streamlined version, shorter and easier to digest. I downloaded ours with fractionally more interest than usual.

Only to find I didn't understand a bloody word of it.

Not that there were actually many words. The document consisted of pages filled with little graphs, arrows, dotted lines and mathematical signs. One page was covered with so many overlapping squares and crosses it looked as if somebody had been playing battleships, given up, and trodden all over it. Instead of being easier to read, it was totally and utterly incomprehensible. I had no idea whether my school was going up, down, sideways, or hovering, bewildered, in educational limbo. I couldn't find a single sentence I understood, apart from 'This is your school PANDA'. At least the old style document said things like 'Your school is above average in maths compared with similar schools.' I could cope with a sentence like that.

Even when I attended a PANDA training course, which was supposed to show you how to interpret these things meaningfully, I was lost after five minutes. The bloke running the course had previously been a headteacher, but I later discovered he was so obsessive about data crunching, pictograms and bar charts he spent most of his week poring over a computer, and his staff hardly saw him. When he did emerge from his room the children wondered who he was. His headship only lasted two years, though. The DfE knew a boffin when they saw one and he was soon offered a top job in their statistics department.

Why did we have this awful obsession with analysing data, I asked the tutor? The answer reminded me of a final line in The Stepford Wives, when Katherine Ross, trying desperately to rescue her children from an old dark manor house where there are frightening and mysterious goings-on, suddenly realises that she is going to be reborn into one of the 'perfect' Stepford wives. 'Why?' she implores evil scientist and misogynist Patrick O'Neill in utter desperation, 'Why?' 'Because,' he says simply... and terrifyingly... 'we can.'

Computers are now so sophisticated it is possible to cram millions of pieces of information into them. You could probably cram it all into a current mobile phone. Schools are required to collect a staggering amount of data on everything it's possible to collect data on; SATS results, children with additional needs, ethnic origins, free meals, pupil movement, absence patterns... and feed it all to the DfE or the local authority. And what do they do with it? Number-crunch it and send back in the form of indecipherable dots and lines purporting to show trends... which frankly, are often questionable to say the least.

Recently, I looked at a document that had been worked on by forty people and was proudly sent to schools as a definitive method for getting pupil targeting and tracking procedures right... and pleasing OFSTED at the same time. It seems 'outstanding practice' occurs when a pupil can access his personal data on, say, literacy and make informed decisions about it, amending his own targets accordingly. My first thought was to wonder if these forty people had ever had a childhood, because young children simply don't behave like that, and with these current obsessions we really are in danger of messing up a vital part of their lives.

A huge number of ex-pupils always wrote fondly to our school website. Why? Because they enjoyed, and now missed, the sheer richness and variety we offered in their primary years. The music, the poetry, the drama, the art, the enthusiasm for writing that came from an inspired teacher, who'd long ago abandoned the constricting Literacy Hour. Nobody, as far as I know, has ever written 'Thank you for ensuring I had appropriate tracking procedures'.

But it wasn't enough to assemble all this useless data. The DfE also wanted every teacher to be regularly checked, to ensure they knew what they were doing. This had to be done by 'managing their performance'. A teaching staff had to be divided into groups, and then senior managers would meet monthly with their group after school to fill in more forms and assess the work they were doing. And for a while, it seemed headteachers were unable to go for more than a month without another performance management advisory document landing on their desks. Usually, it would say that the rules had changed because a working party had found the last set unworkable. Invariably, the new model meant more work.

One circular of this type had me chuckling into my morning coffee, and for a moment or two I thought somebody with a wry sense of humour in the ivory towers of the education authority had created it to lighten my day. But no, as I read further, I realised it was deadly serious. It described the procedural changes in performance management to be made that year.

On the front page, there was a photograph of two people, a teacher and a reviewer, poring over the teacher's performance management document. This wasn't a few sheets of paper though. It was an entire roll of the stuff. It seemed as if the teacher had spent the whole summer holiday scribbling her life story on a roll of anaglypta. Since they were of similar ages, and didn't have leather patches on their sleeves or white PVA glue on their clothing, it was also difficult to tell which one was the teacher. Page two gave details of a course designed to update heads on current requirements, and I quote the opening sentence in full. You'll probably think I'm making it up.

'The new performance management regulations require reviewers to align school development priorities with professional development needs, demanding of reviewers a thorough understanding of the teacher's standards and progression possibilities and the ability to set objectives producing outcomes in the form of evidence upon which the overall performance of the teacher will be judged.'

Then we're told the training course would be run by an 'consultant experienced in performance management.' It didn't mention whether he actually knew anything about schools.

Like so many other initiatives schools were smothered with, the notion of performance management left me cold. If senior managers were properly in touch with the teaching staff and their needs, I saw no purpose in it. I had forty adults… teaching and non-teaching… working in my school, all at different stages of their lives and careers.

Some were perfectly content to carry on doing what they were doing, some were interested in promotion, some wanted to further their careers in other ways. If a teacher or a teaching assistant wanted to sit and chat about their career with me after school, that was fine, and my door was always open.

If I thought somebody should be considering a move upwards, I'd seek them out and have a chat about it. I'd know if a teacher was having problems, or needed practical support, because I visited classrooms daily and I was naturally interested in what was going on. But I wasn't at all interested in putting lots of writing on bits of paper to justify myself.

In fact, I didn't know any good, effective school which undertook performance management exactly as it was supposed to be done. It was a massive amount of work, sorting staff into groups, with harassed team leaders trying to find time to interview them all when their time would have been better spent organising their classrooms. Naturally, there was plenty of form filling to be done if you followed the prescribed path, and then there were follow-up meetings to check if 'targets' had been achieved. Then, before you knew it, a new year would have arrived, and the whole sorry cycle would need to be started again. The benefits? Well, if you were a senior manager who didn't like children, the work load was a good way of avoiding them. And Ofsted would undoubtedly pat you on the back when they saw the size of your file, but frankly I thought that Parkinson's Law had never been more prevalent. Mr P must have been chuckling in his grave.

ICT, of course, rapidly changed the face of education, often in many ways I supported. When my teachers designed lessons involving the electronic whiteboard, I watched with interest as they used an array of media… all immediately available via the classroom internet, DVDs, audio files and other clever ancillaries. Children, I won't tell you how a spider makes its web, or show you a picture in a book, here is a film of a web actually being made….

The downside, for me at least, was the use of computers for educational number crunching. We tell the computer the children's ages, their country of origin, the results of our constant assessments of them, their attendance patterns... everything except their shoe sizes, though it wouldn't surprise me if we're asked to put those in before long. Then we push a button, and the computer juggles all this information. It tells us what levels the child should achieve each year, how the child compares with others the same age, where the child's strengths and weaknesses lie, and it helps us to set 'targets'. People like SIPs and Ofsted love targets. They can check them and rap schools over the knuckles if they're not achieved.

In fact, a computer tells us.... pretty much everything a school should already know!

Yesterday, I spoke to an extremely competent infant teacher. Her school uses one of the highly sophisticated... and extremely expensive... commercial packages for tracking and targeting. Her headteacher, apparently, rarely speaks to a child or visits a classroom, but pop into his room and ask him about achievement and he'll bore you rigid with computer screens and wall charts full of information purporting to show his children are securely 'on track'.

The teacher has a different view. 'Every teacher here spends at least a couple of hours, every week, typing a mass of information into the computer. In reality, much of it is unreliable, because we're dealing with unpredictable little human beings. Then the computer prints out lots of pretty lines, graphs and pie charts to tell me where my children are at. It pleases the head, and senior management spends hours analysing it. But I simply don't need it. Nor do the other teachers. We already know exactly what our children can and can't do.'

And that, surely, is the point. Any half decent teacher worth her salt will know her children thoroughly. At the start of the year she'll already have talked at length to the teachers who taught the class during the previous year. She'll have looked in detail at their work. She'll know the saints and the sinners, the shy ones and the ones who've always got a lot to say. She'll know which children have additional needs and who has a particular talent that needs nurturing.

But the DfE leans on the local authorities for data and the local authorities then pressure their schools.

When a new form called the *School Workforce Census* arrived, it bounced into school via the local education authority. When she saw it, our secretary's mouth dropped open in astonishment. Ten screens … eighty three questions in all… had to be completed for every adult working in the building. You couldn't duplicate information from one person's file to another, either. It would have been helpful, for example, to call up the screens for your male staff and enter 'Mr' in them all at the click of a button. But no, you had to do them one at a time.

Then I too stared at the questions in disbelief. The first screen asked for a person's initials, surname, salutation, known name, legal surname, maiden name, initials and second name. Then address, e-mail, home phone, mobile, passport, nationality, ethnicity, mother tongue, religion, disability, CRB, ID check, references… you name it, it was all in there, apart from the colour of their shoes. I calculated it would take my admin officer two days just to interview staff and fill in one of these forms, even if she had the time, which she didn't.

And then…. hand on heart I'm not making this up… there were questions about your car. Why on earth would the DfE want to know the make of our cars? And not only the make: they wanted the licence plate number and the colour as well. I suppose they wouldn't be… surely not… intending to market all this information, would they?

Irritated, I phoned a local authority statistics officer. No, he didn't know why they wanted my staff car colours or number plates either, and he suggested phoning the Department for Education. At first nobody at the DfE had any idea which form I was talking about, but after being passed from official to official I was eventually told that they certainly didn't want to know anything about my car, or its colour, or how many gears it had, or if there was enough room in the back for Granny. It must have been the local authority that wanted the info. I phoned the local authority back, suggesting they might have been telling me a porkie, and incredibly, I was told it must have been the school that had added the car questions to the survey. I was speechless, and wrote about it in my weekly Times Educational Supplement column, where it was spotted by a journalist on a national Sunday newspaper. The following week, I was very amused to see that he'd created an extremely amusing leading feature about it.

I had no intention of asking my admin officer to waste her time unless the DfE sent me a letter of explanation. Naturally, I heard nothing more. Although frankly, I was tempted to say every teacher owned a Porsche, the average age of the staff was 105, everybody's religion was Russian Orthodox and the teachers only had qualifications in raffia and Morris dancing. And see what they made of that.

For me, the end of one summer term vividly demonstrated how differently education authorities and schools viewed the purpose of education. We'd had a stunning carnival in which every class created colourful costumes and head-dresses, a hugely successful musical with a cast of eighty, concerts by our school orchestra and our Jazz Group, the Summer Fair, and the annual Leaver's Concert written and performed by a truly delightful Year 6. All things that children love and are an important part of a thriving primary school. The only downside was a slightly snotty e-mail from the LEA, telling us we hadn't forwarded our Key Stage 2 teacher assessments for the SATs and under no circumstances were we to go off on our cruise to the Bahamas without sending them. The statistics department, the e-mail said, was exceptionally busy at this time of year, so kindly get a move on.

How sad, I thought, that data was all the LEA seemed to care about. Then I began to wonder what the authority actually did with all the assessments, so I sent a quick email to the person and asked. Back came a reply saying she wasn't quite sure, but she'd forward my question to a senior member of the team. Unfortunately, this person didn't write back, probably because they didn't know the answer either, so I wrote again. My question was forwarded to an officer in the Research and Statistics department, who told me that teacher assessments were a 'statutory requirement'. Frankly, I always had my doubts about 'statutory requirements'. How statutory were they in reality, I wondered?

But anyway, that didn't answer my question. The officer had sent an attachment with the e-mail, but unfortunately the attachment wouldn't open. I requested it again, but this time the file was corrupt and just displayed a string of funny little boxes. ICT at its most endearing. But this didn't seem to matter, because the officer had added a note saying the guidance didn't mention what the government did with the data, just that schools must send it. And, he admitted, he hadn't seen the data published anywhere in recent years. Curiouser and curiouser....

I asked my secretary to get the form up on screen, and we had a look at it. Unsurprisingly, it wasn't just a case of filling in the teachers' assessment of overall levels for Maths, Science and English. All three subjects had been broken down into learning areas and it meant a considerable amount of extra work. This, when the teachers' efforts were concentrated on all the exciting, child-centred things we were working on. Since we had no idea what use the government was going to make of the data, or even if they were going to publish any of it, I suggested that she should look at the SATs level a child had achieved in a subject, then just fill up all the boxes on his chart with the same level. Nobody, I said, would look at it, let alone bother to question it. And they didn't. As long as the boxes were ticked, the authority was happy.

Sometimes politicians and newspaper columnists spend a lot of time denigrating the teaching profession. What are teachers complaining about? They only work until 3.30pm and are on holiday for thirteen weeks a year. And we'd all like some of that, wouldn't we. We know that isn't true, but it's surprising how many people have sympathy with this notion. This was one of the reasons I was compelled to watch a TV programme called *'Who'd Be a Teacher?'* which examined various points of view in the light of some planned strike action. A journalist, who received much publicity when he setup an independent, state-funded free school, expounded his reasons for thinking that teachers don't really have such a hard time of it. He stated that most schools don't start until 9am anyway, presumably offering this as evidence that teachers could enjoy a good lie-in. Was he really saying that teachers in his school were not required to turn up until 9am? How on earth would they set about preparing their classrooms for the day?

Fortunately, we quickly heard the other side of the story. A teacher was shown organising her two sons early in the morning, before busily gathering everything she needed for the day and setting off to work. We watched her driving anxiously through heavy traffic. We watched her teaching. We saw her running lunchtime and after-school activities. We followed her home, where it was her turn to prepare the family meal. Then she settled down to work again, marking books, planning and preparing teaching aids. She was enthusiastic, dedicated and conscientious, and she stated proudly that, apart from the constant and unnecessary data gathering, she loved her job. But she also made it quite clear that anybody going into teaching and expecting an easy ride would be in for a shock, because it is impossible to do the job successfully without working many hours outside the school day.

I suspect the journalist would have said this teacher was not typical. But in my experience, most teachers are exactly like her and I have met very few who don't want to do the best they can for the children in their charge. They thoroughly enjoy the constant challenges, the fact that two days are never the same, the creativity and inventiveness of the work and the sheer pleasure of being in the company of young people. That's not to say it isn't possible to do a poor job. It is, but I've seen this far more among senior managers than class teachers. There are always going to be the people who prefer to spend much of their time typing up policies, documents and staff instructions instead of coming into contact with any children, the deputies who relish monitoring other people, rather than doing any teaching themselves. But these people certainly aren't the norm. It's the sheer pleasure of the job that spurs teachers and good leaders to give so much of their time. I'm sure they will continue to do so, but it would be nice if their efforts were more readily recognised.

The horrors of Covid and what it did to us have, thank heavens, largely moved on, but at the very least it revealed the life threatening dangers medical staff put themselves in, the determination with which they still carried on with their jobs and cared for their patients, the grief experienced by so many families as their loved ones died alone and in dreadful physical pain, the incompetence of government ministers and the greed of some private firms who were providing personal protection equipment, which sometimes was simply not up to the job. Every Thursday we stood outside our homes bashing saucepans and making a loud noise to show how much we supported the nurses and doctors, as it is always those people at the coalface who have the worst experiences.

But when the Mid Staffordshire NHS scandal broke in 2005, I listened to the reports with mounting horror. After all, in a decade or so I could be needing help and care from the health system that we believed was the best in the world. I could hardly believe that it could have been allowed to go on for so long, and on such a scale. But as I listened to the nurses, medical students, doctors and hospital assistants talking, another concern began to gnaw at me. 'We are in constant fear of speaking out,' one nurse said. 'There is a culture of bullying and our jobs could be in danger. It's easy to see what is going wrong, but few are brave enough to say anything, and if you do, you are ignored or cautioned.'

But wasn't that happening in education, too, I thought? In a recent survey of teachers, a staggering 50 per cent said they had been subjected to pressure or bullying from harassed senior managers.

'It's the awful target and tick-box culture,' another nurse said. 'The constant targets mean that patient care is actually worse. I even have to tick a box when I've put a wrist band on a patient. It's ridiculous. I can see when I've put one on, for heaven's sake.' Isn't education obsessed with the target and tick-box culture, too? Primary schools used to be places where children could be introduced to an exciting array of learning experiences. Weren't they now measured simply by statistics, data, graphs, pie charts and how many level 4s could be squeezed out of Year 6? Is there a school in the country where an inspection team has deliberately not looked at its data, to form an unbiased initial impression? 'The trouble is,' a third nurse said, 'the management has no real interest or involvement with the patients. I was told that targets absolutely have to be achieved. We have even been leaving very sick patients to process minor complaints, to manipulate the target figures. And the paperwork... half of it is useless and simply takes time away from being with the patient, but health-and-safety rules and regulations demand that we do it, and I'm constantly worn out.'

It all sounded so familiar. Heads, deputies and managers moving away from the children and into offices where they can performance-manage overworked staff and make demands that are becoming increasingly unrealistic. 'The number of audits we're subjected to is beyond belief,' an exasperated doctor said. 'When I dared to point out that the audits weren't useful or helpful, I was told by the leader of the team that they had organised a further audit to find out why. He genuinely thought that was a sensible suggestion!'

But isn't that how Ofsted works? If they say a school is inadequate because the data aren't good enough don't they constantly harass the school with mini inspections every five minutes rather than offer helpful and supportive guidance? At Mid-Staffordshire, we had the horrifying statistic of the number of patients who had probably died needlessly. I thought: 'Well, at least teachers aren't in much danger of losing their lives.' Then I remembered Ruth Perry, the headteacher who took her own life, the teacher who was ill on the first morning of her Ofsted inspection but crawled into school and collapsed, dying, on the floor. The teacher in my own school who had such a difficult time with Ofsted inspectors she had a breakdown. And developed cancer shortly afterwards. The parallels seemed rather too obvious.

And that will be the subject of our final chapter.

14

WHO INSPECTS THE INSPECTORS?

The OFSTED Problem

In January 2023, headteacher Ruth Perry took her own life, after her school had been downgraded following an Ofsted inspection.

She had been at the helm of her school for more than ten years, and was a popular and successful school leader. At the inquest, where testimony was heard from colleagues and medical professionals of the mental distress she had suffered during and after the inspection of the school, the coroner ruled that her suicide was contributed to by the Ofsted inspection, The report described the inspection as rude and intimidating, stating that during and after the inspection, Ruth Perry's mental health deteriorated significantly. There was, rightly, huge outrage across the country about her sad death. Just how could a school inspection cause such a devastating thing as this?

Shockingly, Ruth Perry was not the first member of the teaching profession for this to happen to. There have been other deaths and serious mental breakdowns that Ofsted has contributed to, and certainly many more across the country, possibly in their hundreds, that haven't been reported.

A brief glance on the internet reveals the tip of the iceberg. Typically, one senior teacher says his last Ofsted inspection remains a 'trauma'. In the staffroom with other teachers after the inspectors left, having delivered the verdict that the school had plummeted from 'outstanding' to 'requires improvement', he says everyone was 'ashen faced'. His deputy started having a heart attack right in front of him. He explains that this sort of rating sends the school into a downward spiral. 'Funding falls because parents suddenly don't want to send their children to your school, and good staff start leaving,' he says.

It's hardly surprising that Ofsted affects family members too. Partners say the pressure and fear surrounding Ofsted inspections has become completely out of hand. There is sickness, there is extreme worry and teachers often get no sleep at all during their school inspections. Very few headteachers say they are afraid of their schools being put under the microscope. What bothers them is the inconsistency, the poor quality of inspectors, the aggression, the tendency to bully, the fact that primary schools are sometimes landed with inspectors who have only taught in secondary schools, and a report at the end of it all that often doesn't reflect the school at all. There is also a strong argument that heads in inner city schools in rundown areas, with families in crisis and too few social workers, have the odds stacked against them. One headteacher says 'I can keep calling the local authority about referring a particular child who is appallingly behaved or exhibiting sexualised behaviour they might have learnt at home, and nothing happens. If Ofsted turn up and see that, the school will be in special measures.'

Another headteacher, and former inspector, recalls how she took part in an inspection where the head had been in post for just over two weeks. The school was put into special measures before the new headteacher had the remotest chance of turning it around. 'The lead inspector tends to have a view before the team arrives on what the verdict will be,' she says. 'They can make up their minds in ten minutes, and everything else is about justifying that view.' Another former inspector says 'You still have to stick rigidly to the Ofsted framework, and I disagreed fundamentally with what it was measuring. Giving a school a one word judgment and making that public is simply wrong. Schools and communities can be ruined just on the basis of that word.' A youth mental health worker says 'I left teaching because I couldn't sleep or eat during Ofsted inspections. I started losing my hair because of stress. I've seen headteachers physically and mentally broken. I saw one man break down in tears and walk out. He was five years away from retiring, but he didn't ever come back.'

Ofsted costs the taxpayer £150 million a year and it costs approximately £7,200 to inspect a school. 75% of schoolteachers and 82% of senior leaders have now said that inspections negatively impacted their mental health and wellbeing. So what level of fear can possibly cause these outpourings? After all, schools have always been inspected, haven't they? And wouldn't parents, especially, be extremely concerned if they weren't? To find the answers we need to look back at the history of school inspection, before we can come to an understanding of what is happening now.

In Victorian times, teachers also dreaded a visit from the school inspector. If the knowledge and academic performance of the children wasn't up to scratch on the day the inspector visited, or the children were nervous and performed badly, the teacher's wages suffered and she was in danger of losing her job. It was hardly a fair system, but all the evidence indicates that today's school inspection system is probably even worse.

State schools have always been inspected of course, and it is right that they should be. After all, how else will taxpayers be satisfied that the education of their children is of a good enough standard? The possibility of a visit from an inspector is a sure-fire way of keeping a school on its toes, but the manner in which schools should be inspected has always been a matter for intense debate, which is why we are still far from getting it right.

When I began my headship at the start of the eighties, local authorities across the country appointed their own school inspectors. In London at that time, the Inner London Education Authority appointed inspectors centrally and allocated them to the boroughs. They'd often been successful headteachers who would have an intimate knowledge of the borough they were appointed to, and this was important. The needs of a school like mine, in an area of enormous social deprivation, were vastly different from those in a comfortable tree-lined suburb just a few miles away. Because inspectors knew the requirements of their schools well, they always attended headship appointments. Indeed, they invariably knew far more about education, and the school, than the school governors themselves. Then, once a headteacher had been appointed, the inspector popped into the school regularly, until he or she was satisfied that things were running smoothly. The inspector's role was to be supportive, helpful, critical where necessary and to occasionally find a little extra funding for projects that a new head wanted to initiate, especially if the outgoing head had let things slide a bit. Certainly, this had been my experience, and I was grateful for the support I'd received.

Occasionally, I was visited by an inspector from Her Majesty's Inspectorate. HMIs were highly trained and exceptionally astute inspectors who travelled the country and usually only stayed in a school for a day. Nevertheless, in that short time they were able to sum up what was going on with consummate skill. At the end of one in-depth visit several years into my headship, an HMI settled comfortably into one of my chairs after school and said 'Mike, your school is extremely impressive. It's no wonder the children are happy, learning well and involved. But your room is a tip. It's the first port of call for parents and visitors and it really doesn't create a very good impression.' I hadn't even considered it, but he was absolutely right. My room was filled with equipment needing repair, musical instruments we had nowhere to store, sets of books being sorted for classrooms, and even a pile of lost property. I attended to it immediately.

In those days inspectors were often far more of a help than hindrance. The school only saw them a couple of times a year, and even a local inspector with an inflated view of his own importance was little more than a minor irritant who'd be gone by the end of the day. And anyway, I welcomed inspectors. My school was running extremely well and I was proud of it. I enjoyed showing off what we were achieving, the staff were happy and relaxed and the children loved chatting to visitors about their work.

And then, in the early nineties, the method of inspecting schools changed dramatically. Following the introduction of the national curriculum, designed to ensure that every state school in the country followed a prescribed curriculum in each subject, the Conservative government decided it would also be a good idea if all state schools were inspected in exactly the same way. This, it said, would be the fairest way of doing things. Parents already knew exactly what their children were learning, so now, with the new radically revised inspection format, they would also know how their child's school compared with any other school across the borough or, indeed, schools country wide. Increasingly sophisticated computers in schools also meant the gathering of pupil achievement data was rapidly beginning to assume much greater importance, and the government could easily analyse and disseminate it. Every school was already receiving an 'Autumn Analysis Package' detailing exactly how its academic achievement compared with other schools.

But there were very serious flaws in the government's reasoning. Schools vary enormously in ability intake, local environment, social conditions and staffing levels. Some schools are highly selective in their intake, while others achieve exceptional results because the children are extremely able, even if their teachers aren't necessarily of the highest quality. Some schools, working extremely hard with a low ability intake, can appear to be achieving poorly academically even when they are doing the very best they can for their pupils, and actually achieving many good things. Equally, data and statistics can be notoriously unreliable, sometimes giving a very distorted view of a school.... and, whisper it… they can be manipulated.

Nevertheless, the great inspection initiative went ahead, and the Office For Standards In Education, shortened to Ofsted, was born. It was initially decided that schools would be inspected every four years. At first, school inspections lasted a week and a team of at least six inspectors, plus a 'lay' inspector from the general public, would descend on a school and investigate every aspect of it. Since many schools were now being inspected at the same time, contracting companies had to be set up and a virtual army of inspectors recruited, and although some inspectors were very capable the abilities of many were seriously questionable. Simply because so many were needed, it wasn't hard to be selected, and more than a few disillusioned teachers, deputies and heads saw it as an easy escape route out of the classroom or school office. Incredibly, even people not involved with education were also recruited. Schools could therefore be put under the microscope by briefly trained people who had little knowledge of local conditions and who often didn't have enough relevant experience to make valid or worthwhile judgements. To add to schools' concerns, a chief inspector with very little teaching experience had been appointed, and he attacked teachers as never before, saying that 15% of them were ineffective and that Ofsted would be playing a strong role in rooting them out. The number seemed to have been conjured from highly questionable evidence, and it was virtually a mandate to bully. The only upside was that schools would be given more than a term's notice of an impending inspection, at least giving them ample time to prepare for the ordeal.

During my years as a headteacher, my school had four Ofsted inspections. None of them were particularly pleasant, and all were very stressful for my staff. However, one of the inspections was an experience never to be forgotten. Until that point, we had considered ourselves to be a highly successful school. Our reputation was strong, we were very oversubscribed, I had no problem with finding good teachers, the children and parents were happy and satisfied, and so was the local authority. I had no idea that I would soon be experiencing the most worrying and frightening week of my entire career.

Two weeks before the inspection began, the team leader visited us for the day to gather the necessary paperwork, clarify arrangements for the inspection, and introduce herself to the staff and children. The day went well and she was made welcome by everyone in the school. She was impressed on her tour of the building and commented positively on the colourful displays in the classrooms and around the school, stating that we obviously had much to be pleased about. We showed her our latest exciting project, an environmental park area being built at the far end of the junior playground. As she left the school she was asked how she had enjoyed her day and she said that our children seemed exceptionally well behaved and hard working. Then, after the evening meeting with the parents, mandatory at the time, she telephoned to say that they were highly supportive of the school's work. It all sounded promising, but one thing nagged at me. When we'd first met, I'd asked the inspector why she'd left headship to join Ofsted, and she'd replied that she'd become bored with being a headteacher. This seemed very odd to me. I didn't understand how anybody could find the job less than fascinating. I was also concerned that the lay inspector would be a farmer's wife. I hoped her knowledge of the workings of a tough London primary was greater than my knowledge of milking a cow.

On the first day of the inspection the sky was formidably dark, the rain torrential and the forecast was for more of the same. We were obviously going to be suffering wet playtimes and lunchtimes, meaning a greater likelihood of the children being fractious. One of the inspectors arrived fifty minutes late, saying that she'd travelled for hours in the rain and traffic to get to the school. There wasn't a great deal of sympathy; my teachers had all been in school since the crack of dawn, despite the appalling weather. The manner of the lead inspector seemed to have changed too. There was a stiff formality, apparent in our first assembly. Since every child in Key Stage 2 played at least one musical instrument, we had prepared a short concert and the children were excited about showing how well they played and sang. The inspector, however, seemed unmoved. Some of the children, she felt, were 'over blowing' their recorders. How, I wondered, could anybody not be impressed by such a large group of small children playing the Chorus of the Hebrew Slaves, not an easy piece by any means, with so much passion?

After assembly the teachers hurried the children back to their classrooms. I'd forgotten how quiet the school is during an inspection. For the teachers it had been the culmination of many weeks of preparation and the children caught the air of urgency and anxiety. The morning passed slowly and then, at lunchtime, the lead inspector said she'd like to talk to me in my office. I left my lunch untouched and hurried upstairs. 'I'm afraid we've seen a great deal of unsatisfactory teaching this morning,' she said. 'We're being generous, but from tomorrow we shall be very rigorous indeed.' I was stunned. I knew my teachers well, and there had been hardly any staff changes since the last inspection. Then she talked about the dangers of the loose bricks on the building site in the playground, and it took me a moment to realise that she was referring to our burgeoning environmental park area. I explained that the bricks were going to be built into plant beds within a few days, but she said that until they were cemented into position it would be possible for the children to throw them around. I said that my children weren't prone to throwing bricks around, but I would ask the premises officer to organise extra barriers to make sure. After school the lead inspector visited me again, saying that more unsatisfactory lessons had been seen and I might want to tell my staff to be very diligent with their lessons from Tuesday onwards. I pressed the issue, asking her to explain which lessons had been unsatisfactory, and why. She quoted three, all taught by experienced teachers, running the lessons down in a casually destructive manner. She expressed doubts about one teacher's ability to be the literacy co-ordinator for the school... and yet that teacher's work had been chosen as a model by the local authority.

The inspectors left for the day and staff flocked to my office. They complained that inspectors had often only seen parts of lessons because they'd arrived late, or early, or not at all when they'd promised they would. Some had arrived fifteen minutes into a lesson and then left shortly afterwards, missing the beginning and end completely. On entering the room labelled The Nursery Class, an inspector had asked how old the children were. Although clear documentation had been given about the layout of the building, a Year 1 class had been confused with a Reception class, Year 2 work was mistaken for Year 1, and a Year 4 class was thought to be Year 5. Teachers also felt the inspectors deliberately sat in unnecessarily conspicuous positions and in one case actually at the teacher's desk, shuffling through everything on it, even though a chair had been placed discreetly at the back of the classroom. Feedback had been promised and not given, and only one inspector had spoken to any children. The day ended moodily with many teachers disgruntled, one in tears, and the weather forecast promising heavy rain for the rest of the week.

We managed to grind through Tuesday, the staff looking more ashen by the hour, and then on Wednesday the lead inspector informed me that something would have to be done about the 'building site'. The additional barriers wouldn't keep the children away, she said, and one of the inspectors had seen a child throw a brick during the lunch period. I was astonished. The children were extremely enthusiastic about the park area and although the bricks had been there for a month, nobody had touched one. Her tone suggested the inspection might stop if the matter wasn't addressed and I spoke quickly to our premises officer, who immediately hired a skip to remove all the bricks from the site. He was upset and very angry, since we'd need to buy another consignment before the builders arrived or we'd have no plant beds.

The situation quickly deteriorated further. One of my teachers had been with me for many years and had proved herself an outstanding teacher, much respected by younger staff and parents. Now she looked drawn, tired and extremely upset. Her history lesson had been savaged the previous day, although only a small part of it had actually been seen. Then her gymnastics lesson had been grudgingly labelled satisfactory, the inspector saying that no words of encouragement had been given to the children, an accusation she strongly denied. Anxious and distressed, she asked if I would be a witness in any future observed lessons.

I called an emergency staff meeting after school. Complaints tumbled out. Children's work had been sent to the inspectors on Monday and most of it still hadn't been returned. Some inspectors didn't appear to know whether they were supposed to offer feedback to the teachers. Inspectors had yawned through parts of lessons. Much school documentation either hadn't been read properly, or had been misinterpreted. The inspector covering religious education had stated that the school didn't celebrate all the children's religions, although she was forced to retract the comment when the teacher responsible for our RE curriculum gave her a list of the readily visible work displays in the classrooms.

Following the meeting, the teacher of the history and gymnastics lessons spent an hour crying in her room. Two other teachers were in tears, and for the first time in my career, I had no sleep at all that night, worrying about my staff. I was extremely tempted to halt the inspection, call in the contractor, and refuse to co-operate further, but then the school would have been forced to start the inspection again, and there was no guarantee that a replacement team would be any better than the one we were enduring. The following day questions were often aggressively suspicious, and many teachers felt that the inspection was all about trying to catch them out rather than assess them constructively. Towards the end of the week the staff had raised so many issues I called the lead inspector into my room and told her I intended to lodge a formal complaint, and that from now on I would not speak to any of the inspectors without a witness present. It was bitterly disappointing, as just a week earlier we'd been so optimistic.

Four school days had never passed so slowly. I hadn't the slightest faith in the inspectors, and I wouldn't have employed any of them. I had never seen my teachers so angry and upset, and on the Thursday evening, after the staff had gone home tired and anxious, I sat dejectedly in the staffroom with my deputy, waiting for the verdict. When it finally came, at 7.45, it wasn't as bad as we'd feared. But then a comment, almost an aside, immediately heightened the tension again. Under the current regulations, we were told, the inspectors had to decide whether we fell into a category known as 'coasting', because their interpretation of the data showed that our test results had been slipping slightly for the past four years. We were astounded. It wasn't true, and after the meeting I hastily scoured my filing cabinets for information to prove it. Right until the last moments of this inspection, we felt we had been fighting an unfair battle just to prove our worth. I went home miserable and depressed. Schools rarely complain about their Ofsted inspections, however unfair they are, and for understandable reasons. It is far easier to accept the verdict, try to bring the school back to normal as quickly as possible and leave the bad memories behind, rather than challenge a huge piece of government machinery. Especially as it would be another four years before they came again.

Now I began to understand why the chief inspector had proudly stated that schools were more than happy with the current form of inspection, because only three percent had ever complained. But neither I, nor my staff, were willing to leave things as they were. What we had experienced was unfair, and if nothing was done about it we knew the same team could move on to other schools and cause the same distress. I had told the lead inspector we were going to complain formally, and now we had to see it through to the bitter end, however long it might take.

Fortunately, the Easter holiday followed our inspection, and it was a much needed break for everybody, although I had little chance to rest. I spent most of it assembling a lengthy document, collating all the grievances that staff and governors had raised and showing how I felt the Ofsted guidelines for the conduct of inspectors had been clearly breached. I also decided to ask for the names of the last three schools inspected by senior members of the team, as it occurred to me that a precedent might be established. A meeting of the governing body had been arranged at the start of the new term, to discuss the inspection, and I knew it was going to be important to have the governors onside. Those who had been in school during the inspection knew very well what we, and they, had experienced and they were supportive of our complaint, apart from Anthony, who always had a great deal to say but rarely followed it with any action.

'There is no precedent for a complaint like this,' he said. 'I can't give my support unless I know in detail what went on.'

'You were invited in during the inspection,' I replied. 'But you said you were having a very busy week. And you have all the documentation in front of you. That has all the detail you need.'

'Well, perhaps so, but I haven't had time to read it yet. We need a working party to examine all the relevant issues.'

One of the parent governors groaned audibly. 'I don't agree. We don't want a time-wasting working party. Mr Kent and the teachers are obviously very angry and unhappy, we all know this is a popular and successful school, my children love it here, and I think it is important that we help'.

There was a murmur of agreement and the chair of governors turned in my direction. 'I think we're broadly supportive of what you want to do, Mike, but you need to be aware of what you'll be up against. From what I've read, you'll need to deal with the inspection contractor first, and then Ofsted if you get no satisfaction. If that doesn't work you'll need to go to the independent adjudicator, and then if you still receive no satisfaction, to an ombudsman. Frankly, I don't think there'll be much chance of success.'

'I know,' I said. 'But I can't let this go without trying.'

'Then do it. But keep us closely informed.'

The following morning I posted my document to the inspection contractor, expecting to wait a while for a reply, but it came within days. There was concern that we'd been upset by our inspection and my document would also need to be passed to the lead inspector for her comments. The contractor's own principal inspector would then make a considered judgement. And sorry, but it wasn't within their brief to tell me which other schools had been inspected by this team.

Three months passed, and I jogged the contractor's memory. I was told that a reply was on its way, but the lead inspector was very busy on another school inspection and a complaint document as detailed as mine had never been received before. I pointed out that I was very busy too, probably even busier than the lead inspector, but I'd managed to put my document together quickly and I saw no reason why a reply should take so long. It arrived soon afterwards and I handed copies to my staff. The response simply increased their anger. It was clear the inspectors' versions of events were completely different from our own and in some cases we couldn't even recognise the scenarios they were describing.

Then, after a random but not very optimistic search on the internet, I couldn't believe my luck when I discovered a school that had also been inspected recently by members of our team, although I hesitated before calling the headteacher. Would she tell me the conduct of the inspectors had been fine? Had her school received glowing praise? Was I wrong in my assessment of our own school? I needn't have worried. The school had gone through a very similar experience to us and the written reports were almost interchangeable. The staff, just like mine, were thoroughly demoralised afterwards.

'My teachers work their backs off, and so do I,' the headteacher told me when I phoned. 'I'm working all hours trying to keep up with everything. This was never an easy school, but we've turned it around considerably in the last three years and I simply couldn't do more. Then this happens.' Two months later, I learned that the headteacher was taking early retirement, still angry and upset over what had happened. Her teachers were distraught, and it made me even more determined.

Shortly afterwards, we were sent our Ofsted report to read through before it was published. There were spelling and grammatical errors, paragraphs that didn't make sense, sentences that contradicted each other, and serious factual errors. I sent it straight back, insisting it was altered and re-typed before I would look at it again. Then, out of the blue, I received a letter from an Ofsted official. Serious complaints had been received from the inspectors about the 'hostility and intimidation' they had been subjected to by me and my teachers. In a vaguely threatening manner, he stated that he would be sending a copy of his letter to the chief inspector. Then, towards the end of the school year, we received a letter from the contractor's senior administration officer. Our views had been carefully examined, together with the responses from the inspectors, and he had made a brave attempt at sifting the wealth of detail on all the issues raised. He explained that he was replying in place of their principal inspector, who was on long term sick leave. Since the teacher worst affected by our inspection was also now on long term sick leave, it seemed a bizarre case of tit for tat.

The administration officer visited a fortnight later. He'd been a policeman in South London, a lay inspector, and a chair of governors, and he had a passionate interest in primary education. After an intense hour of discussion we had to inform him that we were still dissatisfied with the contractor's responses, and now intended to pursue our complaint through Ofsted itself. Our dossier, now over an inch and a half thick, was posted to the Ofsted complaints department the next day. I heard nothing for weeks.

When I eventually phoned out of sheer frustration, an official apologised and said they had no knowledge of the dossier, although the name of the school did 'ring a bell'. He would look into it and phone back. Half an hour later a different person phoned and said that although it had arrived, it had unfortunately been accepted by a temporary staff member and left underneath a pile of documents. Nevertheless, it would be attended to as soon as possible, although due to their heavy workload this could take up to three months. I pointed out that it was already more than nine months since our inspection.

Another five months passed, and Ofsted's tactics were becoming clear. Each time I phoned, I could never obtain the person I had previously spoken to, and there were lengthy delays before any letters were replied to. Also, the contractor's administration officer was now denying what he'd said to us, and I suspected he'd been instructed not to comment further. Tired of this seemingly deliberate prevarication I wrote and then telephoned again, demanding that the dossier was passed to the independent adjudicator without further delay. An official wrote back, apologising for the delay, but assuring me that our complaint was receiving Ofsted's full attention and that the dossier had now indeed been passed on.

A full fourteen months after our inspection, the final response arrived. On many of the issues, sympathy was expressed but the adjudicator had been unable to make a judgement because the versions given by both sides were so different. Nevertheless, just over half of our complaints had been upheld and this, she said, would be brought to the registered inspector's attention. The team would be allowed to continue inspecting, but there would be careful monitoring by an experienced HMI to ensure it was undertaken correctly.

We had made our point, and it was a victory of sorts, when Ofsted was in its relative infancy. In common with teachers across the country, our hope was that Ofsted would change, adapt and improve its practice through meaningful professional discussion with people at the chalkface. Unfortunately, it has done nothing of the sort. The inspection system has now been in existence for over a quarter of a century, the public has been conditioned to judge a school by its current Ofsted report, and each year with government backing Ofsted has tightened its stranglehold on education... regularly altering its inspection criteria so that teachers are constantly wondering whether they are up to date with current requirements, although there are plenty of firms out there making a buck by offering to tell you. An Ofsted inspection is now the thing most feared by schools, to the extent that the whole of a school's agenda is often geared towards pleasing the inspectors.

During the last twenty years, schools were required to provide vast quantities of data on children's progress. An Ofsted team would examine this before coming into a school, and then look for evidence that corroborated what the data seemed to be saying. It was an absurd way of judging a school. Data can be manipulated, it is often highly unreliable, and children are not... however much the government would like them to be... merely outcome units on a sales curve.

One headteacher, whose school was enormously popular and very successful, suffered a difficult inspection because her Year 6 cohort had many children with special needs in it, and one child had died in a traffic accident during the final term, causing the other children considerable distress. The inspection team, led by a lawyer with no teaching experience whatsoever, thumped her fist on the desk while asking questions, had little sympathy and gave the school a poor and eminently unfair report. The headteacher was so distressed she hid behind a clothes rail while shopping in Marks and Spencer, to avoid being recognised when she spotted some colleagues from a neighbouring school.

Stories of bizarre comments and actions from inspectors are legion. The inspector who told a languages specialist that primary school children should spend lots of time writing Spanish down, not speaking it; the inspector who instructed a headteacher to conduct the pre-inspection briefing by mobile phone... because she needed to walk her dog; the school that almost failed its inspection because the team was offered coffee before being asked for identification; the inspector who told the head of a country school that the small scattering of autumn leaves in the playground was a serious health and safety hazard; the inspector who yawned her way through every lesson she saw and then, when her rudeness was pointed out, said she had a medical problem which caused her to take occasional gulps of air. In fact, there's a rich vein of bizarre comedy to be had from school inspection reports. Not laugh-out-loud comedy, but some of the statements are so questionable the reader can only grin and say, in true John McEnroe fashion: 'You cannot be serious.'

'Where teaching and learning was successful, the teaching was good and the children were purposefully occupied.' Read that sentence twice and you immediately realise what a statement of the utterly obvious it is. How many teachers wouldn't know that in order for their children to learn, they have to teach well? And that if the teaching is good, the children will naturally be purposefully occupied? The report might just as well have said: 'Where the teaching and learning was poor, the teacher had no control and the children were jumping on the tables.' Another said: 'The school can improve further by ensuring that teachers plan lessons that are closely matched to every pupil's needs, so that every child is effectively challenged.' Think about this for a minute. Doesn't the average class have thirty children in it? How could a teacher possibly cater for all their individual needs? You'd need an army of teaching assistants, thirty six hours in the day and the patience of a saint. No teacher could do it. All they can do is arrange the children into groups of ability and then aim to find successful tasks for each group level. Even that is difficult, because in many schools there is such a huge range of ability among the children.

Here's one more: 'Opportunities should be provided for pupils to check their own work and other pupil's work so that they have responsibility for their own learning.' This statement is simply daft. Can you imagine a child of average ability trying to find the mistakes in his own essay? If he had known they were there, he wouldn't have made them in the first place. And should he really be checking the work of very clever Simon, who sits next to him? It seems to me the responsibility for the children's learning should lie primarily with the teacher.

Today, schools are given only one day's notice of an impending inspection... a far cry from the many weeks they originally had. The short notice should, in theory, give a much more accurate vision of a school. In practice it often doesn't, because the inspectors are in the school for just two days... barely enough time to make a worthwhile or accurate assessment. Though far greater importance is now, rightly, attached to high quality teaching and learning, Ofsted was unable to resist creating its own format for what a good lesson should look like, and how marking should be done, seriously stunting a teacher's creativity and freedom. When a school close to mine was inspected, eight of its teachers were graded good or outstanding and one was told she was merely 'satisfactory'. Four years later, in the subsequent inspection, the satisfactory teacher was told she was good, and six of the others were given a 'notice to improve', simply because the ground rules for a 'good' lesson had changed. One teacher appealed and demanded to be reassessed, and by carefully following the tickbox guidelines for a successful lesson, he was suddenly 'outstanding'. Another teacher was told her lesson was superb, but she couldn't be given an outstanding because the class was too well behaved and the inspector was unable to see how she dealt with challenging children... one of the tick box requirements.

In another school, a class teacher was told that the aim of a lesson should always be written clearly on the whiteboard before the lesson began, and that the children should copy it down. Wouldn't this spoil the excitement the children might have experienced in wondering where the lesson was going? What if the lesson went off at a slight tangent when one or two children raised interesting queries? And what about poor old Simon, who sits near the front, hasn't great eyesight, and takes ages to copy anything down. He could be spending much of the lesson just copying down the aim of it...

There is no sense in all this, just as there is no sense in trying to prescribe a format for a perfect lesson. Looking back to my youth, many lessons stand out in my mind. I remember Mr Johnson, who told us in a history lesson how Louis Pasteur stayed up night after night struggling to develop a vaccine for curing a nine year old who'd been mauled by a rabid dog. Mr Johnson's lesson didn't have a beginning, development or, for heaven's sake, a plenary. It was just Mr Johnson talking, from start to finish... but I still remember everything he told us. And we didn't write anything down in Miss Davis's music lessons either, but her enthusiasm fired my lifelong love of classical music. I've never forgotten the lesson in which she made us plug our ears tightly, told us to try composing some simple tunes with the instruments we had in our classroom... and then played what Beethoven had achieved when he was stone deaf and wheeling an ear trumpet around in a pram. Sadly, none of this would be acceptable today in our Stepford designed, Ofsted-aimed primary school lessons. Mr Johnson with his lesson about Louis Pasteur would presumably be out on his ear.

Near my home, a local primary school hired a huge advertising hoarding in the main road to promote its Ofsted rating of 'outstanding.' This in itself seems an extraordinary waste of money, but the comment the school had chosen to highlight stated that 'every child makes exceptional progress.' Since an Ofsted team is now in school for just a couple of days, it seems pertinent to question how the inspectors found time to discover that four hundred children were all making exceptional progress. Furthermore, it raises the question of how an 'outstanding' school should be defined. Another local school was recently rated outstanding, but over a period of three consecutive years nineteen teachers left, due to the stressful conditions and bullying attitude of the senior leadership team. In their final year, the children had no lessons in the arts at all. Instead, they were subjected to a diet of practice tests to ensure the data read exceptionally well. It's not a school I would want a child of mine to attend. No system of school inspection can be perfect of course, but we seem to have come full circle and reached a stage where, just as in Victorian times, good teachers and leaders fear for their jobs following the visit of an often inadequate team. Pleasing inspectors seems, once again, to be the purpose of education.

I suppose, given the animosity Ofsted raises, it was hardly surprising that some schools tried a few little dodges to help them outwit the inspection process. There were stories of giving difficult children monetary bribes to truant, hiring quality artwork displays, less than top notch teachers being told to take sick leave, an advanced skills teacher 'bought in' for the duration of an inspection…

The national press loved it, of course. After all, who's interested in knowing that the vast majority of teachers work exceptionally hard under increasingly trying conditions? Far more interesting to tell the world how good old Ofsted, that bastion of inspection integrity and fairness, is trying desperately to raise educational standards in the face of frustration from these devious, conniving teachers who only work nine till three, for heaven's sake, and anyway, look at the long holidays they get. It's not hard to see the reasons why some teachers resorted to a little cunning, and I can imagine the scenario…

'You wanted to see me, headmaster?'

'Ah, come in Mrs Smith. Thank you for bringing Tommy. I wanted to mention that we're sending him to the school allotment on Tuesday.'

'That's fine. His class goes there for an hour sometimes.'

'I know. But we're sending him there for a few days. With some children very similar to Tommy.'

'Sorry headmaster, I don't understand…'

'Could you both sit down please. Now, Mrs Smith, watch closely as Tommy sits… What did you notice…'

'He travelled a long way down…'

'Yes, he did. That's because he's a very large lad. He's what we call obese. And that's a shame, because our teachers spend lots of time talking about healthy eating.'

'Oh, he knows all about that. Ask him anything about food and he knows what he should eat. It's just that he prefers kebab and chips.'

'Well, everything's fine in moderation, but he needs to

balance his diet with fruit and veg as well. And exercise of course.'

'I know. I've told him. But you can't tell kids anything these days, can you?'

'The trouble is, Mrs Smith, there's a knock-on problem for the school. We have quite a few children like Tommy who are overweight, and now Ofsted has got involved. You've heard of Ofsted, haven't you?'

'They come into school and frighten teachers, don't they?'

'That's right, and they're arriving on Tuesday. They'll be checking on overweight children and blaming us if we've got too many. Our inspection report could suffer as a result. If we become a failing school, my mortgage could be on the line.'

'But I thought inspectors came to see if children are making progress in lessons?'

'Ah, that's what used to happen, when the Government had oodles of money for five day inspections. Things are leaner now.'

'But hasn't the government said standards in schools are rising?'

'It has, and they are. But if standards keep rising, there won't be much need for a mighty organisation like Ofsted.'

'And inspectors would have to be laid off?'

'Exactly. Thousands of them. They might even... have to return to the classroom. After all, the world of education is littered with dubious and expensive consultants, so they won't find much work in that direction...'

'So they've decided to inspect overweight children like my Tommy, as well as educational standards...'

'Correct, Mrs Smith, The more things they can inspect, the easier it is to persuade the government not to disband them.'

'So it's the school's fault if the pupils are fat?'

'Yes, and bored. You see, they're also blaming us if pupils are bored in class. Which brings me to the next point. Tommy's teacher spends hours making her lessons creative and exciting, but Tommy keeps falling asleep.'

'It's because he's on his Playstation till late. I tell him to turn it off, but as soon as I go out of the room he turns it back on again.'

'I see. Well, here's a little suggestion, then. Take it out of his bedroom.'

'But he'd never forgive me! It wouldn't be worth the aggro.'

'And that's why we're sending him to the allotment, Mrs Smith. Killing two birds with one stone, you see. Tommy can do some energetic double-digging and some vegetable growing.'

'He won't like that, headmaster. He's not keen on carrots. Or cauliflower. Or exercise.'

'No, but at least he'll be out of the way until Ofsted's moved on.'

After all, what happens when the inspection call comes? As a booklet circulated by a headteachers' association put it... 'You'll have been expecting it, because you'll know when it's time for Ofsted to call again. Nevertheless, however well prepared you are, your stomach will turn a somersault, your brain will instantly remember all the things that aren't up to date because you've spent time dealing with those funny little things called children, and your heart will thump mercilessly with fear.'

The booklet was meant to be amusingly helpful, but I don't imagine many headteachers were laughing. Unless you're the sort of head who swans off on courses every five minutes and your school is sliding down the tubes, should the call really engender *fear*? Then you tell your staff, who will sense your panic and spend the entire weekend beavering away in their classrooms, dawn till midnight, checking every possible fault line has been sealed and worrying endlessly about any that haven't. Throughout the inspection days, everyone survives on panic and adrenaline.

The rationale for Ofsted borders on the insane. Create a system that inspects every school in exactly the same way. Use inspectors who might not have been teaching for years. Allow people who've only had secondary school experience to inspect the under-fives. Let retirees from other professions inspect schools after a couple of week's training. (like the retired police officer who inspected my nursery and said it would be okay, because he'd had three weeks intense training. Under that rationale, I said, would I be an expert thief taker if I'd spent three weeks at Hendon?) And if a school is found wanting, hound it to pieces. Is it any surprise that so many good, child-centred teachers have been driven from the profession? And is it any wonder that a very real anger has motivated many schools to employ whatever means they can to survive this aggressive and demoralising method of inspecting them?

After a telephone call one afternoon, I agreed to appear on Radio 4's *Today* programme. I'm very wary of the media, but I said yes, primarily because the news item was going to be about Ofsted and here was a chance to remove another brick from its foundations. A charming young 'news gatherer' arrived at my school the next morning, armed with a tape recorder and a list of questions. The viability of Ofsted was going to be discussed at the coming weekend's teaching union conference, she said, and since she knew my school had fought Ofsted all the way to the independent adjudicator, would I care to give my views on the subject? I spoke to her for a little under an hour, and she went away with a tape full of information, while I waited with bated breath for the broadcast. It came on air two days later. Well, twenty eight seconds of it. The remaining time was given to the head of Ofsted's former chief inspector, who said the public and profession supported it, and people like me should stop making crass and uninformed comments about it.

One winter afternoon, an education adviser went to a large school near me to give a talk about primary education and I went along to hear what he had to say. Did he discuss good classroom practice, techniques for making sure the children behaved well, ways in which lessons could be made exciting and relevant, or the range of experiences it was important for a child to have at primary school? No, he discussed current Ofsted requirements, and how to make sure the school passed its inspection. It's hardly surprising that this happens all over the country. Schools are bombarded daily with e-mails daily from companies, consultants and consortiums eager to get into a very crowded market by showing how any school can achieve greatness pandering to the latest bits of Ofstedian diktat. Meanwhile, Ofsted constantly bats away any criticism, saying it receives very few complaints, that most headteachers find inspection an invigorating process, and that its inspectors are highly trained, courteous and competent. This is blatantly and demonstrably not true, although its views have obviously been modified a little since Ruth Perry.

It seems that the current breed of headteacher is strongly encouraged to be something of a whip wielder. Trusting your teaching staff to know what they're doing is naïve, and if you don't keep a watch on them they are liable to slacken off. Headteachers, or their senior leaders, constantly need to make them accountable. They need to realise they will be monitored and assessed regularly, with frequent classroom clipboard visits and a performance management session a couple of times a year. It's almost as if they were the enemy, and an increasing number of heads are becoming aggressively demanding.

Recently, I read a piece by a headteacher about to retire. He was writing about his final Ofsted inspection, and it seemed the lead inspector, while addressing the staff on the first morning, had told them she believed intensive Ofsted inspections were vital in forcing standards up, and that Ofsted had made a massive difference. That was the reason, she said, why she intended to inspect with the utmost rigour. The staff apparently sat cowed, slumping lower in their seats as she spoke. Although the school actually came through the inspection reasonably well, I felt that with such a display of staggering arrogance the lady should have been seen off the premises at that point. How dare the woman, who obviously had a highly inflated view of her own importance, start an inspection in that manner?

Whenever a change was made to the inspection process, such as the move to much shorter inspections with the corresponding short notice, I dutifully attended any courses which promised to keep me fully acquainted with what was happening. The shorter inspections were introduced alongside a self-evaluation form known as a SEF. Since the new inspections were to last only a couple of days, the self-evaluation forms would assume huge importance, because that's where the inspectors would get all their information about your school. They could stick a pin at random in your document and say, 'Ah, it says all your teachers have attended professional development courses in the last eighteen months. Please show us the folder where you've kept the records of these.' And if you couldn't come up with the evidence, you'd have a problem, because we all knew headteachers weren't trusted any more. If you hadn't got a fully documented record of absolutely everything you were doing, then sorry, they'd say, you can't be doing it.

But the form was an electronic one with the usual raft of confusing instructions. And once you'd got past those and reached the boxes, it wasn't clear how much information should be typed into them. Well, how long is a piece of string? The boxes expanded into infinity, and from the examples the course leader gave us to look at, some heads had obviously decided to pour out their entire life stories. Write too little, and the inspectors would think you're not doing anything. Waffle at length and you'd be giving them a million things to home in on (and you'd have a million boxes of evidence to prepare). By mid-afternoon, we'd shuffled through nearly 100 sides of A4. We'd looked at best practice, satisfactory practice and pretty dubious practice. We'd been through model answers with a fine-toothed comb, and we'd realised we were in for half a term's worth of form-filling weekends, carefully weighing every word we wrote.

Afterwards, I stayed to talk to the course leader. Surely, I said, there are simpler ways of assessing a primary school? After all, any parent can spend half an hour in a school and know whether they want to send their child there. What do they look for? Simple. Are the classrooms busy and purposeful? Are the teachers enthusiastic and happy? Is children's work everywhere, and is it of a high standard? Is there a wide and interesting curriculum? Is there progression in the work from year to year? Is the head always present, and knowledgeable? It's hardly rocket science, and never has been. In many ways, I suspect nothing much has changed over the years. Inspiring leaders will run exciting schools, just as they always have, while mediocre leaders will produce mediocre schools. And trying to turn heads into paper-churning, meeting-intensive business managers who have little contact with children is precisely the wrong way of going about things. He shrugged, and said that he was merely outlining the current procedures, not suggesting alternative ways of judging a school.

Newspapers can often have a lot to answer for too, with misleading headlines about schools and the inspection process. 'Coasting schools slammed for failing pupils,' shouted one. 'Far too many schools coasting,' shouted another. Naturally, Ofsted was behind these lurid stories. Thousands of state schools were apparently failing to provide a good standard of education. Thousands? Where on earth could that figure have come from? Or was it just the latest Ofsted ruse to show the public how indispensable it is?

And there was more. 'Schools blamed for making class assistants a risk to pupils,' said another headline in the same week. Apparently schools risked damaging children by leaving teaching assistants in charge instead of qualified teachers. I haven't found one teacher who supports the idea of teaching assistants supervising classes, good though they may be, and very many of them are. But what was the real story behind this headline? And shouldn't Ofsted have pointed out that it was the government's idea to use classroom assistants to support the half day of planning and preparation time it wanted teachers to have. Why? Because they're cheaper than fully qualified teachers. And here's an interesting statistic. At any given time, forty per cent of schools advertising for a headteacher have difficulty in appointing one. Forty per cent is a frightening number, but the reasons are obvious. Long hours, poor behaviour from parents and children, endless and meaningless paperwork, not enough money in the budget, initiatives that seem to come along weekly, and always the dead hand of Ofsted waiting round the corner, ready to pounce on the slightest weakness. No wonder people prefer to stay lower on the promotion ladder.

But undoubtedly, two days of Ofsted was always going to be more bearable than five. The trouble is, as soon as the inspection process undergoes the slightest change, the usual industry springs up around it. Need to write your self-evaluation form? Don't worry, there's an army of consultants out there, willing to show you how to produce one that's Ofsted-proof. Of course, their work isn't cheap, but it's hardly surprising that a lot of schools take up the offer. Almost as soon as the changes come into play, questionable practices quickly come to light. Two headteachers recently told me how, on the day they got the call to say Ofsted inspectors would be arriving the next day, they were told to put aside an hour after school to discuss their SEFs on the telephone. The discussions turned out to be intensive grillings. Even worse, they were told they weren't 'obliged' to answer all the questions. The inspector might just as well have added 'But if you don't, an assumption will be made and could be used in evidence against you'.

Eventually, after a great deal of concern, Ofsted found it necessary to look more closely at the quality of its inspectors, and it found that 40% were not up to the required standard. Put another way, that meant nearly half of Ofsted's inspectors hadn't measured up. It seems the rejects were unable to assess schools effectively, couldn't write meaningful, accurate reports or, incredibly, didn't have qualified teacher status. It beggars belief that inspectors could have been appointed without QTS. Did they craftily omit that piece of information from their CVs?

Other inspectors with a strong conscience have left Ofsted because they were extremely unhappy about the way they were required to inspect. One that I knew personally... a superb headteacher... returned to headship because he believed it was a far more honest and worthwhile job. Another couldn't stand the sight of teachers quaking when he walked into a classroom. A third couldn't accept his point of view being summarily dismissed by a vitriolic lead inspector.

And then the Ofsted rules changed again. Schools were notified that 'contextual value-added'.... A system whereby certain allowances were made for schools in particularly challenging areas... was disappearing, putting schools in tough areas on a level footing with schools down leafy lanes. In other words, force Emily, second in a family of five, whose mum does drugs and whose dad has long since disappeared from the family home, through a level four hoop... or else. And these days, there are rather a lot of Emilys. One headteacher said 'My school was delivering the curriculum we knew was absolutely right for our children. But I can't afford to do that any longer. I've got to join in the game.' Why did he feel the need to do this? Because he could be in danger of losing his job, that's why, and so could members of his undoubtedly capable staff. Years ago, the primary schools around me were rich in diversity, often inspired by the interests of the headteacher. One school sent chess teams all over the country, another had mini gardens everywhere, including the rooftop, a third put on incredible art exhibitions, a fourth achieved exceptional results in sports. My own school offered an amazing amount of music... including a full 30 piece orchestra... because I feel music is absolutely essential for young children.... but headteachers these days are wary of creating an individual flavour for their schools.

It's undeniable that most teachers fear Ofsted inspectors. Instead of arguing with their loonier comments, they suffer in silence and simply sigh with relief when the two days are over. And what if one of those days is a nightmare? The inspectors knock on your door at eight o'clock. It's the middle of winter, and two of your best teachers have succumbed to flu. The supply agencies have no teachers left, so the two teachers crawl in because they don't want to let anybody down. Mr and Mrs Evans are coming to see you this morning about Cynthia being bullied. Again. The auditor is due in, and he'll need your room, and your computer. The staff room fridge has leaked all over the floor during the night. You need to interrogate Charlie and his mates urgently to find out who set the fire alarm off yesterday. The cook has just announced that no vegetables have arrived. What are the inspectors going to do? Sit in the staff room until you've got time to get everything on an even keel again?

At the beginning of this chapter, I stated that it was important for schools to be inspected. But having looked at Ofsted closely, how do we come to a decision on how it should be done, competently, at reasonable expense, and to the satisfaction of both teachers and parents? I believe we should return to a system of using local authority inspectors who know the area well, have been outstanding and highly regarded leaders themselves, and who can make reasoned and balanced judgments on whether the school is serving its pupils well, based on simple and straightforward criteria. Ofsted has stated that it is now training its inspectors to recognise stress in teachers and school leaders, and offering guidance for making a good relationship with a headteacher when they arrive at a school. Frankly, this shouldn't even be necessary, because good, strong leaders do not have to be taught how to make relationships and if there is the slightest hint of bullying from an Ofsted inspector, it should be called out immediately.

I'm not optimistic that a great deal will change. For years, schools have almost been encouraged to be in competition with each other, headteachers and senior managers are expected to hassle rather than encourage, and many inspectors, it seems, have taken almost a bizarre pleasure from intimidating people. And schools who have been labelled 'outstanding' are hardly likely to complain about the system, even if some of their staff have been placed under a great deal of stress. The problem will come in the future, when nothing much has changed except the inspection criteria and the school has dropped from 'outstanding' to a much lower rating.

Fighting Ofsted is dispiriting and difficult, as I discovered. But if unions, school governing bodies and headteachers took a much stronger stand, I believe this unacceptable form of school inspection could rapidly change or, hopefully, be removed altogether.

15

AFTERWORD

At the time of writing this book, we are living through difficult times.

We have experienced a terrifying world pandemic. There are dreadful wars and suffering in many countries across the world, and at home we are ground down by the daily events on the news. The health service needs much re-organisation and possibly a different structure. It is difficult to get an appointment with a doctor. The police no longer have the support of the public and we don't have anything like enough policeman. Police stations are a rarity, as are local community officers. Prisons are full to overflowing and the probation system hardly works. Seashores, rivers and lakes are contaminated with sewage and litter, while the water companies are making outrageous charges to their customers and outrageous payments to their shareholders. There are regular shocking scandals; the post office scandal, the contaminated blood scandal, tower blocks that catch on fire and kill people because their exteriors are covered in poor and cheap cladding.

Many people on very low incomes have no option but to resort to food banks so that they can feed their families. Shop lifting is at an all-time high, and the cost of it is wearily built into the prices charged to customers. Energy prices are out of control. Trains don't arrive and strikes go on for years. Children... even primary school children... have access to the most appalling images on their mobile phones and it seems almost impossible to do anything about it. Climate damage... even though progress is being made... continues on its deadly path.

And we have endured questionable prime ministers and politicians, many of whom have an inflated level of self-interest and a lack of any real capability beyond anything we have experienced in the past.

It is not all bad news of course. Medical science is on the verge of creating a vaccine for cancer, tailored to a patient's specific requirements. Wind power has overtaken gas to become Britain's largest source of electricity. There are amazing improvements to medicines and surgery which wouldn't have been dreamed of a decade ago. Modern cars are a pleasure to drive, petrol cars are being phased out and all kinds of travel are safer than ever. It is easy to holiday abroad and experience other sights and cultures. We can have a huge variety of food and even cooked meals delivered to our door. We can stream a massive variety of music directly to our homes. We can choose from a staggering range of films and TV programmes and watch them instantly in the highest quality, we can use the internet to buy almost any book ever published or download any book onto an electronic device and if our eyesight isn't great, easily change the size of the print. We can fit our own bathrooms and kitchens with a minimum of skill, and carry out repairs if we've a mind to. My father, with his small toolbag of six tools, would be astonished if he could see the array of hand and electric tools in my shed. And most of us are living longer than ever before.

So it is essential that we educate our children in a way that will make them grow into mature, responsible and thinking adults. Sadly, a fair number won't, but there is no reason why most shouldn't. Sometimes it seems that schools are up against impossible odds. Even very young children can be difficult and demanding. Parents no longer have the respect they once had for any public service. Only the NHS continues to receive uncritical affection. Notices are placed in many public buildings stating that the people working there will not accept poor behaviour or abuse, and it says something that these notices have to be put up in the first place. Even the pupils themselves are often questioning the validity and relevance of their schooling, as perhaps in many cases they should, and there's no doubt that schooling occupies some of the most important and formative years of their lives. If it is done well, it can have a lasting impression and relevance that helps to steer them through their adult lives.

Most teachers today are vastly more skilled than they were when I was a teenager. Probably the only reason I didn't rebel more than I did was because I grew up in an age of much greater deference. But undoubtedly, there is work to be done and many things still need to change. As a teenager, I had access to a wide range of interesting activities through scouts, youth groups and locally organised activities. Many were physical activities, because this is what young people need and thoroughly enjoy. By cutting back on these we are creating large groups of disaffected youngsters who are inevitably drawn towards the excitement of criminal activities.

The social aspect of schooling is also essential. During my headship, a local secondary school had a small extension built, where groups of six teenagers at a time could stay for several days, including a weekend. They had to cook, clean, garden, arrange their own activities and entertainment, learn to get along with each other and sort out any problems that arose. It always seemed to me an excellent idea. The more life skills children experience at school, the better prepared they will be, because aspects of life will always be difficult and challenging.

The daughter of a friend is currently training to be a teacher at a secondary school in the East End of London. It is a very difficult school to work in, and she has witnessed some very poor behaviour and teachers occasionally bursting into tears. But she loves the job and relates extremely well to the youngsters she is working with. She copes with their depressions, their anxieties and their occasional challenging behaviour. She listens to them, engages with them, laughs with them, and achieves a great deal of respect in return. She is the kind of teacher we need. One pupil asked how many GCSEs she had. 'Quite a few' she replied, but you can achieve it too if you put the right amount of work in.' 'Not me, Miss,' the youngster replied, 'I've got a life to live!' The art will be in persuading her 'that life can be lived' alongside storing up some good exam results for the future.

Although I have now retired from education, I am still in touch with many of my teachers. I know that we gave children the finest possible start to life, in a strong, controlled but exciting school environment. We didn't write a ridiculous 'mission statement'. We didn't pander to any ludicrous diktat from the government or local authority. Our aim, not necessarily spoken or written down, but shared by every person in the building, was for our children to wake up in the morning and hopefully say 'I can't wait to get to school today, because…'

I still receive regular letters and emails from past staff and pupils, telling me how lucky they were to be at the school. One of them came this morning, from Belinda. It said…

> *I was the young girl who came from Uganda, age 6, mid-term and I'd not been in the country for very long. I was quiet, but I worked hard. You taught me to play the guitar and harmonica and I learned that chess was nothing like as boring as it first seemed! Through the amazing teachers in the school, I learned so much more beyond the classroom curriculum which has helped me to excel in many ways and contributed to who I am today.*
>
> *Times have changed, but the memories remain and I will be forever grateful that you accepted me into the school and for your dedication to your profession. There are a multitude of other young lives you and your teachers have shaped, and who remember you, and who, I know, would also thank you.*

You really couldn't ask for more than that.

This book is printed on paper from sustainable sources managed under the Forest Stewardship Council (FSC) scheme.

It has been printed in the UK to reduce transportation miles and their impact upon the environment.

For every new title that Troubador publishes, we plant a tree to offset CO_2, partnering with the More Trees scheme.

MORE TREES
LET'S PLANT A BILLION TREES

For more about how Troubador offsets its environmental impact, see www.troubador.co.uk/sustainability-and-community